Praise for Bulli

Peter Oborne – J

"Sam Bright, one of our fine

has written a superb book which conveys

stench of the Johnson era in all its horror."

Annette Dittert – ARD London Bureau Chief & *New Statesman* columnist

"A fascinating tour de force on how privileged elites keep plundering Britain."

Musa Okwonga – Author

"Essential. A precise, thorough and devastating indictment of Britain's social and political elites."

Carol Vorderman – Broadcaster

"Bright scorches a path through the moral corruption of government in recent years. I have been shocked by its revelations."

Peter Reid – Football manager; former England and Everton player

"A brilliant book that reveals exactly how our political system is corrupt and broken."

Jolyon Maugham – Director of the Good Law Project

"Sam Bright is one of a handful of journalists who have held a steady gaze on what history will reveal to be, likely, the greatest corruption scandal modern Britain has ever seen."

FIRST EDITION

BULLINGDON CLUB BRITAIN

SAM BRIGHT

FOREWORD BY JOHN MITCHINSON

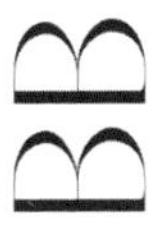

LONDON, UNITED KINGDOM

Byline Books

London, United Kingdom

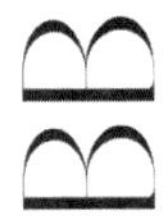

First published in the United Kingdom of Great Britain and Northern Ireland by Byline Books, 2023

Cover design by Steve Leard

Layout by Prepare to Publish

Printed in Great Britain by Short Run Press Ltd

ISBN: 978-1-8384629-6-3

CONTENTS

PREFACE

PETER JUKES

When Boris Johnson was nominated for a BAFTA award in 2004 for his appearances on the BBC's *Have I Got News for You* comedy quiz show, I had a suspicion that something was going badly wrong with the culture of this country.

It wasn't until Johnson won a resounding election victory as Prime Minister in 2019 that the horror dawned. A whole swathe of the population was fooled by him. Even worse, many actually admired him. It was as if they had read *Tom Brown's Schooldays* and seen the upper-class bully embodied by Harry Flashman not as someone to abhor, but something to emulate.

This era that I called 'Bullingdon Club Britain' is a mirror of our national disgrace. Every supposed British gift or virtue has been transformed into a curse or vice. Our alleged tolerance? A license to make snobby or sexist or racist jokes. Our history of liberalism? An excuse for lockdown breaking and lawless libertarianism. Our sense of humour? They have been laughing at us, not with us.

Somehow the ethos of a university drinking club has invaded and taken over a political party, which in turn has transformed back again into a private party, which we paid for but couldn't attend, and that broke the laws we had to obey.

Like an old story of some cursed fairy-tale kingdom, Bullingdon Club Britain went from being a state of mind to the mind of our state. It will take decades to wash away the shame, and to rebuild our country free from its taint.

FOREWORD: CONFESSIONS OF A REFORMED BULLINGDON CLUB MEMBER

JOHN MITCHINSON

> "You never know what is enough unless you know what is more than enough."
> – William Blake

Almost 37 years ago, a group of young men I didn't know entered my university college room, violently overturned over my desk and chair, sprayed champagne over my bed and record player and bundled me, in a semi-dressed state, to a waiting car outside. I don't remember the rest of the evening clearly: I ended up at someone's house, drank more champagne and was deposited back at my college alongside another equally dazed victim.

That, in case you've ever wondered, is how you 'join' the Bullingdon Club, the University of Oxford dining society known for its dedication to gourmandising and mindless vandalism, and more recently for offering a temporary berth to two prime ministers (David Cameron and Boris Johnson) and a chancellor (George Osborne).

I wish I could tell you that I was appalled and angry and reported my intruders immediately to the college authorities, but I wasn't and I didn't. I joined up and went the whole hog, even getting measured up for the elegant dark blue tailcoat, with its ivory silk lapels and 'BC' monogrammed buttons.

My flirtation with 'the Buller' ended several months later with my fiancé and I being asked to leave a wine bar after a fellow member of the club had emptied a jug of port refilled it with his own piss and sent it back to the waitress, saying the port was 'off'. That was enough for me. I moved on and buried the memories of my poor choices as deeply as I could.

As it turned out, the Bullingdon hadn't quite finished with me. There were the photos of course – those infamous posed shots on college steps in full club outfits, with unsmiling faces desperate to project hauteur and privilege. 'My' 1986 photo (with Johnson centre stage) first gained notoriety in 1993 when Boris's long-time friend Darius Guppy was jailed for staging a faked jewel robbery.[1] It was superseded in 2007 by the one showing Johnson and Cameron together, but mine reappeared in 2022 when the excellent Led by Donkeys campaign group created a potted biography of Johnson and featured it as part of his charge sheet. I shared the film on social media many times before realising I was in it, staring out of the screen at 00:56 – my bit part role in a nightmare that went on to engulf a country.

Every time I saw Johnson stumble his way through a press conference, or ruffle his thinning mane, I felt culpable – as though, somehow, I'd put him there. I don't mean that 23-year-old me should have somehow found the cunning and the will to sabotage Johnson and so prevented Brexit and the COVID shambles (although that fantasy has occurred over the years). More, that my susceptibility to what the Bullingdon Club represented contains a dark and uncomfortable truth, one that still disturbs me four decades later.

I joined because I was intrigued. It felt like I was penetrating the mysterious heart of something uniquely English. The nuances of class and privilege weren't things I properly understood then – I had arrived at Oxford from the vigorously anti-elitist state schools of New Zealand and was only elected because no one knew who I was or where I'd been to school (remember, this is the club that nicknamed George Osborne 'oik' because he hadn't gone to Eton or Harrow).

But I'd read Evelyn Waugh and wondered if the 'Bollinger Club' of *Decline and Fall* could still exist half a century on, with its "epileptic royalty from their villas of exile; uncouth peers from crumbling country seats; smooth young men of uncertain tastes from embassies and legations; illiterate lairds from wet granite hovels in the Highlands; ambitious young barristers and Conservative candidates."

Well, yes and no. In my year there was a glut of future investment bankers, mixed in with ambitious journalists and manipulators like Johnson, the future prime minister of Poland, some notable sociopaths, and a British Indian entrepreneur who drove a decommissioned fire engine. A very '80s version of mad, bad, and much less interesting than it sounds.

As a natural optimist with a weakness for good wine, there was part of me that hoped I had stumbled into a parallel dimension where I would finally see how the road of excess led to the palace of wisdom. But, in fact, the opposite was true. The excess felt forced, the violence more embarrassing than scary, the misogyny feeble and pitiful. When I hit my limit, as the shame of being ordered out of the wine bar engulfed me, it felt like the moment in a folk tale when the land of plenty is suddenly revealed to be a barren and blasted heath.

That feeling has never left me. As the years passed, whenever I saw Johnson's face contorting to its best impression of Winston Churchill, on his remorseless rise to the very highest office, I remembered the jug of piss and saw the skull beneath his pudgy skin.

Because these student banalities turned out to have real-world consequences. The Bullingdon Club I joined was a purpose-free institution where lies went unpunished, and a large stack of cash could always be summoned to make problems go away. It had a brazen and amoral quality that felt strange to me back then. Now, as *Bullingdon Club Britain* demonstrates so clearly, it's the reality we all live in. The idiots in tailcoats braying about being 'players' have been in power for well over a decade. When I turned my back on them, little did I know I was turning my back on my country's future. We have all been deceived by the slick equivocations of Cameron and the outright lies of Johnson. My secret shame is now a national disgrace.

I'm tempted to end with F. Scott Fitzgerald's beautiful lines from the *Great Gatsby* about careless people: "they smashed up things and creatures and then retreated back into their money or their vast carelessness or whatever it was that kept them together, and let other people clean up the mess they had made."

But there's no closure in that. In fact, their carelessness, their ineptitude cloaked by bluster and lies continues to inflict daily damage on Britain's reputation and its economic prospects. The Bullingdon generation of politicians built no empire, won no wars, effected no social transformations, left no permanent monuments to their vaulting ambition. They lied to gain power and money and had no clue what to do with either. History is unlikely to be kind to them.

In its admirable combination of forensic research and moral clarity, this book explains why.

1 THE STATE WE ARE IN

"Like Cincinnatus, I am returning to my plough," Boris Johnson declared on the steps of Downing Street as he tendered his resignation to the nation on 6 September 2022. After failing to prepare for the pandemic, supplying nurses with too little PPE, turning care homes into hermetically-sealed COVID hotspots, locking down too late, partying through the whole thing, and lying to the nation about it, Johnson used his departing address for one last act of ego-mania.

Cincinnatus – the person whose story Johnson invoked – was a retired Roman statesman and farmer, called on to save Rome in 458 BC, after which he returned to the fields.

Having read Classics at Oxford, the habit of adorning his language with arcane references has stayed with Johnson throughout his life and political career.

However, there is one such noun that I don't remember Johnson ever using, which perfectly describes him.

Sophistry is used to describe the clever use of arguments that seem true but are substantially false, in order to mislead people. Indeed, this is precisely why Johnson deploys such ornate language – both in his writing and his public appearances. It is a distraction technique – a proven and successful one – designed to conceal his hazy attention to detail.

"The thing about Latinate words is they're evasive," Johnson admitted at a Latin-themed charity event in 2007, yet the media has lapped up this act ever since.[2]

Other politicians are not as talented at *sophistry* as Johnson. His successor, Liz Truss, spoke to the nation through awkward, hesitant, bland prose – a marked departure from Johnson's beguiling oratory. However, she still appeared capable of deception.

Soon after taking the top job, Truss spoke of an "anti-growth coalition" standing opposed to economic reform. She said this included "Labour, the Lib Dems, the SNP, the militant unions, the vested interests dressed up as think tanks, the Brexit deniers, and Extinction Rebellion."

And yet, in her first three weeks in office, UK markets lost $500 billion in value – largely the product of Truss's self-destructive 'mini' budget released on 23 September, which promised radical tax cuts for the rich.[3] This economic ideology was incubated by the free market think tanks that line Tufton Street in Westminster – opaque organisations that are backed by big corporations that have a vested interest in tipping the scales further towards the rich.

This sort of wilful deception is happening with increasing frequency in Britain and across the world. Assisted by social media, which amplifies gripping myths over sombre facts to create a whirlwind of distortion, expedient politicians have been able to plant 'fake news' and watch it spread like Japanese knotweed, with fact checkers straining to pull these falsehoods out of public discourse.

With the Brexit campaign and the elections of populists Donald Trump, Jair Bolsonaro in Brazil, Giorgia Meloni in Italy and Narendra Modi in India, this seems to be a feature of world democracies, not simply a passing bug.

This democratic crisis is mutually reliant on an economic crisis that has been suffered by Britain – and many developed countries – for the last 15 years.

Economic growth has stalled, inequalities have widened, working life has become more precarious, and identity-based divisions have festered – while, in the UK and elsewhere, governing parties have insisted that others are to blame, typically immigrants and nebulous liberal agitators, for our sad situation.

The 2008 financial crash and the subsequent rise of populist, anti-immigration politics in the form of UKIP and then Brexit; brutal austerity cuts to state spending; the UK's high economic and health toll from the COVID pandemic. All of these events are interrelated, and have been the consequence of economic and political choices. While they are often written up in the media as freak events – a 'once in a 100 year pandemic' – they are not simply an anomaly or an accident. They are repeated, interlinked, and compounding.

Populists have therefore been fed by many justified anti-establishment grievances – notably the growing realisation that while most people have suffered, some have thrived. The number of billionaires in the UK reached its highest number ever during the pandemic.[4]

In the UK, MPs and those close to power have been among those cashing in while imposing austerity on the rest of the population and our public services. Seeking to replace the income lost in the wake of the expenses scandal of 2009, when it was revealed that parliamentarians were funding often lavish personal items from the public purse (in one case using taxpayer cash to clean their moat), MPs turned to second jobs.[5]

In November 2021, this second scandal detonated, when the public learned of the lucrative consultancy positions enjoyed by their MPs. Private service had once again trumped public service – MPs earning more than £17 million from their second jobs between 2019 and 2022.[6] Conservative donors and associates, meanwhile, hoovered up £3 billion in Government contracts during the pandemic.[7]

The question is therefore: what is so fundamentally and structurally wrong to have caused this condition; this sickness of democracy and economy in modern Britain?

Much like the Bullingdon Club, the infamed Oxford drinking society described by John Mitchinson in the foreword, Britain is suffering from the actions of an elite whose loyalty to self and the old school tie vastly outweighs its belief in the collective good.

It has been alleged that Bullingdon Club newcomers are asked to burn a £50 note in front of a homeless person as an initiation ritual – a claim that, due to the secrecy of the group, hasn't been widely corroborated, but also wouldn't be surprising.[8] Confirming John's account above, a former Bullingdon membership 'scout' told *The Observer* that "every time someone was elected, they had to have their room smashed to pieces," saying that Bullingdon members "had an air of entitlement and superiority."[9]

This book is not a history of the Bullingdon Club – nor is it focused purely on the handful of Bullingdon Club graduates, notably Boris Johnson, former Prime Minister David Cameron (2010 to 2016) and his Chancellor George Osborne (2010 to 2016), who have sauntered into high office. It is a study of how the sort of mindset epitomised by the Bullingdon Club has infected British politics, business, and high society.

Indeed, the walls of privilege surrounding the Bullingdon Club are high, closely guarding the intimate details of this depraved syndicate – making a full history of the organisation virtually impossible. In a profile of Boris Johnson produced by the BBC in

2013, it was noted how "members of the Buller feel bound by strict vows of *omertà* [a code of silence] – and normally refuse to speak publicly about the club."

Johnson even mutters "omertà, omertà", according to the journalist Sebastian Shakespeare, whenever he is asked about his youthful transgressions in the Bullingdon.[10]

Tackled about his former membership of the club, Johnson was presented with an awkward fact by BBC reporter Michael Cockerell: that, according to his fellow Bullingdon alumni, he still greets them with the primal chant: "Buller, Buller, Buller".[11]

Johnson didn't deny the claim, though was visibly taken aback by the breach of *omertà* by his Bullingdon brethren.

This lack of detail has fed the imagination of journalists and scriptwriters, including Laura Wade, whose film the *Riot Club* dramatised an elitist Oxford dining society, portraying its members trashing a pub and violently assaulting its landlord.

However, these fictional and semi-fictional narratives have been fed by the occasional stories that have escaped from the Bullingdon Club's vault of secrets.

The former Bullingdon scout – who rubbed shoulders with the group in the mid-1980s, when Johnson and Cameron were members – has claimed that female sex workers were asked to perform sex acts at lavish dinners, that women were routinely belittled, and that intimidation and vandalism were its hallmarks.[12] "The whole culture was to get extremely drunk and exert vandalism," she told *The Observer*. "People talk about the Bullingdon Club 'trashing' places, but it was serious criminal damage."

She added that "Boris was one of the big beasts of the club. He was up for anything. They treated certain types of people with absolute disdain, and referred to them as 'plebs' or 'grockles'... Their attitude was that women were there for their entertainment."

Her claim about the club's use of prostitutes was corroborated by former Bullingdon member Ralph Perry-Robinson in an investigation into the club by Tom Mutch in 2016.[13]

Those recruited to the club are typically heirs to fame and fortune. They are (exclusively male) members of rich dynasties who attended the most prestigious private schools.

Think of it like Crufts, but without the awards for good behaviour.

Mutch manages to find a set of club rules from 1850, which describes the penguin costumes – the "Blue Coat, Brass Buttons, Buff Waistcoat [and] Blue Trousers" – worn by its members to this day.

His investigation also notes that the Bullingdon was "ordered not to hold any meetings within 15 miles of central Oxford in 1894 after smashing all 534 windows in Peckwater, a quad in Christ Church, the grandest of Oxford's colleges."

As reported by the *New York Times* in 1913, Queen Mary demanded that her son – the future King Edward VIII – relinquish his membership of the Bullingdon, due to its raucous reputation.[14] Mutch says that, over a 50-year period during the 20th Century, the club's alumni included a prime minister, a chancellor of the Exchequer, three foreign secretaries, five first lords of the Admiralty, some 50 members of Parliament and more than 100 peers of the realm.

The Bullingdon Club's influence is so pervasive that one of its annual photos has been erased from the internet, featuring two lofty-looking future prime ministers (Johnson and Cameron) – though the Conservative Party denies that it was involved in its erasure. Two heads have also been scrubbed from another of these yearbook portraits, giving them an eerie mystique.

"It is a truly shameful vignette of almost superhuman undergraduate arrogance and toffishness and twitishness," Johnson said to Cockerell about the club – failing to acknowledge or appreciate how he had become the political embodiment of the infamous society. As Asher Weisz so aptly puts it in the *Oxford Student*: Johnson began his career "smashing up restaurants with the Buller and has now progressed to smashing up the whole country."[15]

This is the point; the central premise of *Bullingdon Club Britain*. Namely, that our institutions of power continue to be populated by individuals who are drawn from privilege, who have perpetuated a politics of destructive elitism. Just as Oxford was a playground for Johnson and his contemporaries in the 1980s – their enjoyment derived from the vandalism of both people and property – the ruling elite (including but not confined to Bullingdon alumni) are now ransacking Britain.

A decade of grinding austerity and stagnant wages

has been accompanied by the enrichment of political and corporate elites. In this way, the political, social and economic establishment in Britain is effectively acting as a private club for the privileged, dedicated to its own gluttony at the direct expense of ordinary people. Money and power are hoarded among this alliance of aristocrats, oligarchs and their butlers – and you're not invited.

Far from being marked by stable, 'conservative' governance in recent history, Britain has been afflicted by instability – stoked by expedient actors who have pivoted to populism in order to harness public rage with the status quo.

The Bullingdon Club elite has fractured the nation – demonising welfare claimants, trans people, immigrants, and 'liberals' – to retain their psychological grip on the nation; to direct the anger of the masses towards the vulnerable, rather than those in power.

As Tom Nichols writes in *The Atlantic*, in a description that could equally apply to Boris Johnson: "Donald Trump is central to this fraying of public sanity, because he has done one thing for such people that no one else could do: he has made their lives interesting. He has made them feel important. He has taken their itching frustrations about the unfairness of life and created a morality play around them, and cast himself as the central character. Trump, to his supporters, is the avenging angel who is going to lay waste to the 'elites,' the smarty-pantses and do-gooders, the godless and the smug, the satisfied and the comfortable."[16]

As they demonise their 'woke' opponents, populists in Britain and elsewhere have used this smokescreen to tip the economic scales even further towards the rich and powerful: reducing taxes for the highest earners; cutting local government spending in half; outsourcing public contracts to well-connected insiders; and dismantling the regulations that keep capitalism functioning for ordinary people rather than merely shareholders and rentiers.

The result has been the evolution of a great British *plutocracy* – a state in which political leaders are dependent on, or are heavily under the influence of, wealthy individuals who derive their growing riches from the decisions taken by their accomplices in high office.

Rampant immorality is permitted by the system – even facilitated by it – as the perpetrators in power shrug off their transgressions with the chameleon charm learnt in their boarding school dorms. If you think this is a stretch, think of the way in which Cameron avoided culpability for the 330,000 excess deaths caused by his austerity policies, or how Johnson clung onto power while the "bodies piled high" due to his COVID policy failures.[17]

To many of these politicians – the ones who have jumped on the conveyor belt leading from an elite private school, to Oxbridge, and then to Parliament – democracy is simply a game. Whether a former member of the Bullingdon Club or not, they share, or have learned, the mentality – seeming to have no real concept of the harm they can cause. Their only understanding of politics is through frivolous, theoretical slanging-matches at student debating societies.

One of Johnson's fellow former inmates at Eton – the upper-class private school – recalls to Sonia Purnell in *Just Boris* that the school's debating society was "probably the most influential forum of [Johnson's] life."[18]

Cameron said in his post-premiership memoir, by contrast, that the Bullingdon Club, "haunted me for most of my political life". Yet, if the former Prime Minister hadn't been coated in this balm of privilege, would he have made it into Downing Street?

Famously, on 15 June 1988, Conservative Central Office received a phone call from Buckingham Palace, answered by the deputy director of the Conservative Research Department.

"You are about to meet a truly remarkable young man," the royal errand said. "I have tried everything I can to dissuade him from wasting his time on politics, but I have failed."

They were referring to Cameron, who was about to be interviewed for a job in the research department. Unsurprisingly, he was offered the spot.[19]

Likewise, the process through which Johnson decided to support Britain's departure from the EU, writing two *Telegraph* columns arguing opposing points of view, was eerily reminiscent of the protocol at the Oxford Union, the university's illustrious debating society. You argue for or against a particular motion, regardless of which you think is correct.

As Simon Kuper notes in *Chums* – his psycho-analysis of the pathway from Oxford to Westminster

– Johnson pretended to be a Social Democrat in order to win the coveted Oxford Union presidency.[20]

Not only does this attitude breed an ignorance towards the suffering borne from political decisions, but it also encourages an arrogance, and a sense of impunity, among these sons of privilege who have won their own private political parlour game.

Johnson "inhaled his legacy before he'd created it", says venerated constitutional historian Peter Hennessy. This is echoed by Andrew Rawnsley of *The Guardian*, who sagely argues that, "The character of organisations is immensely influenced by the example set by the person at the top. When that person is Mr Johnson, you get a culture of selfish, arrogant, entitled, amoral, narcissistic rule-breaking that combines, in the true spirit of the Bullingdon Club, snobbery with yobbery."[21]

Exploring Hennessey's theory, which suggests that British democracy has relied – due to its weak democratic conventions – on 'good chaps' behaving with a sense of personal morality, Rawnsley says: "We now need to adopt a 'bad chap' theory of government, which presumes that some politicians will behave abominably unless they are prevented from doing so by robust laws that are vigorously enforced."

The rules of British democracy have been premised on the conviction that our leaders belong to a paternal, benign bourgeoisie. There is no need for checks and balances on their power, such is the case in America, for example, because our morally superior leaders are governed by higher laws.

This was always an illusion. Legislation to introduce welfare provision and strengthen workers' rights was an act of necessity to prevent popular revolt (and often implemented by Liberal and Labour administrations), rather than a demonstration of aristocratic altruism.

Yet, an underlying sentimentality towards the aristocracy is still prevalent today, perpetuated by the newspaper editors drawn from this social stratum. It is epitomised by their fawning attitude towards royalty; their daily idolising and showcasing of a handful of people who represent centuries of privilege.

A compliant, innately conservative press helps to cover up the crimes of the elite – as witnessed during the 'Partygate' scandal, during which right-wing newspapers actively attempted to downplay the stories of Johnson and his advisors spilling wine at sweaty Downing Street lockdown raves.

Those who call for wholesale change, meanwhile, who say it's a bad thing that thousands of people needlessly died during austerity or COVID, are derided as unserious or accused of spreading conspiracy theories.

This burying of bad news – the denial and distraction tactics of the Bullingdon Club elite – is witnessed across the political system, as wrongdoing is masked beneath a toothy, hollow grin.

The motto of the Royal Borough of Kensington and Chelsea (RBKC), emblazoned on its coat of arms, is the Latin *Quam bonum in unum habitare* (how good it is to dwell in unity). Yet, in 2017, the police said that it had "reasonable grounds" to suspect that RBKC committed corporate manslaughter for its role in the Grenfell Tower fire, in which at least 72 people died.[22] RBKC has faced accusations that it ignored a catalogue of warnings over fire safety, downplaying the concerns of the working class tenants.

As former Kensington Labour MP Emma Dent Coad has catalogued, the borough is one of the most unequal in Britain – the only area of London with three wards in the top 20 least deprived and three in the top 20 most deprived.[23]

Bullingdon Club Britain is a study of how this has happened, unpicking the ways in which power operates in modern Britain – from the dark money think tanks that provide the faux-intellectual grounding to right-wing political campaigns, to the media outlets that carry these distortions to the public. This is a tour of the corridors of power from someone who has investigated money and influence in British politics – from Brexit to COVID – pretty much every day since 2016 (minus a few stints in politics rehab, on a beach).

You would be correct in pointing out that elitist rule, of the sort described in this chapter, has been a feature of British politics for centuries. As George Orwell wrote in *The Lion and the Unicorn* in 1941: "England is the most class-ridden country under the sun. It is a land of snobbery and privilege, ruled largely by the old and silly."

However, something has intensified in recent years. The number of political scandals hitting the headlines has multiplied, while their scale has steadily enlarged. Now, barely a week goes by without a new Conservative donor being appointed to a public position or awarded a state contract. The Cabinet is equally as socially exclusive, measured by the proportion of ministers having attended private school, as during the early 1990s.[24]

And while a hereditary elite is entrenching its wealth and power, the economy is flatlining for the majority of Brits. No longer is the British class system softened by the universal growth in living standards experienced in the post-war 'age of affluence'. Taking inflation into account, real disposable incomes doubled in Britain from 1950 to 1970. The 2010s, by contrast, saw living standards in the UK grow at their slowest rate since the Second World War.[25] What was formerly a fact of life, that you would be better-off than your parents, is now a fool's paradise.

Meanwhile, the British aristocracy – those born into wealth and privilege – which seemed to be in retreat during the 1980s and 1990s, has evolved and resurged. It has forged a pact with new money oligarchs from the East and West who have provided new sources of finance to Britain's hallowed, old money institutions. This includes the right-wing press – controlled by a narrow-band of ideological billionaires, spearheaded by Rupert Murdoch.

Any lingering sense of national duty has evaporated among the elite, replaced by the thin, two-faced facade of nationalist populism. Our ruling class laments the retrenchment of Britain's role in the world, not because this process has been accompanied by the stagnation of living standards for the average person, but because these elites no longer have an imperial power to govern.

In fact, they blame Britain's relative decline on the evolution of the welfare state – which has protected Brits from hunger, disease and deprivation – and the social democratic consensus that emerged in the post-war years. Truss, her Chancellor Kwasi Kwarteng and their *Britannia Unchained* co-authors wrote in 2012 that the stagnation of the British economy is characterised by "the draining of effort from our psyche, replaced by a sense of entitlement."[26]

This Bullingdon Club mentality, at the heart of the Government's ethos for much of the last 13 years, is based on the idea that the nation's future prosperity should be built on the backs of working-class people whose current comfort is strangling the success of supposed 'wealth creators'. The attitudes of the British Empire have been brought home, with state-sponsored capitalist exploitation draining the spirit and the affluence of the majority, while a small segment of society dines on the wealth of a nation.

2 THE GREAT PROCUREMENT SCANDAL

Two days before the 2019 General Election, on 10 December, Boris Johnson decided to put on a final show. Grinning hysterically, like Mr Blobby in a wig, Johnson ploughed through a wall of polystyrene boxes forming the word "Gridlock". The then Prime Minister was sat in a JCB tractor emblazoned with a Union Jack, its front loader carrying the Conservative election slogan, "Get Brexit Done".

The media, kept at a safe distance (from Johnson) by a series of pedestrian barriers, lapped up this performance, while he hastily exited through a side door without answering a single question from the assembled media pack.

There is no better symbol for recent British political history than this pointless, vain, chaotic stunt. Politics has been reduced to a macho pantomime of three-word slogans, paid for by corporate interests, broadcast to the nation by a click-hungry media establishment. JCB, the ubiquitous construction equipment firm that hosted Johnson's playground antics, is owned by Lord Anthony Bamford, whose family has donated some £13 million to the Conservative Party in recent years.[27]

Bamford helped to fund Johnson's wedding to Carrie Symonds (now Johnson) in the summer of 2022 after the newspapers caught wind of the plan to host the bash at Chequers, the taxpayer-funded home used by our leaders. Accommodating the wedding at the Georgian country home Daylesford House in the Cotswolds cost the Bamfords some £24,000 – while, after leaving Downing Street, the Johnsons have been accommodated, free of charge, at the Bamfords' £20 million London townhouse – a feat of generosity that was matched by Johnson during his time in high office.[28]

On a visit to India in April 2022, Johnson personally opened a new JCB factory in Gujarat.He called it a "world-leading factory" and a "living, breathing incarnation of the umbilicus between the UK and India".[29] He didn't mention the millions given by the Bamford family to the Conservative Party.

This is the political culture instituted by the Conservative Party since 2010, and especially since 2016. Big money takes precedence over ethics.

And when this populist pageantry came into contact with the greatest health emergency in 100 years, the consequences were devastating.

Downing Street's response to the COVID-19 pandemic was woeful in various different respects. A total of 275 people per 100,000 have died with the virus – some 200,000 overall, at the time of writing – compared to 230 per 100,000 in France and 176 in Germany. The Government failed to spot the danger of this deadly disease, repeatedly locking down too late and opening up the economy too early, risking the creation of ever-more-lethal variants and disregarding the risk to the clinically vulnerable – 2.2 million people.

Perhaps the most damning aspect of the Government's response, however, was in its procurement of essential products for frontline health workers – in particular personal protective equipment (PPE).

"Contrary to the official line, Britain was not in a state of readiness for the pandemic," write investigative journalists George Arbuthnott and Jonathan Calvert in *Failures of State*, their forensic account of the Government's failures during the pandemic. "Emergency stockpiles of PPE had severely dwindled and were out of date because they had become a low priority in the years of austerity cuts."[30]

This became clear just a few months after the emergence of the disease. In a detailed report by the National Audit Office (NAO), the Government's independent spending watchdog, in November 2020, it stated: "The [PPE] operating model was not designed to respond to a pandemic."[31]

In fact, the situation was dire. The Government's stockpile contained enough PPE to provide for the health service for just two weeks, with some items in dangerously short supply. There were only aprons to last six days in the national stockpile, the report suggested.

What's more, the stock was not exactly accessible. Much of the PPE was housed in "deep storage", which led to delays in ferrying it to the frontline. Some of the equipment had passed its expiry date or did not meet safety standards, including six million respirator masks that had to be tested and relabelled.

Delays were compounded by an archaic IT system, meaning it was impossible to add new PPE storage warehouses onto the database, to track their stock.

Moreover, the Government was warned, in the crucial few months before the virus arrived on our shores, about the impending threat of PPE shortages – yet failed to act.

PPE supplier Sarah Stoute, CEO of Full Support Healthcare (FSH), told a committee of MPs that she contacted officials in December 2019 – warning of imminent issues with the supply of PPE.

FSH has been a supplier of PPE to the Government for many years and had received warnings from hospitals that stockpiles were dwindling due to supply issues in China.

"We started to talk to [the Government] about stock issues in December 2019," Stoute told the committee. "All of the hubs in the country were emptying. There was no stock and hospitals had started to call, to say they were in a panic. It took all of December and January to beg [the Government] to release the Brexit stock as a matter of emergency, while we went to production full-scale in the background, and urged them to place orders on products that were running out."[32]

Stoute called officials and told them that a "major problem" was coming down the track, as some PPE products had almost entirely stopped being shipped out of Wuhan in China. "[You] need to buy everything you can get your hands on," she told the officials.

However, her warnings were not heeded. "The person I was speaking to in inventory tried to escalate that and was ignored," she told the MPs.

While the Government struggled to understand the scale of the crisis, Stoute's company increased PPE production in December 2019 and January 2020.

"We went into production and risked everything, just to get as much on a plane as we could," she said. "So we'd already gone to production for things we couldn't afford to pay for, waiting for the Government to catch-up."

FSH had millions of items of PPE waiting on planes in February and March, she told the committee, but her firm did not receive the go-ahead to supply the Government until April.

"It took senior officials in the Department of Health and Social Care [DHSC] to be put in place to get the wheels moving," she told MPs. "Prior to that it was very slow, very low-level... Weeks went by when nothing was happening."

The NAO report explains this institutional inertia. Despite the vast scale of the looming crisis, the Government still believed in mid-March, when England was about to enter its first lockdown, that its existing stockpiles "would provide most of the PPE needed to manage a COVID-19 pandemic".

By late April, however, the Government's previously held optimism had been fully dismantled. Modelling future demand, the DHSC estimated a huge increase in the need for some types of PPE compared with previous flu pandemic calculations: an 820% increase in demand for aprons, 388% for gloves, and 125% for face masks.[33]

This was too late. The international market for PPE was overheating, with dozens of nations engaged in a desperate bidding war. The NAO claims that if the country had been able to purchase PPE at the same unit prices as in 2019, it would have paid £2.5 billion – some £10 billion less than the Government ended up spending. The pace of procuring these items was also slow. Even by November 2020, the majority of the 32 billion items of PPE procured by the Government still hadn't arrived.

Adding insult to the frontline fatalities, former Health and Social Care Secretary Matt Hancock claimed that there was never a "national shortage" of PPE during the pandemic – a claim that has been widely refuted by doctors and public bodies.[34]

"We are flooded with anxieties and concerns by doctors – it is the single biggest issue at the moment," the British Medical Association's chief Dr Chaand Nagpaul told MPs in late March.[35] Some doctors and nurses even shared photos of themselves wearing bin bags due to a lack of protective gowns.

The Government's solution to this crisis – which it claims was never a crisis – was to institute a haphazard procurement system, awarding billions of pounds to seemingly inexperienced firms, and those seemingly able to benefit from their political connections.

As an investigative journalist, I have to admit that I was sceptical, when these stories first emerged. Massive Government contracts being shovelled towards firms with political links to the Conservatives, and those with seemingly little or no experience in healthcare? It all seemed too brazen; too ridiculous. This sort of thing doesn't happen in the UK, right?

The following few months, from the summer of 2020 onwards, proved my initial doubts wrong – in spectacular fashion.

On 29 July, I published my first story – showing how multimillion-pound PPE deals had been awarded to a bookmaker cited in the Panama Papers (which revealed the offshore wealth of the global elite), a retired soldier, and a fast fashion supplier.[36]

By the end of the year, our team at *Byline Times* had revealed PPE contracts awarded to a hotel carpeting company (£5 million), a naval design firm (£5 million), a Florida fashion designer (£200 million), a four-month-old DNA analysis firm (£120 million), a one-year-old 'micro' firm (£40 million), a small 'luxury packaging' company (£70 million), a one-month-old firm owned by offshore finance specialists (£200 million), a dormant firm (£44 million), and a lifestyle company with no employees or trading history (£25 million).[37]

And that's not to mention the bigger controversy – the dozens of deals awarded to firms with direct ties to the Conservative Party. These contracts were almost all awarded without competition – the Government using 'emergency' procurement procedures to sidestep the rules.

Take Meller Designs – a small UK firm typically specialising in the production of homeware, fashion and beauty products. The co-owner of the company during the pandemic was its namesake, David Meller, who has donated nearly £60,000 to Conservative politicians and the central party since 2009, including £3,250 to Michael Gove's unsuccessful leadership campaign in 2016, serving as its finance chair.[38]

Government records show that Meller Designs was referred to the 'VIP lane' for Government PPE contracts by the office of the Government Chief Commercial Officer, and by the office of the Chancellor of the Duchy of Lancaster – a position held during the pandemic by Gove, who is still a senior Cabinet minister.[39]

The VIP lane was an expedited route used by the Government to award contracts to 'trusted' suppliers that had been referred by MPs, ministers and advisors. A company channelled through the VIP lane was 10 times more likely to win a contract than a firm processed through normal procurement routes – a fact that led the High Court to conclude that its use by the Government was unlawful.[40]

Records show that Hancock was involved in referring four firms to the VIP lane for PPE contracts, while former Conservative Chair Lord Andrew Feldman also referred multiple companies.

Our calculations suggest that Meller Designs won at least £170 million in PPE contracts during the pandemic. The company saw its profits increase by more than 9,000% during the accounting period ending December 2020, from a modest £143,000 to £13 million.[41]

"Turnover increased... reflecting the additional PPE business in the year," the company's accounts say.

Serving as a Health Minister at the time, Lord James Bethell held a meeting with Meller Designs on 6 April 2020.[42] A month later, Government records show, the firm began winning PPE contracts worth tens of millions of pounds.

Indeed, Lord Bethell was seemingly a key facilitator of the Government's cosy relationship with the private sector – including Conservative donors and associates – during the early stages of the pandemic. A hereditary peer and an alumnus of Harrow School, one of the UK's most exclusive private institutions, Lord Bethell was at the apex of this crisis.

In November 2020, the peer was asked in the House of Lords to explain his meeting with Meller Designs, which had also been attended by Lord Feldman.[43]

"The noble Lord must realise that he is in danger of appearing complicit in the stench surrounding these procurements," Labour peer Jonathan Harris said. "What was discussed on 6 April?" he asked, "and will the noble Lord, the minister, publish all documentation relating to every one of these VIP and fast-tracked procurements, including emails or messages suggesting specific contractors, and show how decisions were based on value for money rather than favouritism?"

Lord Bethell responded by saying that the global supply of PPE had "completely collapsed" during the early stages of the pandemic and, as a result, "we relied on a very large network of contacts and informal arrangements in order to reach the people who could manufacture, often moving their manufacturing from one product to another."

This was a confession, in front of peers and recorded *in aeternum* on Hansard, that ministers and officials used their personal "contacts" to urgently supply PPE – eschewing formal procurement procedures in the chaos of this health crisis.

Rounding off the debate, Labour's Baroness Glenys Thornton drew Lord Bethell's attention to the Ministerial Code, which contains specific provisions to deter conflicts of interest.

"Ministers are responsible for ensuring no conflict exists, or appears to exist, between their personal interest and their public duty," Baroness Thornton directly quoted.

Referring to rules about healthcare procurement, she said that a conflict of interest exists when a "reasonable person would consider that an individual's ability to apply judgement or act in the context of commissioning, delivering or ensuring taxpayer-funded health and/or social care services is or could be impaired by another interest they hold."

The baroness questioned whether Lord Bethell had declared the conflicts of interest arising from his meetings and, if he had, where these were published.

Lord Bethell responded vaguely. He said that "transparency is key" and that "I take that responsibility very seriously", though he didn't say how he had adhered to even the most basic transparency requirements.

"We are extremely proud of the role we played at the height of the crisis and managed to secure more than 150 million items of PPE," a Meller Designs spokesperson told *The Times*.

P14 Medical was another firm that benefited from the "informal arrangements" described by Bethell. Owned by Conservative councillor Steve Dechan, the firm – that suffered significant financial losses in 2019 – won contracts worth £276 million for the supply of PPE. After these contracts were awarded, in October 2020, Dechan donated £7,500 to the Conservative Party.[44] Dechan denies that he ever discussed PPE contracts with any MPs or ministers. "We are an expert company that has been in medical supplies for eight years including PPE that has managed to deliver on a big contract that the 'big companies' could not", he said.

Yet, gaining the names of companies that profited from the VIP lane was not an easy task. There was an ongoing legal campaign – led by the Good Law Project – resulting in the Information Commissioner's Office (ICO) ordering the Government to release the names of the 50-or-so firms that had previously been withheld from the public on 'commercial' grounds.

"There was no good reason – but there were obvious bad reasons – for the Government to keep the public in the dark about these links," said Good Law Project director Jolyon Maugham.

The Government has repeatedly maintained that ministers were not involved in the awarding of COVID contracts.

However, while ministers may not have been directly involved – their signatures absent from the formal paperwork – there are numerous examples of companies with links to ministers winning big-money deals. Too many to ignore.

The centre of Newmarket features the monoliths of the modern high-street. Starbucks, Greggs and the local Wetherspoons jostle for position in the cramped market town, best known as the global capital of horse racing.

Nestled in this throng is Newmarket Acupuncture, part of the Chinese Medical Centre. All of its staff have training from the Traditional Chinese Medical University in China, according to its website – including Chunlei Li, who has been practising Chinese medicine in the UK since 2003.

In January 2020, Chunlei Li launched a new venture. On the second day of the new year, he formally incorporated CH&L Limited, assigning himself one share – the company's full allocation. At that time, the Companies House website listed him as a 'receptionist'.

Soon, CH&L struck a big win. On 30 April, the

company was awarded a £14.4 million contract from the Government for the provision of isolation gowns. The contract was awarded without a formal competition process.[45]

How did a small-time acupuncture practitioner from Newmarket with a brand new business secure a PPE contract worth as much as a Premier League footballer?

For starters, Chunlei Li had seen an opportunity to use contacts in his home country. CH&L detailed its business case in May 2020, when applying for financial support. Chunlei spoke to "colleagues and contacts in China" about sourcing "NHS/DHSC PPE items" such as gowns, masks, goggles and face shields, according to information provided to me by an insider about the firm's efforts to obtain PPE contracts.

However, as the Government belatedly set about procuring equipment – attracting thousands of PPE offers – many firms, even those with links to production hubs in Asia, were marooned on an island of chaos and confusion.

This is where Chunlei's business partner appears to have played a crucial role. For the previous 12 years, Chunlei had known the Honourable Frances Stanley "both professionally and as friends", the material provided by the insider stated.

According to information provided to me, Stanley "used her connectivity" to Whitehall purchasing departments and "UK contacts in the Government" in an attempt to secure contracts on behalf of CH&L.[46]

Stanley explained her mindset: "We were not

professionals prior to the worldwide pandemic. As a full-time charity worker it seemed obvious to me that I should turn my attention to this terrible crisis where events have shown that we were able to make a difference by sourcing much-needed PPE at a very favourable price for the DHSC," she told me.

"My primary objective was to procure PPE for our hospitals and care homes facing a healthcare crisis of immense scale. Dr Li provided strategic connections with manufacturers in China and we worked together in the spirit of collaboration for our country."

A well-known contact of Stanley and her family is Matt Hancock. Newmarket forms part of Hancock's local constituency, where Stanley is a director of Newmarket Racecourse.

Frances Stanley's husband Peter Stanley – also in the horse racing business – donated £5,000 to Hancock's office in June 2019. When asked about this donation, Peter Stanley was later quoted as saying that Hancock "recognises that horse racing is more of an industry than a sport" and that "he knows better than most that we are a huge export industry and foreign currency earner."[47]

The commercial alliance of British horse racing, the Jockey Club, is also based in Newmarket and Hancock has been a vocal advocate for the sport in the past. Baroness Dido Harding, appointed by the Government to run the nation's 'Test and Trace' programme, also holds a board position at the Jockey Club – alongside Peter Stanley.

For her part, Frances Stanley appears to have worked with Hancock on various projects related to

Newmarket – sitting on a delegation with the MP about investment in local rail services, for example.

"At no point did I ever talk to Matt Hancock about our plans to help, only DHSC purchasing officials involved in the process," she told me.

Ultimately, the company did not deliver the goods and returned its deposit. "Due to unforeseen logistical circumstances, we weren't able to help and the deposit was returned in full to DHSC," Stanley said.

I understand from the material provided to me that CH&L expected to make a profit margin of 5% (£720,000) on its initial £14.4 million PPE deal – and it didn't plan to stop there. The firm seemingly had been promised subsequent ongoing contracts for isolation gowns after the fulfilment of the first contract, each with a value of between £1 million and £15 million, with an expected five sales a month. These subsequent deals would allegedly have achieved a profit margin of 25%.

Stanley said that the profits arising from the deals would have been used to help expand her charity, Bridging the Gap, "a charitable scheme I had established to fund food purchases for disadvantaged families for the three weeks prior to Universal Credit commencing.

"If all had gone well, I was also aiming to use some of the money to support the new Children's Hospital in Cambridge, for which I am an ambassador," she added.

I don't doubt Stanley's account, or her altruistic intentions. Rather, the example of CH&L draws into sharp relief the actions of the Government during this crisis – whereby it selected a company that seemingly had no prior experience of supplying PPE, owned by someone with political connections, and awarded it multi-million-pound public contracts.

Indeed, I understand that CH&L only had a few thousand pounds in its bank account when it received its £7.2 million deposit from the Government in late April 2020.

But smaller operations weren't the only ones to benefit from the Government's great procurement rush.

The global healthcare company Randox – based in Northern Ireland – was one of the primary beneficiaries of COVID contracts, awarded deals worth more than £600 million for the provision of tests. There were plenty of good reasons for this. As the company repeatedly maintains, the awarding of these contracts, though they didn't go through competitive tender, "reflected Randox's extensive diagnostics capabilities within the UK and 40 years of experience in that field."

However, official records also suggest that Randox may have benefited from its proximity to parliamentarians – and one parliamentarian in particular.

Documents released by the Government show how Owen Paterson – who was at that time serving as a Conservative MP – corresponded with Hancock at the outset of the pandemic about the services that Randox could offer. Paterson was employed by the firm to the tune of £100,000-a-year while sitting as an MP.[48]

The messages show how Paterson recommended at 9:23pm on 26 January 2020 that Hancock should contact Peter Fitzgerald, the founder and owner of Randox.

"Have told him to expect an email from you. Ring anytime if you want to discuss," Paterson messaged Hancock.

Just 10 minutes later, at 9:33pm, Hancock emailed Fitzgerald asking for "more detail" about the services that Randox was able to offer.

The documents show Paterson again contacting Hancock on 25 February, complaining that Randox's tests had not been approved, despite it "now [being] 19 days since [Public Health England] contacted Randox at your request".

Hancock then appears to forward Paterson's concerns to officials, noting that he was "very worried" about the matter and adding that: "If we are treating other companies like this we are failing". It's worth noting that Paterson does not try to conceal his conflict of interest – repeatedly noting in his messages that he is a paid consultant to Randox.

A large contract with Randox was ultimately signed on 30 March and renewed on 30 September 2020. Alex Chisholm, Chief Operating Officer for the Civil Service and Permanent Secretary for the Cabinet Office, noted his "disappointment" at the fact that a competitive tendering process had not been established in the meantime. This meant that directly renewing the Randox contract was the "only viable option".[49] Randox has repeatedly insisted that Paterson had no role to play in the awarding of the contracts.

Once again, the release of these documents was the product of a months-long campaign from politicians and transparency activists – the Government only coming clean when its attempts to defend Paterson's history of private sector lobbying (more on that later) caused a public backlash.

Indeed, prior to the release of the Randox documents, the Government admitted that it had failed to answer eight Freedom of Information requests about the firm's COVID contracts – one of which had remained unanswered for 14 months.[50] The Government evidently had the information on file, but was refusing to release it.

In 2010, the then Conservative Prime Minister David Cameron promised "a transparency revolution" that would make "our Government one of the most open and transparent in the world". A decade later, Cameron's successors in Downing Street have launched a counter-revolution – concealing, denying and distracting from their actions, particularly during the COVID pandemic.

Take Lord Bethell's meetings at the outset of the crisis – clearly and rightly the subject of public and parliamentary scrutiny.

The Government failed to declare 27 of these meetings for 14 months – eight months after they were supposed to be released. The companies involved in these meetings, held between 1 April and 6 April 2020, went on to win Government contracts worth more than £1.1 billion for the supply of various COVID-related products and services.[51]

The meetings were originally omitted from the

official register, the Government said, due to "an admin error".

Likewise, the Government failed to declare a meeting between a number of technology firms and Hancock at the outset of the pandemic. The tech giants at the roundtable went on to acquire public-sector contracts worth £1.3 billion during the crisis. This meeting was eventually published by the Government 21 months late, 25 months after it took place. Its omission was again due to "an admin error", the Government claimed.[52]

In sum, we have calculated that £3 billion in COVID contracts were awarded to suppliers owned or run by Conservative donors or associates. The Labour Party has estimated this figure closer to £3.5 billion. Yet the Conservative Government, previously pious about the need to ensure prudent public finances, has furiously dodged scrutiny about how our money was poured lavishly into the pockets of Tory allies.

People have called this 'cronyism', 'chumocracy', or simply outright corruption. I will leave you to make up your own mind, but there's no denying that billions of pounds made its way into the bank accounts of politically-connected firms in the institutional rush to procure vital equipment and services. That is an irrefutable fact.

The Government has repeatedly claimed that this is justified on the basis that ministers and their subordinates did "everything they could" to deal with widespread shortages of equipment (shortages created by a decade of Government-imposed austerity). Yet, even on this basis, the Government's plan failed.

In total, according to the NAO, the DHSC awarded almost 10,000 PPE contracts with a planned expenditure of £13.1 billion. These contracts are expected to have delivered 37.9 billion items of PPE.[53]

Contracts awarded through the VIP lane, meanwhile, totalled £3.8 billion and are expected to have delivered 7.8 billion items of PPE.

Yet, rather than providing a procurement route for reliable suppliers, the VIP lane appears to have been plagued by problems. Of the £670 million of PPE procured by the Government that flat out cannot be used, half (£360 million) was purchased through the now-notorious VIP lane.

The NAO further notes that 46 of the 115 contracts awarded to VIP lane suppliers did not go through the full eight-stage due diligence process that was implemented by the Government in May 2020.

The purchase price of items yet to be distributed, years after the onset of the pandemic, is £8.6 billion at the time of writing – out of a total planned expenditure of £13.1 billion. To put the spending into context, the UK's Government's outlay on PPE comfortably exceeded the UK's international aid budget in 2021, at £11.1 billion.

By November 2021, it had cost the Government £737 million to store PPE, which included £436 million of penalty charges due to officials being unable to remove items from shipping containers on time.

In total, the Government has written off £8.7 billion worth of PPE that is unusable, has passed its expiry date, or was procured at highly inflated prices – enough to pay for the salaries of a quarter of a million nurses.

The Government also did not consider profit margin when awarding contracts, "meaning it did not know if intermediaries were making significant profits on these contracts." It took this approach because potential contracts were "on the table for hours or a day", so "there was no time to secure a detailed breakdown of costs", officials told the NAO.

In short, the procurement of PPE was a cyclone of incompetence, cronyism, waste and mismanagement that left doctors and nurses at risk of catching and dying from a deadly disease.

The Conservative Party's response to the pandemic was ideologically jarring. Decades of Conservative thought has argued that the 'free market', supposedly rational and meritocratic, is the best way of solving economic problems.

As Margaret Thatcher wrote in an article for *The Telegraph* in May 1978, a year before she was elected Prime Minister: "The free market is the only safe way of ensuring that productive effort is directed towards supplying what individuals actually want, and in a way which secures the dignity and independence of the worker."

However, the modern Conservative Party does not seem to believe in a truly free market. It has cultivated an economic model based on monopolistic corporate control, cronyism and vulture capitalism – exposed by the PPE procurement scandal.

As US President Joe Biden (US leaders, even

Democrats, it's worth noting, are typically more right-wing than their British counterparts) said in September 2022: "Capitalism without competition isn't capitalism. It's exploitation."

This principle is put more elegantly by Tom Clark, former editor of *Prospect*, who argues that, "far from being emancipatory, a lot of the neo-liberal programme can be thought of as akin to the historic enclosures of common land, excluding some in order to strengthen property rights for others."[54]

In part, an expedited PPE procurement process was a necessity during the early stages of the pandemic. In the Darwinian reality of a global health crisis, the UK became acutely aware of its diminished international clout. It could not outbid China or America or the EU – and a market failure risked cutting us adrift, without the supplies that we needed.

And yet the Government's knee-jerk response also revealed its new ideological instincts.

The Government selected its suppliers in a private members' forum; the rigged market superseding the free market. It's as if, faced with an unparalleled crisis, the ruling class grasped for the only mode of governing it really trusts – patronage – which has served as the basis for aristocratic self-preservation for centuries. In other words: the Bullingdon Club mentality.

So, during the pandemic, a new socialism for the rich was born, whereby revenues flowed from the Government into the bank accounts of Conservative allies and donors, while the party received a chunk of the proceeds. In total, at the time of writing, the party has received more than £600,000 from individuals and firms awarded Government COVID contracts worth £400 million.[55] This is the Conservative COVID cash carousel: the enrichment of party benefactors through the public purse, the proceeds of which have trickled down into the Tory war chest.

Despite the free-market mythology favoured by the Conservative Party, which has infected our institutions of power, the party's new economic ideology is concierge capitalism: using state power to tip the economic scales in favour of a small, politically connected elite.

Even away from the vast sums of money spent during the COVID crisis, there is little genuine competition for big government contracts. The procurement market is dominated by billion-pound outsourcing firms that, despite repeated controversies, have captured chunks of the state.

For example, take the outsourcing company Serco, that has 50,000 staff working on UK public services – more than a-tenth of the entire civil service. The firm has a history of controversies regarding its management of asylum accommodation, prompting a government investigation into the behaviour of Serco guards in Yarl's Wood detention centre – who were accused of degrading asylum seekers and of sexual harassment in 2015.[56] Serco says its focus is "decency and respect" for the "residents" of Yarl's Wood and that "we will not tolerate poor conduct or disrespect and will take disciplinary action wherever appropriate."

Despite these concerns, Serco has continued to

win contracts worth billions (more than £2 billion at the last count) since 2010 to run asylum and migrant services.[57]

And then there's Deloitte – one of the 'big four' management consultancies – which acted as a surrogate for the civil service during much of the pandemic, paid £2 million a-day to supply more than 2,000 consultants to the 'Test and Trace' programme.[58] In the year following the onset of the pandemic, contracts worth £510 million were awarded to 35 management consultancies, including £330 million to Deloitte.[59]

These firms act as the agents of concierge capitalism. They are hired to maximise profit at the expense of workers, while their connections allow them to win vast contracts in both the corporate and the political world.

As described by US legal schollar Daniel Markovits in *The Atlantic*: "Management consultants advise managers on how to run companies; McKinsey alone serves management at 90 of the world's 100 largest corporations." Essentially, they advise the owners and senior executives of companies on how to become more profitable. As Markovits describes, their current ubiquity – especially in American and British corporate life – has corresponded directly with "job cuts and the explosion of elite pay."[60]

As witnessed during the pandemic, these firms have successfully advised governments and corporations on how to cut out middle managers, after which they have offered their management services to these bodies at inflated rates.

"That is to say: the administrative techniques that management consultants invented [namely: middle management cuts] created a huge demand for precisely the services that the consultants supply," writes Markovits.

Moreover, although they are portrayed as a steadying influence on the public and private sectors, these firms in reality carry their own histories of wrongdoing, with the biggest winners of consultancy contracts during the COVID pandemic having been punished to the tune of £100 million by regulatory bodies since 2010.[61]

Yet, as described by Aeron Davis in *Reckless Opportunists*, the big four consultancy giants "are present at all the main political party annual conferences and make financial contributions to each of them too... They have become simply too big and too connected."[62]

This is reflected in the attitude of Johnson who has a long-standing reliance on consultancy firms. Indeed, millions disappearing into the pockets of consultants before his notorious Garden Bridge project – the plan to build a tree-lined walkway across the River Thames – was scrapped, while he was London Mayor.[63]

This is the form of capitalism engendered by the Conservative Party, that materialised during the COVID pandemic. State assets, including natural monopolies like rail and energy, have been flogged to politically savvy corporate giants under the vague pretence of competition. Rather than empowering agile, innovative firms, the public realm is dominated by corporate hulks with a talent, above all else, for procuring Government contracts.

Seeing an opportunity to profit from Johnson's moral deficit – combined with the commercial opportunities provided by the pandemic – various corporate interests circled the Conservative Party. During this period, the governing party therefore acted more like a social club for the rich – a frat house for corporate interests – than a democratic body.

In this *brave new world*, the Tories theatrically bow before the god of the free market, adopting the self-righteous language of fairness and open competition, while keeping the rest of us locked at the gates.

This epitomises the Bullingdon Club mentality – a social elite seizing power and imprinting its nepotism onto the political system, haplessly throwing billions at well-connected insiders while nurses and doctors died on the frontline, nakedly inhaling a deadly virus.

3 FLOREAT ETONA! (MAY ETON FLOURISH)

> "Strain every nerve, parents of Britain, to send your son to this educational establishment... Exercise your freedom of choice because in this way you will imbue your son with the most important thing, a sense of his own importance."
> – Boris Johnson, writing for *The Chronicle*, Eton's student magazine, aged 16.[64]

Eton College in Windsor, the world-renowned boys-only private school that educated Boris Johnson and David Cameron, tries its best to avoid public controversy. Though barely a day goes by without its alumni in the news, their backgrounds forensically inspected, the college itself is anxious not to add fuel to the fire – making few public pronouncements and remaining coy with curious reporters.

So, it must have been deeply discomforting when, in September 2019, Eton hit the headlines. With Johnson recently having been installed in 10 Downing Street, various commentators found an Eton entrance exam paper from 2011, in which prospective students were asked to draft a speech from a theoretical Prime Minister, justifying the killing of protestors in London by the army.[65]

It's worth recounting the exam question in full, to give you a sense of what exactly the college was asking of 12 to 13-year-old boys.

"The year is 2040. There have been riots in the streets of London after Britain has run out of petrol because of an oil crisis in the Middle East. Protestors have attacked public buildings. Several policemen have died. Consequently, the Government has deployed the Army to curb the protests. After two days the protests have been stopped but 25 protestors have been killed by the army. You are the Prime Minister. Write the script for a speech to be broadcast to the nation in which you explain why employing the army against violent protestors was the only option available to you and one which was both necessary and moral."

This is a pretty ghastly task to give to any child, but it is made even more disturbing by the fact that 20 of the UK's 57 prime ministers to date (35%) have been educated at the boarding school. This includes two of our last five leaders, governing for nine of the past 13 years.

If these are the ideals being instilled in Old Etonians during their formative years – that they should expect to reach high office and be ready to commit and justify atrocities against their own citizens – should we be shocked by Johnson's blasé response to mass COVID-19 fatalities, or Cameron's willingness to push people into food banks through his austerity agenda?

Cameron and Johnson were not one-offs, however, but rather signify a renaissance of the British aristocracy in politics and business. The meritocratic ideals seemingly embodied by former prime ministers Margaret Thatcher and John Major – the former the daughter of a grocery shop owner; the latter having left school at 16 with three 'O' levels (i.e. GCSEs) – have been wiped from the latest breed of Conservative leaders. The march of the meritocracy has been halted, and in some respects has even been sent catapulting in reverse.

Indeed, the 1980s and 1990s presented a moment of crisis for the aristocracy; its institutional power declining. This occurred both through the Conservative Party – the vehicle of the elite in Parliament, that became more concerned with "middle class interests" in the words of Thatcher – and through the private education system, which "felt a beleaguered form of schooling" during this period, writes Richard Beard in *Sad Little Men*. "In 1982," Beard recalls, "two years after Cameron left for Eton, his prep school closed down despite impeccable upper-class credentials."[66]

However, these private institutions are now booming – with the Conservative Party once again in the thrall of a rejuvenated aristocracy. While

Thatcher, Major and Blair tried to squeeze out this old money elite, it has morphed and returned in a new guise.

As Iain Overton wrote for *Byline Times* in August 2021: "Eton College appears to have become almost pestilent in British public life. Today, almost every single pillar of British society boasts, at its head, an old Etonian...

"These include the [now former] Leader of the House of Commons and Lord President of the Council, Jacob Rees-Mogg; the [former] Chief of the General Staff, General Sir Mark Carleton-Smith; the Archbishop of Canterbury, Justin Welby; the [former] editor of Britain's most influential paper – the *Daily Mail*, Geordie Greig; and a Justice of the Supreme Court, Lord Leggatt – while in 2020 another old Etonian Justice, Lord Robert Carnwath, retired...

"Not to mention our king-in-waiting, Prince William and his brother, Prince Harry, who both attended the school."[67]

As Mark Carnegie, the Australian scion and Johnson's main opponent for his second run at the Oxford Union presidency, remarked to Sonia Purnell: "It became clear to me how powerful Eton is as a manufacturer of cultural capital. It's disproportionately powerful, devastatingly so. It's like the Goldman Sachs of England but instead of financial capture, it has national capture."[68]

Carnegie also came out with the immortal line about Johnson: "Sure he's engaging, but this guy is an absolute fucking killer."[69]

The cultural power of Old Etonians can be traced

in no small part to our innate national deference towards our alleged social superiors. Britain still fawns over monarchy, the aristocracy, and the trappings of privilege. We take a weekend stroll around their properties and watch TV dramas about their gilded lives. There are some 5.4 million members of the National Trust, which looks after more than 300 stately and country houses.

As Beard further observes: "Something immature and boyish survives in men like Cameron and Johnson as adults. They can never quite carry off the role of grown-up, or shake a suspicion that they remain fans of escapades without consequences. They look confident of not being caught, or not being punished if they are. Cameron has his boyishly unlined face and Johnson his urchin's unbrushed hair, and his arch schoolboy's vocabulary."[70]

Rather than balking at these traits, the nation has retained a twinkle-eyed affection towards posh lovable rogues. Despite the language of 'meritocracy' that has pervaded modern politics, there has been the enduring sycophancy towards the likes of Johnson and his brand of idle genius. A working-class politician, for example, would not get away with the tangled hair, baggy suit and slurred speech that has come to form Johnson's wildly successful political brand.

It could even be argued that a sense of entitled self-assurance is essential to the modern politician. In an era when politicians are under the microscope – subjected to daily scandals and needing to persuade a sceptical, apathetic population of their ability to lead

– a dogmatic certainty in one's own calibre (often impervious to reality), is vital to ensuring political longevity.

Aside from delivering good grades, private schools are valuable because they educate students about systems – the ways to navigate the modern world to enhance your power and wealth. Graduates are also endowed with the social manners of the elite – allowing them to assimilate easily into high society (if they were not otherwise born into it).

British institutions of this nature are different to many of those in the rest of their world because of their histories; their sense of superiority spans back generations, with that weight of history loaded onto the egos of the most self-regarding students. Nick Clegg, Nigel Farage, Blair, Cameron and Johnson were all privately educated, all (aside from Farage) attended Oxbridge, and all were (and still are) absolutely certain of their own convictions.

As Overton observes, Johnson has hyperbolically described 'Pop', the Eton society reserved for elite prefects of which he was a member, as "a self-electing elite of almost sickening pomposity and arrogance with a belligerent disregard for the rest of humanity."

Former Prime Minister Theresa May was also privately schooled, but she corresponds more with former Prime Minister Gordon Brown and Labour Leader Keir Starmer – all of whom are politicians less comfortable in the limelight. There's an awkwardness to them, an uncertainty – if only in public – created by the absence of pestilent privilege.

Instructively, May and Brown are known, above all else, for their public services ethos – May holding back tears on the steps of Downing Street when, in her resignation speech, she said that she loved her country. Brown, meanwhile, has devoted his post-parliamentary life to public service rather than personal enrichment.

This defies traditional class stereotypes, formerly epitomised by the noble aristocrat willing to sacrifice it all for King and country. The working classes, such as the key workers who kept the country running during the pandemic, are the ones guided by patriotic altruism.

"One thing that has always shown that the English ruling class are morally fairly sound, is that in time of war they are ready enough to get themselves killed," George Orwell said in *England Your England*, during the Blitz of 1941.

Simon Kuper backs up this claim in *Chums*, quoting contemporary accounts of Oxford lecture theatres left deserted after times of war, such was the appetite of dons to march into battle. Seven Oxford Union presidents died during the First World War; three during the Second.[71]

This spirit has evaporated, at least among the aristocrats in public life. Though Johnson thought of himself as a Churchillian leader, writing a bad biography of the wartime Prime Minister, he instinctively clung to self-interest over the public interest. Most infamously, Johnson missed several key emergency planning meetings at the outset of the COVID pandemic, preferring to spend the time at

Chevening, a 17th Century mansion in Kent typically used by foreign secretaries.[72]

His former chief aide Dominic Cummings has likewise claimed that Johnson was distracted during this period, the early months of 2020, by his divorce from Marina Wheeler, his engagement to Carrie Symonds (and the expected arrival of their first child), "and his finances and all that sort of stuff".

Johnson shares an *alma mater* with former Prime Minister Harold Macmillan, the Old Etonian who served as Prime Minister from 1957 to 1963, but there is a key difference between the pair. Macmillan fought in World War One and was badly injured as an infantry officer, something that you can't imagine of Johnson, who combines the blithe incompetence of *Blackadder*'s Melchett with the vanity of Lord Flashheart.

Part of the reason that Johnson was able to persuasively express his 'make Britain great again' philosophy was because he embodied the past: he was and still is the Bertie Wooster of Westminster – Bertie being the affable English gentleman created by early 20th Century author PG Wodehouse – merely stripped of Bertie's bashful naivety.

Johnson and his political acolytes embody old aristocratic privilege, yet alongside an abandonment of old aristocratic ideals of public service.

Infamously, however, even aristocrats of Macmillan's era didn't always enact the most publicly-spirited policies, despite their public-services virtues – a contradiction that can be traced back to the private-school system. The oldest and most socially exclusive private schools in particular bred individuals for imperial management – a form of national service that involved the exploitation of vast numbers of people.

The nature of British capitalism, and the private school system, was historically designed to "extract wealth from the countries within the British Empire, which has now been enshrined in corporate law and how the neo-liberal economic system functions," Labour MP Clive Lewis has suggested. However, now that Britain has lost its empire, "these same laws and principles have been used to extract wealth domestically".[73]

This imperial mindset is sustained at the University of Oxford, writes Kuper, who says that the history and architecture of the university produces an obsession with the past, and a misplaced assumption that the British state (and state of mind) is more powerful than it actually is. This is why the likes of Johnson were obsessed with entering high politics, Kuper says; they wanted to reinvigorate the age of empire, with them ruling the world.

This is epitomised by *Britannia Unchained* – the libertarian manifesto for Britain, authored in 2012 by Liz Truss, Kwasi Kwarteng, former Home Secretary Priti Patel, ex-Foreign Secretary Dominic Raab, and the Conservative MP Chris Skidmore.

It states that: "Britain has lost confidence in itself, and what it stands for. Britain once ruled the Empire on which the sun never set. Now it can barely keep England and Scotland together... To avoid decline, Britain needs to look out to [sic] rest of the world and learn once again what it seems to have forgotten."[74]

The industrial-imperial era was the nation's high point, this reading of history contends, when Britain led the international rat-race.

However, in modern Britain, hard work and innovation are being stifled by the warm embrace of the welfare state and regulation, the authors suggest. As the book's most infamous quote states: "Once they enter the workplace, the British are among the worst idlers in the world. We work among the lowest hours, we retire early and our productivity is poor."

They consequently suggest that insecurity is a necessary bed-fellow of economic dynamism. At one juncture – pushing this ethos to its most extreme – *Britannia Unchained* suggests that Brazil's favelas are an example of an environment in which entrepreneurship can thrive. "As a sheer experiment in what the poorest entrepreneur can achieve, when nearly all society's strictures are relaxed, the informal economy is pretty hard to beat," it says.

In this perverse cosmology, our 'beating' of other countries in the era of empire is more important than the material gains experienced by the majority of people during the post-imperial evolution of the welfare state and the institution of workers' rights. Or, to put it another way, things were better in Britain before the creation of the modern welfare state.

Britannia Unchained is therefore a reflection of the country that its authors would like to govern – a neo-imperial power. Thankfully, most of the authors are no longer in positions of power, but the book pitches a manifesto for the sort of society that would be most enjoyable for the rulers, not the citizens they govern. It is a form of private-equity politics – ruthlessly extracting as much economic output from national resources, no matter what the toll on workers.

Yet, the challenge for the aristocracy – in an open, supposedly meritocratic Britain – has been in persuading the public that it deserves to rule a neo-imperial power.

In his 2012 Conservative Party Conference speech, Britain's Eton- and Oxford-educated former Prime Minister David Cameron remarked: "It's not where you've come from that counts, it's where you're going."

This notion of meritocracy hasn't really changed since 1958, when it was first theorised by political scientist Michael Young (the lefty father of Toby) in his seminal dystopian text, *The Rise of Meritocracy*. Young suggested that meritocracy is based on a simple algorithm: *IQ + effort = merit*.[75]

In other words: to achieve what you want to in life, all you need is hard work and talent. Anyone can succeed, regardless of their background, if they simply have enough brains and grit.

As constitutional historian Peter Hennessy writes in his pamphlet, *Establishment and Meritocracy*, "the preoccupation with merit, I think, is... the wish, the almost indignant expectation that those who make it into the establishment enclosure are propelled there by their abilities and powers of application rather than shimmering in thanks to birth or social connection."[76]

This idea – that members of the elite are deserving of their riches – has sustained the inequalities of the modern era, with many politicians continuing to flog their knock-off version of the American dream. As the authors of *Britannia Unchained* suggest, the only thing holding back the working class is a lack of graft. Those at the top of the pile are simply superior and are thus deserving of their power and riches.

A footnote to this fable arrived in the summer of 2020, when the Government used a standardisation formula, taking into account the expected performance of students at certain schools, to award grades to A-level students whose education was disrupted during the pandemic.

There was a strong correlation between local deprivation and exam results, exposing what we already knew: that social background is a central force in the performance of students. Private schools saw the proportion of their students achieving A and A* grades lifted by 4.7% – more than double the uplift experienced by comprehensive schools.[77] The algorithm moderation process was also more likely to downgrade the performance of students from poorer backgrounds. There were stories of high-performing students from disadvantaged backgrounds being downgraded from A*s across the board, to Bs and Cs.

Essentially, the algorithm created a hyper-exaggeration of a system that already exists, whereby kids from good schools and good homes generally go to good universities, while a few of their peers from less advantaged backgrounds follow them.

These exceptions are typically used by conservative thinkers as supposed proof that anyone can make it, regardless of background.

However, as Akala writes in his book *Natives*, in the context of race: "A few successful black people also do very little to alter the race-class dynamics of the UK, and can even help to cement it. These successes can and will be used... to beat other poor people that 'didn't make it' over the head. They can be used to pretend that the system is just and there are enough seats at the table – 'if you just work hard and pull your socks up you can be like me' – rather than simply being honest about the way things actually work."[78]

In 2020, the 'exceptions' – the teenagers who got the grades despite all of their social and economic barriers to success – were forced to conform to the rule. Their grades were dragged down, because the algorithm judged, correctly, that people from their station typically under-perform.

There is plenty more evidence that educational performance relies heavily on social background; that people, more often than not, are small sculptures of their hometowns.

The 2018 *Access to Advantage* report conducted by the education charity the Sutton Trust, which examines social mobility in Britain, noted that, over a three-year period, eight of the UK's top schools received as many Oxbridge acceptances as 2,894 schools and colleges combined, three-quarters of the total number of applicable institutions.[79]

The Sutton Trust also highlighted how

independent school students are seven times more likely to get places at Oxbridge than students from non-selective state schools, and more than twice as likely to go to a Russell Group university. Likewise, you are approximately half as likely to go to Oxbridge if you're an applicant from the north or the midlands, compared to if you're an applicant from the south.

The report unsurprisingly concluded: "In the UK, whether someone goes to university, and if so at which institution they study, is highly impacted by an individual's socioeconomic background, the school they attended and where in the country they are from... Whether looking at Oxbridge, the Russell Group or top tariff institutions, our most highly regarded universities are not equally accessible to all young people in the country."

While the exam fiasco was galling, it was simply an amplification of the insidious sorting process that sees the rich and privately educated miraculously succeed every single year. There has been an algorithm that has sorted children for centuries – it just wasn't created by a computer.

And so, for all the rhetoric of social progress that has emanated from the Conservative Party, the idea of meritocracy has counter-intuitively sustained the quiet and continued preservation of a hereditary elite in business and in politics.

Indeed, some 70% of Liz Truss's first (brief) Cabinet was educated at fee-paying schools. This included the Chancellor, Foreign Secretary, Home Secretary, Deputy Prime Minister (who also served as Health Secretary), Defence Secretary, Justice

Secretary, Business Secretary, Education Secretary, Levelling Up Secretary, and Transport Secretary.[80]

Each holder of a great office of state (aside from Truss herself), was privately educated.

This compares to just 7% of the population overall who are educated privately and 29% of MPs elected in 2019. Some 41% of Conservative MPs elected in 2019 were privately educated, compared to 14% of Labour MPs.[81]

In fact, ever since the Conservatives gained a clear House of Commons majority in 2015, the holders of high office have been drawn from increasingly elite school backgrounds. Around 50% of Cameron's 2015 Cabinet were privately educated, falling to 30% among May's 2016 Cabinet, before soaring to 64% under Johnson in 2019 to 2020 and then 70% under Liz Truss. It stands at 61% among Prime Minister Rishi Sunak's first administration.[82]

For context, 71% of Major's 1992 Cabinet was privately educated, while 91% of Margaret Thatcher's Cabinet in 1979 had attended fee-paying schools.

Yet, despite this elevation of the privately schooled into Thatcher's Cabinet, she was also credited with tackling the dominance of a few elite private schools in the upper-reaches of politics. Tory journalists called the Thatcher years "petit-bourgeois triumphalism" – the supposed victory of the middle class over the old aristocracy (and the working class) – prompting *The Atlantic* to claim in 1999 that, "Under Thatcher the Tories finally became a meritocratic and populist party, for better or worse".[83]

Equally optimistically, *The Guardian* noted in 2005 that, "There are still, to be sure, Etonians in the Tory party; but what Alan Clark called 'government by means of the Old Etonian cabal', appears distinctly passé nowadays."[84]

Thatcher's sacking of four Old Etonians in 1983 seemed to herald the death of the institution's stranglehold on Conservative politics. It was a moment that prompted the derisive (and antisemitic) comment from former Prime Minister Macmillan that there are "more Old Estonians than Old Etonians" in the upper ranks of the Government. Nine alumni of the school were Cabinet ministers in Macmillan's 1956 Government.

Then along came Cameron. Although he attempted to encourage greater diversity among Conservative backbenchers, his inner circle drew heavily from his *alma mater*. The then Education Secretary Michael Gove was even motivated in 2014 to say that the number of Old Etonians in Cameron's top team was "preposterous".[85]

These included Oliver Letwin, who at the time served as Minister for Government Policy; Jo Johnson, head of Cameron's policy unit; Edward Llewellyn, his Chief of Staff (now a Lord); and Rupert Harrison, then Chancellor George Osborne's Chief of Staff.

Boris Johnson is of course an Old Etonian – and a former member of the Bullingdon Club – who has also been known to rely on the counsel of social elites. Johnson appointed Old Etonian and seasoned Foreign Office diplomat Peter Wilson to run his private office in March 2022. He also installed Harry

Mount – a fellow former Bullingdon Club member and author of a book on Johnson's "wit and wisdom" – as the individual responsible for overseeing new House of Lords appointments.[86]

Truss's Chancellor Kwasi Kwarteng and the former Business Secretary Jacob Rees-Mogg – the two figures who were (briefly) tasked with steering the country through the cost of living crisis – are both Old Etonians.

The regional divides within Truss's first Cabinet were also stark. Truss took the opportunity at her first Prime Minister's Questions (PMQs) to chide Labour for its last two leaders holding seats in north London, yet she neglected to mention that 30% of her first Cabinet were born in the capital. Just 13% of the overall UK population lives in London.

Meanwhile, not a single attending member of Truss's first Cabinet represented a seat in Wales or Northern Ireland (with a solitary member drawn from Scotland). Almost 60% of the MPs in her Cabinet represented seats in the south of England.

This has wider significance, beyond the hypocrisy of the meritocracy and the inability of working-class people to reach the highest political offices. Namely: a politician's background informs their view of society and economics, and therefore their decisions. The disproportionate clustering of the privileged in positions of power typically creates a disconnect, some would say a disregard, for the circumstances of the poorest – who are dismissed as feckless and anti-aspirational.

This has been the rhythm of the Conservative

Party's rhetoric throughout its recent history. "To look at everything through the lens of redistribution, I believe, is wrong," Truss has said. "Because what I'm about is growing the economy. And growing the economy benefits everybody."[87]

Truss has similarly claimed that lower economic output outside London is "partly a mindset or attitude thing" – a libertarian conviction widely used to justify restricting state support for the poorest people.[88]

While Truss is not an aristocrat, she appears to have been captured by the elitist politics that flows from aristocratic rule – fuelled by the belief that those at the top of society have not succeeded due to their cultural capital or inherited wealth, but instead through genetics, intelligence, and hard work.

This mindset, which pervades our collective understanding of 'meritocracy', has justified successive Governments pilfering the lunch money of the poorest and giving it to the rich.

Indeed, the very private schools that have educated generations of Conservative Cabinet ministers – including those currently governing the country – benefit from tax exemptions to the tune of £3 billion every year, according to academic estimates.[89] Ergo, the UK's 1,300 private schools gain tax advantages equating to more than 6% of England's total state school budget.

These tax benefits include the process through which private schools run institutions abroad – typically using private subsidiaries and gifting the profits to their UK charities, incurring no corporation tax.[90]

Moreover, the profits and capital gains (profits on the sales of investments including shares, land and facilities) of private schools are exempt from income tax, capital gains tax and corporation tax. Meanwhile, in England and Wales, private schools receive an 80% discount on business rates and can claim an extra 25% from the Government on all donations received.

These tax exemptions were created in the early 20th Century and have not been amended since. In return, private schools must fulfil a charitable purpose, providing a public benefit with their resources – mainly in the form of fee remissions to relatively poorer students. However, the rules applied to these remissions are vague.

A court case in 2011 set the basis for the charitable support required by independent schools – stating that they must provide remissions to those of "modest means" – defined as those who could not afford the school's full fees. However, given the drastic inflation in private schools' fees in recent decades – more than doubling in the last 25 years – these institutions are now able to deliver on their charitable requirements by offering financial assistance to relatively well-off pupils.

"The vast majority of children from families with more modest incomes are excluded by this fee spiral from enjoying such facilities – which should, by law, be available for public benefit," say the academics at Cardiff Metropolitan University, as well as Monash University and Tampere University, who produced the research.

In the 2018 to 2019 academic year, UK private schools awarded fee remissions totalling more than £1 billion to 176,234 out of their 537,315 students. Of this £1 billion, some £440 million was means-tested. The means-tested £440 million was shared between 44,395 students – an average of around £1,000 a-head. Just 6,118 – 1.1% of all private school students – received a full scholarship, and a further 2.1% received fee remissions in excess of 75% of fees.[91]

As mentioned, private school graduates also disproportionately attend university – particularly the most prestigious, with more than 31% of Oxford students being privately educated in 2020. Since universities are subsidised by the Government, the higher education of the privately schooled is therefore effectively being paid for by the state educated.

The inflation of private school fees – locking out all but the super-wealthy – has partly been propelled by the burgeoning wealth of Britain's super rich, particularly concentrated among an international elite.[92]

There are some 2,300 Russian children currently studying in UK private schools, and a report by Transparency International found that between 2004 and 2014 there were 327 'laundromat' payments – cash flows designed to hide illicit wealth – to independent schools in the UK, amounting to £2.8 million.[93]

"Whether it's those with Kremlin connections or individuals accused of corruption, sending children to private schools can be a stepping stone towards integrating into the British establishment and laundering reputations," says Ben Cowdock of Transparency International. "Independent schools should be aware that they are exposed to high levels of risk and may even be accepting tainted funds."

Currently, however, these schools are not legally obliged to report suspected money laundering, and their assets continue to multiply.

In *Sad Little Men*, Beard talks of the demise of private schools in the 1970s and 1980s. "Even to a child of 12, by 1979 private education felt a beleaguered form of schooling," he writes. "A dwindling number of parents saw the attraction of withdrawing small children from regular life for months on end, as if abducted by aliens, and leaving them in dormitories until their brains had been suitably modified. This rarefied experience was shared in 1978 by only 4.5% of the population, and decreasing, because schools that were private and isolated would inevitably lose out to those that were public and comprehensive. Britain would become a more open, meritocratic nation that could look to the future with confidence."[94]

Beard is describing the demise of old money – to be replaced in the 1990s onwards by the spoils of oligarchy, when the world's rich were allowed, without many strings attached, to buy visas and even UK citizenship.

Consequently, some of Britain's 'elite' private schools are heavily populated by the global super rich, allowing these institutions to sidestep the waning cultural and economic clout of the old aristocracy and become immensely wealthy institutions in their own right. The Dickensian imagery of draughty dorms and tweedy tutors could not be further from the truth in this globalised education system.

The top nine 'elite' private schools in England – the so-called 'Clarendon Schools' – increased their assets by 44% or almost £600 million from 2015 to 2020. The total consolidated assets (minus liabilities) of the nine schools rose from £1.36 billion to £1.96 billion in this period. All of these institutions possess charitable status.[95]

One of these schools, Winchester College, is the *alma mater* of Rishi Sunak and the recipient school of £100,000 from the Prime Minister and his wife. The school has increased its net assets by more than £70 million, from £276 million in 2015 (equivalent to £312 million if inflation is taken into account) to £385 million in 2020. Over the course of the last decade, meanwhile, the school has seen its assets double. It costs £43,335 a year to attend Winchester, a boarding school that before September 2022 only accepted boys.

Meanwhile, Eton charges £44,000 a year for attendance – comfortably more than the average full-time salary in the UK, which stood at £38,000 in 2021. The published financial accounts of Eton and Winchester College show that they possess total reserves of £323,000 and £526,000 per pupil respectively.[96]

Private schools are "subject to little or no accountability with regards to the effectiveness or equity with which they use this cash", according to the academic research mentioned earlier. Indeed, many of these institutions invest in new luxury facilities, which further inflate school fees.

Eton's science department, for example, was given a £20 million makeover in 2019, while the construction of an aquatics centre – boasting a 25-metre pool with a moveable floor – has recently been completed.

St Paul's all-boys school, with annual fees at £40,000, likewise recently polished off a 10-year building project, costing £114 million. According to the high society magazine *Tatler*, the results are "fabulous". They include an award-winning science building, a new drama centre with "possibly the best school theatre in the UK", and a "rare books room".

This all signals a wider trend: 'elite' institutions, with few formal regulations governing their conduct, serve an increasingly narrow, international upper class that has seen its wealth and influence swell in recent years. Meanwhile, persistent economic and political crises are suffered by the rest of the population.

As the institutions of democracy, academic learning and wealth creation are increasingly captured by this elite, the country appears to be betraying its commitment – however distant – to meritocracy. Instead, it appears that we are moving closer to plutocracy – a ruling class whose power is derived from its wealth.

A key feature of this ruling elite is that it is extractive and rootless – international vagabonds lacking a sense of loyalty to a particular place –

happy to dine in New York one night and bet against the pound in a London hedge fund the next.

This is the predominant attitude among the Johnsonian political elite – educated at private institutions that preach 'king and country' but teach the art of service to money and power. In the modern world, their graduates have dispensed with archaic ideas of patriotism and instead flow with the gold rush as it sweeps across the globe, collecting properties, companies and allegiances in multiple jurisdictions before safely protecting them in an offshore tax haven.

A Very British Coup, the 1982 political fiction drama originally written by the journalist-turned-Labour MP Chris Mullin, is an instructive analogy. In this tale, a staunchly left-wing Labour Prime Minister is hampered and harassed in office by the British establishment: the media, the financial sector, and the security services. These institutions are all portrayed as being instinctively conservative – a power bloc united in the effort to sabotage a socialist administration.

This tale was inverted by Johnson, who played the aggressor, launching a coup against the institutions of the British state, compromising their authority and integrity in an attempt, albeit ultimately futile, to preserve his own power.

Johnson's coup had been set in motion for several years, initiated by his unlawful prorogation of Parliament in late 2019, when he attempted to shut down Parliament early to avoid scrutiny of his Brexit negotiations. It was accelerated, however, during the 'Partygate' scandal – culminating in the publication of the Sue Gray report, showing how Downing Street binged while the nation followed Johnson's orders and retreated indoors to avoid the spread of COVID.

The Prime Minister was indicted in this crime. Gray reiterated the initial conclusions that she released in January 2022, describing a "failure of leadership" in Downing Street, and saying that "the senior leadership at the centre... must bear responsibility for this culture".[97]

However, rather than take responsibility, the "greased piglet" – in the words of Green Party MP Caroline Lucas – attempted to squirm out of his political bind, ploughing a path of destruction through the architecture of the British state.

In Johnson's imagination, it was everyone else's fault for the Partygate affair and his eventual demise as Prime Minister: low ranking civil servants, the media, invertebrate Tory MPs, but never the Prime Minister himself.

"I [have been] as surprised and disappointed as anyone else in the House [of Commons] as the revelations have unfolded," Johnson claimed, after the publication of Gray's report – suggesting that his staff were ultimately to blame.[98]

On the eve of his eventual resignation, in July 2022, Johnson even suggested that he was minded to defy a no confidence vote in his leadership from Conservative backbenchers. He claimed that he still had a mandate from the 14 million people who had voted Tory at the 2019 General Election, despite the fact that comfortably more than 15 million people voted for other parties.

Johnson attempted to subvert the will of Parliament and the Conservative Party to preserve his own lofty status; to continue to satisfy his childhood craving to be 'World King'.[99]

This, in many ways, is the Old Etonian spirit. The school is the pulsating nerve-centre of the British establishment, and its status imbues the college and its creations with a sense of exceptionalism – a belief that the institutions of power exist to serve their interests rather than vice versa.

At the school in the 1990s as one of its only black pupils, Musa Okwonga writes in his Eton memoir, *One of Them*, "I look at the school's motto, 'May Eton Flourish' [*Floreat Etona*], and I think, it is not right that you flourish, and will continue to flourish, at the expense of so many others."[100]

This is echoed in *Chums*. "This generation had ambition without a cause," Kuper writes about Johnson and his peers. Quoting Rosa Ehrenreich, Kuper notes that, essentially, these Oxford graduates accepted society as it is currently formed – with all its hierarchies and inequalities – and that the offer of their education was that "maybe someday you will be on top of the heap yourself."[101]

As many have commented, Johnson took a temporary break from writing newspaper columns in order to be Prime Minister. He is a polemicist who considers his "real boss" to be the *Daily Telegraph*, according to Dominic Cummings.[102] And, predictably, Johnson's Downing Street served the media, not the masses.

Thus, perhaps to a greater extent than at any time

in recent history, journalists were forced to deny and distort the truth to serve the partisan interests of their man in power. Johnson delivered the miracle of Brexit and produced a vaccine for COVID, all while leading a harmonious existence with his beautiful wife and newborn. This was the narrative plastered on the frontpages, even as the internet sagged with the weight of article showing his enduring laziness, his fatal missteps on COVID, his unethical reliance on donor-funded treats, and his lockdown law-breaking.

The lies used to absolve Johnson of blame, often having germinated on the front pages of the papers, were then carried to Parliament by the Prime Minister – perpetuating the already pervasive belief that no politician can be trusted to tell the truth.

Yet, Johnson was not an isolated figure. A host of Cabinet ministers were willing to lie and deceive on his behalf – people who would pull the same tricks if they were stood in Johnson's shoes. This is therefore not an anomaly but a new psychology of power in Britain, whereby a rampant, destructive elite is willing to ransack democracy for its own gain.

There may be many legitimate reasons to be 'anti-establishment' in modern British politics. Our constitutional norms, our electoral system and the rules governing the individual conduct of MPs are desperately in need of reform – and that's just for starters.

Boris Johnson's form of anti-establishment politics, however, accelerated the downward moral trajectory of Westminster.

To some extent, this democratic demolition-job has been instinctive – Johnson's genetic survival code, programmed through years of privilege and impunity in the face of his personal and political transgressions. Yet, while Johnson imposed his spirit of rampant individualism on Westminster, he was not a lone ranger.

Holed up in the townhouses of Westminster, a number of interconnected groups have spent years tainting the state – particularly attempts to intervene in the economy. They have perpetuated an ideology that proposes shedding the tax and regulatory burdens that constrain the elite and Conservative leaders, to a large degree, have merely been their useful idiots.

4 TUFTON STREET

Libertarian (adjective)
Denoting a political philosophy that advocates only minimal state intervention in the free market and the private lives of citizens.

Tufton Street is a place that knows how to keep a secret. Set in a maze of streets flanking the Palace of Westminster, the red-brick townhouses are anonymous; no corporate logos attempt to catch the curiosity of passers-by. In fact, the street itself is usually deserted. It is an ideological workshop cloistered quietly in the heart of power.

Tufton Street has been the primary command centre for libertarian lobbying groups – the 'Tufton Street network' – for the last decade or more. Shahmir Sanni, who worked for the Vote Leave pro-

Brexit referendum campaign, originally based out of 55 Tufton Street, has described a co-ordinated nexus of policy wonks and media whisperers, working towards collective aims.

At least nine such groups were based on this street in 2018, regularly holding meetings at 55 Tufton Street to "agree on a single set of right-wing talking points" and to "[secure] more exposure to the public," Sanni says.[103]

"Discussion centres around a simple idea," he claims, "that anything funded by the state is wrong."

Tufton Street is much like Fleet Street – the former habitat of the newspaper industry. While the titles that were once based there have now scattered across London, Fleet Street is still used as a shorthand phrase for the industry – much like Tufton Street in the context of the world of libertarian politics.

These organisations are bound by their support for Brexit, and their vigour for low taxes, free markets, and a smaller state. They are the civil servants of the Bullingdon Club elite – the backroom nerds who have been commissioned to formulate and popularise the political ideas that will ensure the continued success of this elite.

As Peter Geoghegan notes in *Democracy For Sale*, while rich individuals have donated extensively to right-wing politicians in recent years, this hasn't been their most effective tool in sponsoring a libertarian agenda. Rather, their true victory has been scored in "[owning] the ideas that dominate the political conversation".[104]

This has been achieved through Tufton Street

and its old fashioned political lobbying, media whispering and high-minded, pseudo-intellectual posturing. These tactics have allowed it to develop a mass market, at least in Westminster, for otherwise fringe, radical libertarian politics.

Few libertarian groups have been more successful than the TaxPayers' Alliance (TPA) and its founder, Matthew Elliott. Founded in 2004, presenting itself as an independent, grassroots pressure group representing ordinary people concerned about the misspending of their tax receipts, the TPA has garnered widespread and uncritical media coverage of its small-state agenda, which has portrayed even essential state spending as wasteful and needless.

Elliott went on to spearhead the campaign against reforming the Westminster voting system, the subject of a national referendum in 2011, and the Brexit campaign in 2016 (serving as the CEO of Vote Leave) – both of which he won.

The TPA claims that, in 2020, it raised £815,000 from 3,000 supporters – though the names of those donors are kept private.[105] *The Guardian* revealed in 2018 that the organisation had received £223,300 in the previous five years from big US-based donors, including the Atlas Network – an ensemble of more than 500 likeminded, libertarian institutions worldwide. The Atlas Network awarded the TPA a $100,000 prize for campaigning for lower taxes, notably the cuts to corporation and income tax initiated by David Cameron's Coalition Government.[106]

"From its early days, the Alliance's

pronouncements were invoked by news outlets more or less as the impartial mouthpiece of the hardworking taxpayer," writes Owen Jones in *The Establishment*. "What was more, the Alliance had from the outset a highly professional relationship with journalists: a press officer available 24 hours a day, and TV-friendly spokespeople available for rolling new channels at a moment's notice. Rather than publishing long policy papers that hard-pressed journalists working to deadlines would ignore, the Alliance issued snappy research notes that got straight to the point."[107]

I witnessed this first hand as a naïve young reporter, in 2016, when applying for a job at an ostensibly 'impartial' political news website. Pulled in for a trial shift, I was asked by the editor to write up a TPA press release, critical of a major rail project, as a news story. Keen to get the job (which I ultimately turned down), I duly obliged.

These tactics have been shared, through the institutional osmosis described by Sanni, with the other members of the Tufton Street network. Spokespeople for these organisations will be familiar to even casual consumers of BBC political programmes, such has been their ubiquity in recent years. The Institute for Economic Affairs (IEA), the Centre for Policy Studies (CPS) and the Adam Smith Institute (ASI), have all been featured regularly on our national broadcaster and elsewhere, despite still-unanswered questions about their major donors.

These think tanks – the most opaque in Westminster – have received £14.3 million in the last two years alone. Indeed, the TPA, IEA, CPS and ASI have all been given the worst rating for think tank funding transparency by *openDemocracy*'s 'Who Funds You?' project – which campaigns for greater openness in this sphere. None of these groups openly declare their donors.[108]

From what we know, however, there appears to be a close relationship between big corporate interests and the Tufton Street network. The IEA, for example, has received funding from the energy giants BP and Exxon Mobil, as well as British American Tobacco.[109] Multiple groups belonging to the Tufton Street network have also received money from organisations linked to American fossil fuel interests.[110]

The head of the IEA, Mark Littlewood, was recorded in 2018 telling an undercover reporter posing as a donor that, in exchange for substantial donations, they would be able to attend "intimate" private dinners and lunches, at which attendees "get to know Cabinet ministers on first name terms".

Littlewood explained that meeting with the agriculture minister would provide him and his client with the opportunity to "bend [their] ear about beef".

Speaking to the BBC about these allegations, Littlewood defended his actions, saying that: "My job is to meet other free-market people to try and persuade them to give me some money so my institute can conduct free-market research so that we can influence debate and opinion in society... I have no power over ministers. I'm not a chief whip or a leader of a party. We can't promise people any access at all. The IEA has done spectacularly well in engaging with politicians."[111]

Littlewood seemed to be simultaneously boasting of the IEA's ability to influence the public sphere, while downplaying the specific allegations – a precarious balancing act.

A wealth of other evidence exists, however, showing how these groups have become deeply embedded in the Conservative Party. The board of the CPS includes – at the time of writing – ex-Tory Treasurer (and major party donor) Lord Michael Spencer, chair of the Conservative 1922 Committee Sir Graham Brady, aforementioned major party donor Lord Andrew Bamford, former Conservative Party Chair Ben Elliot, editor of *The Spectator* magazine Fraser Nelson, and co-author of the 2019 Conservative Manifesto, Rachel Wolf. Her fellow co-author, Robert Colvile, is the director of the CPS.

The CPS website proudly claims that it "was responsible for developing the bulk of the policy agenda that became known as Thatcherism" and contributed towards "the curbing of the power of the trade unions, the privatisation revolution, the shrinking of the state and Britain's embrace of entrepreneurship."

While these outfits maintain a facade of intellectualism, in order to lend gravitas to their economic radicalism, the Tufton Street network is also well-trained in less cultivated methods of attack.

The media mouthpiece of the network is *Guido Fawkes* – a scrappy right-wing blog founded in

2004 by Paul Staines, with a reported 50 million visits to the site in 2017.[112] *Guido* is unashamed in its libertarian ambitions – it is "anti-politics", according to its website, which adopts a tabloid style as a "deliberate and necessary step towards becoming popular". The blog has become infamous for publishing gossipy, biased and occasionally intrusive articles to embarrass anyone not on the hard-right of the political spectrum. Staines set up a pro-Johnson campaign – 'Boris on the Ballot' – prior to the 2019 Conservative leadership election, and *Guido* stubbornly refused to report on the endemic cronyism and waste committed by Johnson's Government, despite its libertarian tastes.[113]

And, largely thanks to the efforts of Liz Truss, the Government has in recent years been infiltrated by the ideas and the personnel of well-funded Tufton Street think tanks.

In October 2020, for example, *Guido* gleefully reported that Truss, at the time serving as International Trade Secretary, had appointed "a swathe of free market think tankers" to her "refreshed Strategic Trade Advisory Group" – a forum of businesses and academics, which meets regularly to consider the UK's international trade policies.

These appointments included: Littlewood, the aforementioned director general of the IEA; Matt Kilcoyne, former deputy director at the ASI; and Colvile, the aforementioned director of the CPS.[114]

Lord Daniel Hannan, one of the forefathers of Brexit, had also been appointed as an advisor to the Board of Trade – a commercial body within the Department for International Trade – a month earlier. His Initiative for Free Trade was formerly based at 57 Tufton Street, sharing the address with Colvile's CPS, based around the corner from the IEA.

A month before Hannan's appointment, in August 2020, Truss had recruited eight advisors to recommend locations for new, post-Brexit 'freeports'. These are areas of the country where normal tax and customs rules do not apply. Two of these advisors were senior members of Tufton Street think tanks. One was Tom Clougherty – head of tax at the CPS. Clougherty was previously executive director of the ASI, as well as managing editor at the libertarian Reason Foundation in the US.

The freeports policy, a libertarian fascination, is said to heighten the risk of money laundering and tax evasion.[115]

This Tufton Street alliance continued when Truss entered Downing Street, with core members of her team drawn from the Tufton Street network.

Sophie Jarvis – previously head of government affairs at the ASI – was a special advisor to Truss at the Department for International Trade and the Foreign Office. Jarvis worked on Truss's Conservative leadership campaign, and was hired immediately as her Number 10 political secretary.

Hugh Bennett, formerly news editor of *Guido Fawkes*, was also a fellow traveller on Truss's leadership campaign, before moving with her to Downing Street. Bennett first left *Guido* to work as an advisor to Jacob Rees-Mogg, before being appointed as an aide to Boris Johnson and then moving to the Foreign Office. Prior to joining *Guido*, Bennett was a Vote Leave staffer and also the deputy editor of the *Brexit Central* blog, itself based out of Tufton Street.[116]

Truss's first chief economic advisor, Matt Sinclair, spent six years working for the TPA, eventually serving as its CEO. In 2010, Sinclair edited and co-authored the book *How to Cut Public Spending (And Still Win an Election)*.

Other Tufton Street alumni who made the jump to Downing Street under Truss included Caroline Elsom, hired as the Prime Minister's health advisor, previously head of education and enterprise at the CPS; and Ruth Porter, hired as Truss's deputy chief of staff, who was formerly communications director of the IEA. A further nine Tufton Street graduates were scattered in senior positions across Whitehall, after Truss's brief elevation to the top job.[117]

Indeed, the alliance between Truss and Tufton Street goes back more than a decade, with the IEA's Littlewood – an old university friend – claiming after her selection as Conservative leader and Prime Minister that Truss had spoken at IEA events more than "any other politician over the past 12 years".[118] Just a year after entering Parliament, Truss created the 'Free Enterprise Group' of backbench Conservatives "to renew the case for genuine free markets and free enterprise" – an endeavour that was supported by the IEA.[119]

And the political philosophy of Tufton Street was on full display during the then-Chancellor Kwasi Kwarteng's mini budget on 23 September 2022.

It announced an income tax cut for those earning more than £150,000 a year – a policy subsequently reversed – as well as halting national insurance rises, cutting stamp duty, and proposing low-tax, low-regulation zones across the country.

As former Downing Street advisor Tim Montgomerie said in the wake of Kwarteng's statement: this was "a massive moment for [the IEA]. They've been advocating these policies for years. They incubated Truss and Kwarteng during their early years as MPs. Britain is now their laboratory".

At its most essential, fringe ideologues with radical, free market views on economics have been paid to become professional libertarians, likely by big corporations and billionaires – people and firms with a vested interest in a smaller state, less regulation and lower taxes.

The latest British Social Attitudes survey showed that 58% of people in the UK are economically left-wing, while 67% of people agree that ordinary working people do not get their fair share of the nation's wealth and even 46% of Conservative supporters back increased government spending.[120]

Yet, the 2020 Tax Commission produced by the TPA, chaired by *Sunday Telegraph* editor (and Truss fanboy) Allister Health and edited by Matthew Sinclair, proposed the abolition of inheritance tax and the creation of a single income tax band fixed at 33%. This would replace the current progressive tax system, whereby higher incomes are charged higher rates of tax.[121]

In other words, there is no silent majority for the

uncontrolled free market, yet the political system has been rigged by dark money donors who have inflated the influence of radical, right-wing ideas.

The economic theory behind these libertarian policies is to boost the income of supposed 'wealth generators' who will be able to invest and spend more – ultimately growing the size of the economy and increasing tax revenues. It is also hoped that diminished financial and bureaucratic restrictions on planning will increase the supply of homes and infrastructure.

The mini budget borrowed from the most radical strain of right-wing thought; a clear departure from the Johnson era of state spending and 'levelling up' left behind parts of the country through government intervention.

As a result of the tax measures outlined by Kwarteng, the Government effectively proposed handing £1 billion to just 2,500 people, each of whom have an income in excess of £3.5 million. People earning £1 million a year were expected to benefit by £55,000 a-year – twice the average UK salary.[122]

Households in London and the south-east were likewise expected to gain three times as much on average (£1,600) from the mini-budget as those living in Wales, the north-east of England and Yorkshire (£500). A 50-year-old earning £1 million a year, it was predicted, would have been forced to pay a lower marginal tax rate than a 28-year-old earning £50,000 (largely due to the latter's student-loan repayments).[123]

In less than a fortnight, Truss and Kwarteng

dismantled Johnson's post-2016 political project – abandoning the promise, however vague and insincere, of greater economic equality. These libertarian policies caused market chaos, with the pound plummeting to new lows against the dollar. Ironically, the new and short-lived Prime Minister and Chancellor had violated one of the core principles of *Britannia Unchained*, that they had co-authored a decade earlier, "Governments that lose control of their finances eventually lose control of their own destiny."[124]

Truss and Kwarteng wrote *Britannia Unchained* in the wake of the financial crash and the Coalition Government's subsequent imposition of tough austerity policies. And, in keeping with this small-state spirit, Truss was an enthusiastic supporter of restrained public spending throughout her Cabinet career.

In her first week as Foreign Secretary, she signed off drastic foreign aid cuts to war-torn states, while reducing funding on the environment and gender equality. Syria received £48 million in overseas aid in the 2021 to 2022 financial year, compared to £154 million the previous year. Yemen, still suffering from a civil war that began in 2014, saw its budget cut from £221 million to £82.4 million.[125] It has been estimated that more than 80% of Yemenis now live below the poverty line and that half of the population face a clear and present danger of imminent famine.[126]

In total, overseas aid to Commonwealth countries has been slashed by £500 million, despite claims made during the Brexit campaign that leaving the

EU would strengthen our ties with its 53 member states.[127] Indeed, in October 2019, Truss told Commonwealth ministers and high commissioners that "we can and must seize the opportunity Brexit presents to take advantage of new partnerships with some of our oldest allies across the Commonwealth."

Cuts within the Foreign Office were also approved by Truss, with the department reportedly set to reduce its staff numbers by 20% in four years – a move former Foreign Office Permanent Secretary Lord Ricketts has called "completely incompatible" with the Government's rhetoric about 'Global Britain'.[128]

This mirrored Truss's approach to public spending cuts in 2015 when, as Environment Secretary, she was one of the first ministers to accept the reduction in departmental funding proposed by then Chancellor George Osborne. Her department faced funding cuts of between 25% and 40%, but Truss insisted that it was "a big opportunity".[129]

As a result, £24 million was cut from the fund that ensured the surveillance of water companies, to prevent the dumping of raw sewage into our waterways.[130]

At the time, *Guardian* writer and environmental journalist George Monbiot described Truss as "impervious to argument, facts or experience".[131]

"I'm probably one of the more ideological among my colleagues... that's what motivates me," Truss told *Politico*, justifying Monbiot's analysis.[132]

A small state ethos is built on the false conviction – proven repeatedly in recent history – that the free market, unencumbered by the interventions of fat-fingered bureaucrats, is both moral and rational. Capital is king in the Tufton Street worldview, subjugating ordinary people and even democracy itself.

As political scientist Francis Fukuyama now argues: neoliberalism, of the sort advocated by Truss and her Thatcher devotees, has produced "grotesque inequalities" by hardening the belief in free exchange to the point where "the doctrine becomes, so to speak, doctrinaire".[133]

The 'free' market is not liberating; it is inherently biased, exploitative and unfair.

Nor does it create economic growth – the golden yardstick that Truss has set as her personal, political mission. Though David Cameron is considered by the media to be a relatively centrist Conservative, his austerity agenda was a more concerted and damaging iteration of the free market philosophies continued by Truss. By shrinking the size of the state and limiting borrowing and investment at a time of record low interest rates, Cameron and his chancellor George Osborne hamstrung the economy. If our economy had grown at its pre-austerity rate it would be a third larger in 2027 than it is otherwise expected to be.[134]

As argued by left-wing economist James Meadway: "Austerity was the biggest, most sustained economic policy error any British government has ever committed. It was stupidity piled on stupidity, a self-inflicted, self-imposed disaster."[135]

Yet, impervious to facts, free market ideas have continued to find fertile ground in Westminster.

This is partly due to the institutional power of Tufton Street – a battering-ram for corporate interests. Underpinning the obdurate popularity of libertarianism on the Tory benches, however, has been the entanglement of 'freedom' philosophies with a conspiratorial mindset, demonising the experts who have anticipated and tracked the failure of free market austerity economics.

This process has also been witnessed in the realm of healthcare, during the COVID crisis. While there was near-universal support for the first lockdown in March 2020 – all politicians and commentators agreeing that we needed to protect vulnerable people from this novel and deadly threat – lockdowns soon became a 'wedge' issue for the right; a cause through which they could signal their zeal for small government.

It is now a common belief on the right of the Conservative Party (and all those even further to the right) that it was a mistake to impose lockdowns. Lord David Frost, for example, a thought-leader on the radical-right of politics due to his affinity with Brexit, has said that they were a "serious public policy mistake".[136]

It has been estimated by the National Institute of Health and Care Research that national lockdowns saved more than three million lives in Europe during the first wave alone.[137] Yet, anti-lockdown hysteria was growing rapidly during the autumn of 2020, just after this unparalleled international effort to save lives.

On 31 August 2020 there were 1,406 new cases of

COVID logged in the UK. By Saturday 19 September, this figure had climbed steeply to 4,422.

Boris Johnson was faced with a recurrent dilemma – either impose restrictions early and aggressively, as the Government's advisors recommended, or attempt to confound the virus with a series of creative yet epidemiologically questionable half-measures.

So, the Prime Minister sought counsel. The Government's official experts, the Scientific Advisory Group for Emergencies (SAGE), recommended a rapid, time-limited 'circuit breaker' lockdown to restrain the growth of the virus. This option, according to reports, was backed by Johnson's chief aide Dominic Cummings and senior Cabinet minister Michael Gove.[138]

Then-Chancellor Rishi Sunak, architect of the nation's 'eat out to help out' binge, disagreed. According to reports, he organised a summit between Johnson and several lockdown-sceptic scientists, to broadcast another point of view.

Government records have firmly confirmed the existence of this meeting – and reveal its full cast.[139]

First on the guest list was Professor Carl Heneghan, director of the University of Oxford's Centre for Evidence-Based Medicine. Speaking to Sky News on 20 September, Professor Heneghan warned against a circuit-breaker, claiming that lockdowns slow down the progression of the virus "slightly" and then lead to a "resurgence". Instead, he advocated allowing COVID to pass through the population to build up natural levels of immunity, while in theory shielding the vulnerable.[140]

This strategy, commonly known as 'herd immunity' has several fundamental flaws. Namely: in a highly mobile society, it is virtually impossible to shield the vulnerable. That's why deaths remained high, even during lockdown. There's also a lack of evidence about the endurance of immunity levels after infection, and whether people can be reinfected with the disease. What's more, a rampant virus increases the likelihood of variants emerging that evade immunity and vaccines.

Yet some scientists still subscribed to the herd immunity mantra – including Sunetra Gupta, professor of theoretical epidemiology at the Department of Zoology, University of Oxford – who was also present at the 21 September summit with Johnson and Sunak.

On the same day as the meeting, Gupta and Heneghan had co-authored a letter, published by *The Spectator* magazine – formerly edited by Johnson – calling on the Prime Minister to "urgently rethink" his COVID strategy.[141]

It said that Johnson's approach, of suppressing the virus until the development of a vaccine, was both "unfeasible" and would lead to "significant harm across all age groups".

Instead, the letter proposed, the Prime Minister should apply "targeted measures" to protect the vulnerable – such as people in care homes – while avoiding lockdowns. The letter did not explain how or why the authors believed care home residents had not been protected during the pandemic up to that point, or what more could be done.

Gupta was one of the three lead signatories to the Great Barrington Declaration – a document that codified the antipathy of some scientists towards lockdowns – and a bible for lockdown-sceptics across the West. The Great Barrington Declaration was incubated by a libertarian think-tank based in the US – the American Institute for Economic Research – partly funded by the Charles Koch Foundation.[142] One of the infamous Koch brothers, Charles is the 13th richest person in the world and the CEO of the second largest privately owned business in America, invested heavily in fossil fuels.[143]

The Great Barrington Declaration proposed "shielding" the vulnerable, likewise without explaining how exactly this could be achieved. It said that the virus should be allowed to pass through the rest of the population – theoretically avoiding lockdowns.

An international outlook was provided at the Downing Street meeting by Sweden's chief epidemiologist, Anders Tegnell. Under the direction of Tegnell, Sweden was an international outlier during the pandemic and imposed only relatively mild public restrictions.

At this pivotal moment in Britain's supposed war effort against COVID, it was these three scientists who lobbied the Prime Minister and the Chancellor – joined on the call by SAGE member Professor John Edmunds, and Professor Dame Angela McLean, chief scientific advisor to the Ministry of Defence.

We don't know what was said during the meeting – the minutes are not publicly available – but we know the outcome. Not for the first time during the crisis, the Prime Minister's pendulum swung.

Rather than favouring a short, sharp lockdown, Johnson spoke to the nation on 22 September and announced peripheral alterations to the Government's rules – banning more than six people from meeting and announcing a 10pm curfew on pubs and restaurants. The latter policy was soon ridiculed, after hundreds of people were seen flocking onto pavements and trains at closing time, like school children bouncing out of a classroom.

Johnson was later quoted as saying – though this has not been firmly verified – that he would rather have seen "bodies pile high" than take the country into another lockdown. According to Cummings, in testimony provided to MPs, Johnson believed that he had made a mistake in applying strict lockdown restrictions during the early pandemic. "I should have been the mayor of *Jaws* and kept the beaches open," Johnson said, according to Cummings.[144]

During the autumn period, a new, more contagious variant of the disease – first identified in September – made an appearance in the south of England. Left to multiply in the fertile conditions of stuffy London pubs, the variant fuelled burgeoning daily case rates, standing at 35,028 on 20 December, when thousands of people were pictured desperately evacuating the capital ahead of Christmas.

On 4 January 2021, the Prime Minister announced a new national lockdown. Daily deaths peaked two weeks later at 1,251.

Contrary to the beliefs of Heneghan and Gupta,

suppression and mass vaccination has ultimately been the only course of action available to the Government, to stave off unconscionable death and the implosion of the NHS.

Without a vaccine, herd immunity was not achieved, nor was it ever going to be.

Yet herd immunity had familiar roots: emerging from newspapers and opaquely funded think tanks set up to defend the interests of the ruling class – presented both as intellectually robust and an expression of popular will – lapped up uncritically by politicians cut from the same cloth, carried into Downing Street and imposed on the nation.

In an additional quirk of the autumn wranglings, the Prime Minister spent the days before and after his non-announcement on 22 September 2020 meeting with right-wing newspaper editors and proprietors – one of the most vocal lobbies against lockdown restrictions. After all, people don't buy newspapers if they don't leave the house.

From 18 to 23 September, Johnson met with Rupert Murdoch, Rebekah Brooks and Victoria Newton (of News Corp, owners of *The Sun*, *The Times*, talkRadio and Talk TV), Lord Rothermere (owner of the Mail Group) and *Daily Mail* editor Geordie Greig, Aidan and Howard Barclay (owners of *The Telegraph*) and the paper's editor Chris Evans, and editor of *The Spectator* Fraser Nelson.[145]

The BBC was the only other outlet to gain access to Johnson in this period – via a meeting with director-general Tim Davie and director of BBC News Fran Unsworth.

Yet, a whirlwind of bile is directed at those who suggest that there is a well-funded and well-connected group of think-tanks, journalists, publications and politicians whose primary ambition is to promote radical anti-government, pro-capital politics.

Certainly, this was the reaction faced by *The Observer* journalist Carole Cadwalladr, who was subjected to prolonged and visceral abuse when she exposed how this network was working in lockstep to deliver Brexit and the election of Donald Trump as President of the US.

In actual fact, Donald Trump's 2016 campaign chief and White House chief strategist, Steve Bannon, tried to buy *Guido Fawkes*, the platform that has led the demonisation campaign against Cadwalladr for her work in exposing the wrongdoing of Cambridge Analytica.[146]

Guido is fervently supportive of Brexit, a supposedly patriotic project, yet the publication is not actually based in the UK. Instead, "the hosting is in the United States of America under the protection of the First Amendment to the Constitution," its website states. The first amendment guarantees the right to freedom of speech.

This is particularly ironic, given that *Guido Fawkes* has repeatedly mocked Cadwalladr for being sued for defamation by Arron Banks, a major funder of the Leave.EU referendum campaign. *Guido* appears to have attempted to liberate itself from the UK's draconian libel laws, that have for decades favoured the ruling class over truth tellers, and yet has no shame in deriding a journalist who was taken to court under these laws.

Guido Fawkes editor Paul Staines has confessed that Bannon made an offer for the publication that was ultimately rejected.[147] The value of Bannon's offer for *Guido Fawkes* is not known, nor do we know when Bannon made the offer. The deal "fell through over price," Staines told the *Press Gazette*. "I never could work out whether we were talking dollars or sterling".

This process would have been easier if Bannon had bid in 2022. Thanks to the reforms implemented by Truss and supported by Staines, at the time of writing the two currencies are basically the same value.

Prior to formally joining Donald Trump's 2016 election campaign, Bannon was the co-founder and executive chairman of *Breitbart*, a US-based news and opinion website that he has called "the platform for the alt-right".[148]

Bannon was also the co-founder and vice-chairman of Cambridge Analytica, the disgraced big-data firm that harvested the information of Facebook users – without their permission – to build psychological profiles of voters so they could be targeted with political adverts.[149] Cambridge Analytica was owned largely by the Mercer family, which also co-owns *Breitbart*.

Back in December 2013, both Staines and his news reporter, Harry Cole (now political editor of *The Sun*), attended a weekend conference hosted by the libertarian Young Britons Foundation in Cambridge, alongside Bannon.[150] According to the whistleblower Chris Wylie, Cambridge Analytica's former head of research, the big data firm was at this time launching a temporary office in the university city.

Cambridge Analytica was ultimately based in London and led by Alexander Nix – educated, like Johnson, at Eton. A decade younger than Johnson, the Cambridge Analytica CEO was a sharp dresser and a smooth talker – picture a less approachable Tom Hiddleston (incidentally also an Old Etonian) – his sharp jaw and quick tongue ripped straight from the pages of Ian Fleming.

Yet, as in the case of Johnson, Nix's superficial charisma masked his murky dealings. His charmed life was upended when journalists secretly filmed Nix and his fellow executives claiming that Cambridge Analytica had campaigned in elections across the world, boasting about using stings, ex-spies, fake IDs and sex workers.[151]

In one exchange, when asked about digging up material on political opponents, Nix said that they could "send some girls around to the candidate's house", adding that Ukrainian girls "are very beautiful... I find that works very well."

The company, which folded in May 2018, claimed that it had not in fact used these tactics in real political campaigns.

Cadwalladr reported that Cambridge Analytica worked on the pro-Brexit campaign, with Leave.EU's former communications director Andy Wigmore saying that Cambridge Analytica was "more than happy to help... we shared a lot of information."[152]

The official Vote Leave campaign, fronted by Johnson, also spent a substantial amount of its online campaigning budget through the Canadian agency AggregateIQ (AIQ), a spin-off business linked to SCL, Cambridge Analytica's parent company. AIQ managed Cambridge Analytica's technology platform – Ripon – and its databases.[153]

Cambridge Analytica's managing director, Mark Turnbull, was captured talking about the company's approach to digital campaigns – saying that "it's no good fighting an election campaign on the facts, because actually it's all about emotion."[154]

Turnbull boasted of disseminating sophisticated, negative attack adverts through proxy organisations in order to assist their favoured candidates. Nix added that: "it sounds a dreadful thing to say, but these are things that don't necessarily need to be true, as long as they are believed."

For his part, Bannon left the White House in August 2017 and subsequently claimed that he was advising Johnson in his attempts to wrest control from then Prime Minister Theresa May.

Filmed on the day of Johnson's first speech after resigning as May's Foreign Secretary, Bannon said that: "Today we are going to see if Boris Johnson tries to overthrow the British Government. He's going to give a speech in the Commons... I've been talking to him all weekend about this speech. We went back and forth over text."

Bannon further claimed that he spent time with Johnson after the 2016 US Presidential Election when he was working as Trump's chief strategist. "Right after we won, Boris flew over. Because their victory was as unexpected as ours. I got to know him quite well in the transition period," he said.[155]

There is now a large body of evidence proving the existence of a trans-Atlantic libertarian coalition. Indeed, the playbook for the rolling maul that has bundled free market philosophies into the heart of British politics was imported from America.

"A tiny group of American plutocrats [has] invested billions in think tanks, universities and election campaigns over the last four decades," notes Peter Geoghegan.

"Before this methodical and precisely targeted spending spree, libertarians had been largely thought of as cranks. Afterwards, the limited space within which policies are created and publicly discussed was filled with proposals that they wanted. The deregulation of Ronald Reagan and George H. and George W. Bush often came straight from blueprints drawn up by libertarian institutes," he adds.[156]

This notably includes the ideas sponsored by the Koch brothers, described by Jane Mayer in *Dark Money* as 'the Kochtopus': a "multi-armed" assembly line that has promoted radical, anti-tax, anti-regulation, anti-state politics "from idea creation to policy development to education to grassroots organisations to lobbying to political action."

The Koch brothers and their ideological allies have formed a "new generation of philanthropist, bent on using billions of dollars from their private foundations" to "remake America along the lines of their beliefs," Mayer writes.

The institutions they have funded, she claims, have lobbied for "drastically lower personal and corporate taxes, minimal social services for the needy, and much less oversight of industry, particularly in the environmental arena."

The brothers "said they were driven by principle," Mayer writes, "but their positions dovetailed seamlessly with their personal financial interests."[157]

Tufton Street think tanks and their ideological allies have raised at least $9 million from American donors since 2012, *openDemocracy* has estimated.[158]

And there are plenty more nodes in this radical, libertarian alliance – on full view on 30 January 2020, when a host of 'journalists' and activists met at a Mayfair hotel to celebrate a historic political moment: the UK's departure from the EU. Each table cover was decorated with a commemorative programme, emblazoned with the words, "The Brexit Battalion (Media Corps)", which listed the names of those present.

Every right-wing publication was well represented on the list, with some of their most prominent journalists essentially admitting that they were campaigners for a political cause rather than objective purveyors of the truth.

Meanwhile, as the Brexit forever war continues to crackle in the margins of British politics and COVID recedes from public debate, the radical right has adopted a new campaign: climate change scepticism.

Former Prime Minister David Cameron attempted to repackage the Conservative Party as an environmentalist movement in 2006 – encouraging

Britons to "vote blue, go green" while changing the party's logo to a tree. However, their words have not always translated into deeds.

Johnson in particular has flirted with climate denial; he once wrote that "there is no evidence that the planet is suffering from the extreme weather patterns associated with climate change." Yet, in typical Johnsonian fashion, he later bounced headlong into the environmentalist camp, pledging to make Britain the "cleanest, greenest country on Earth".[159]

But now, in the post-Johnson era, that green ideology is falling by the wayside – at a time when it is most needed. After Johnson's resignation from Downing Street, Environment Minister (and fellow Old Etonian) Lord Zac Goldsmith warned that most of the likely Conservative leadership contenders "couldn't give a sh*t about climate and nature".[160]

Indeed, while outright climate scepticism has been unfashionable in mainstream politics, prominent right-wing think tanks and media outlets have been building a campaign against the green consensus.

The right-wing broadcasting platform *GB News*, which boasts close links to the Conservative Party – several of its MPs being *GB News* presenters – regularly platforms people who cast doubt on climate science.

Former Vote Leave stooge and right-wing activist Darren Grimes delivered a self-described "ode to oil" on his show, while fellow presenter Dan Wootton has accused the Intergovernmental Panel on Climate Change, a scientific group assembled by the UN to examine global warming, of "spreading terror".[161]

A *GB News* segment during the summer heatwave of 2022 – in which the presenters told a meteorologist to stop doom-mongering about the climate – was widely compared to a scene from the Netflix satire *Don't Look Up*, which is based on the widespread denial that a comet is set to destroy Earth.

The *Daily Mail*, likewise a lodestar for Conservative thought, published a front page around the same time claiming that "sunny day snowflake Britain" was having a "meltdown" over the threat of rising temperatures. The next day, images of burning buildings in London led its front page.

This process – of influential right-wing thinkers and publications questioning mainstream scientific opinion – has echoes in the lockdown-sceptic movement.

Indeed, while the rationale for locking-down was accepted universally at the beginning of the crisis, a slow tide of resistance grew as the pandemic unfolded.

It appears that the same process of gradual radicalisation and science scepticism is taking place in relation to the climate crisis – with the consensus of opinion now fracturing on the Conservative benches. An investigation by *The Independent* in November 2021 found that one-in-15 Conservative MPs have expressed views that suggest they do not believe that climate change is real.[162]

This climate dissent has once again emanated

from Tufton Street and the elaborate network of lobbying groups whose tentacles stretch far into the Conservative Party.

Important to this story is the Global Warming Policy Foundation (GWPF), which overlaps with the Tufton Street lobbying groups that have such influence over the Conservative Party. It is dubbed the UK's "principal climate science denial campaign group" by *DeSmog*, a news outlet dedicated to combatting climate misinformation.

Founded by former Conservative Chancellor Lord Nigel Lawson, the GWPF posted a gross income of £387,490 for the year ending September 2021 – up from £374,330 in 2020, despite a drop of 21.9% in funds from lay members.[163]

The GWPF has said that it seeks to debate the supposedly "contested" science of global warming and is "deeply concerned about the costs and other implications of many of the policies currently being advocated."

In the past 11 years, the organisation has received £4.2 million in funding, while the group's income from big money donations dwarfs that of any other type. From membership fees, £134,000 has been raised since 2010, compared to almost £4 million from individual donations.[164]

The GWPF is based in 55 Tufton Street – the command centre of Westminster's libertarian lobbying groups – and does not openly declare its donors.

As we already know, Truss is closely associated with various libertarian think tanks, and endorsed their environmental stances during her short tenure in Downing Street. One of her first moves when she entered the top job was to remove the ban on fracking – the environmentally-controversial practice of drilling for gas and oil. This echoed the IEA's championing of the practice.[165] She also proposed banning solar farms on agricultural land and expanding North Sea oil and gas drilling.

This apathetic attitude to the climate emergency has been echoed by other Tufton Street think tanks, portraying climate policies as another way in which the state is seeking to extend its power.

"Any serious effort [to push on net zero] will be beset by vested interests – both people pleading for money for their pet projects and the 'green blob' seeking to lure the Government into ever more interfering, meddling, regulating and taxing in the name of saving the planet. And nothing will ever be enough for Greta, who will continue to howl green murder," CPS director Robert Colvile wrote for the *Sunday Times* in January 2020.[166]

Within Parliament itself, Conservative MP Steve Baker has been close to the GWPF, joining its board of trustees in May 2021 and receiving substantial donations from Neil Record, chair of the GWPF (and the IEA).[167] An ideological ally of Truss, Baker left the GWPF board to take up the role of Northern Ireland Minister, but not before establishing a new frontier in the battle against Britain's net zero carbon emissions targets.

In July 2022, Baker hosted a relaunch event for the Thatcherite-era campaigning group, Conservative

Way Forward (CWF), that attended by Conservative leadership hopefuls Suella Braverman and Nadhim Zahawi.

CWF was originally launched in 1991 to "defend and build upon the achievements of the Conservative Party under Margaret Thatcher's leadership, and to adapt the principles of her era in government to modern concerns and challenges."

Baker stated that his ultimate objective for CWF was to "redefine the territory on which the Conservative Party operates" – cementing the libertarian wing as the new "centre ground" of the party.[168]

Both Braverman and Zahawi publicly backed a 'Charter for Tax Cuts' promoted by CWF, written by 'independent economist' Julian Jessop. While now self-employed, Jessop was, until December 2018, the chief economist at the aforementioned IEA.

The CWF pamphlet calls for expansive tax cuts, reductions in fuel VAT, and the suspension of green levies on energy bills designed to fund renewables.

CWF favourite Braverman openly committed to scrapping the Government's net-zero plans during the Conservative leadership contest, stating that: "In order to deal with the energy crisis we need to suspend the all-consuming desire to achieve net zero by 2050. If we keep it up, especially before businesses and families can adjust, our economy will end up with net-zero growth."[169]

The UK has some of the highest public levels of concern in the world regarding the climate crisis, with 81% of people 'believing' in the climate emergency, and 77% saying that we must do 'everything necessary, urgently as a response'. The climate crisis consistently ranks in polls as one of the British public's top concerns.[170]

Despite their endless hand-wringing about 'the will of the people' after the Brexit vote, these libertarian forces are in fact attempting to override British democracy. Funded by opaque donors – likely, as the evidence has shown, by big corporations and vested interests – they are attempting to bounce politicians into supporting a range of ideas that are not popular among the British public.

Voters want to see a more active state dealing with regional and wealth inequalities, while acting aggressively and immediately to ensure the sustainability of the planet. The Tufton Street cabal advocates the opposite: rolling back the frontiers of the state and in turn increasing levels of poverty in Britain, dropping our net-zero targets, and dismantling the social democratic consensus that gave birth to the welfare state.

This is the agenda of the Bullingdon Club elite, disseminated across Westminster by groups that are paid for – insofar as we know – by the very people who have a financial interest in exacerbating inequalities and staving off climate action.

It has been said that 'Global Britain' Brexiters were attempting to turn Britain into Singapore-on-Thames, but I think it's more accurate to describe their end goal as Texas-on-Thames. The American affiliations of Tufton Street think tanks and the policies that they advocate signal a yearning for the deregulated neoliberalism of the US, with its insurance-based health system, its elevation of corporate interests above the common good, and deep structural inequalities between rich and poor.

Tufton Street provides the philosophical facade for a ruthlessly self-interested agenda. It acts as the buffer between the corporate elite and policymakers; an ideological laundering service for the super-rich. Moreover, although the influence of these think tanks may diminish after Truss's departure from Downing Street, the Bullingdon Club elite will still seek to preserve its wealth, and will always find new projects to fund – ones that will continue to argue for rampant libertarianism, regardless of its cost to the nation.

5 POLITICS, PRIVATISED

Big business has been exalted by successive governments seemingly under the belief that a large company can run public services better than the state.

Meanwhile, ministers have swallowed the fallacy that the private sector thrives when the state departs the playing field altogether, taking bureaucracy and regulation with it.

So, partly due to this idolisation of the corporate world – and the propensity of our lawmakers to value self-interest above public interest – democracy itself is increasingly being captured by private interests. Politicians are no longer the policemen of a corporate elite; they belong to it.

Washington DC, the US capital, is often portrayed as a playground for billionaires, with parties and candidates engaged in a constant fundraising cycle, flogging their future political influence to businessmen and lobbyists.

Because the US system is so indebted to corporate interests, Westminster is generally seen as a place relatively free from the corrupting influence of big money. Yet, private wealth does swirl around the UK political system, and – in recent years – it has largely ended up in the coffers of the Conservative Party.

The 2019 General Election campaign attracted roughly £19 million in donations from individuals and £6.5 million from companies, £19.4 million (76%) of which ended up with the Conservative Party. Much of the rest, £4.2 million, was funnelled to Nigel Farage's Brexit Party.[171]

Labour, by contrast, received little more than £350,000 from individuals and private enterprises.

Tory donors evidently seek to further the party's ideological cause. However, many donations are unlikely to be purely altruistic, especially given that rewards – such as access to senior ministers – are offered in exchange for financial generosity.

The Conservative Party has created a system of incentives for big-money donors, offering perks to individuals who donate the most.

More than 80% of Conservative funding in the first week of the 2019 election campaign came from members of the 'Leader's Group' – an elite dining society reserved for the most generous Conservative donors. Its members are those who have donated at least £50,000 to the party in a single year. In exchange, they can attend exclusive events with senior Cabinet members and Conservative grandees.[172]

OpenDemocracy revealed in November 2019 that Boris Johnson had attended at least six meetings of the Leader's Group since 2016, while the summits were regularly held at official government residences.

"A little bit of money goes a long way," ex-Conservative MP Guto Bebb is quoted as saying, in Peter Geoghegan's *Democracy For Sale*. "We are not America. You don't have to spend half a billion on a general election campaign."[173]

But membership of the Leader's Group is not the highest honour that a Conservative donor can expect. As the *Sunday Times* reported in February 2022, a group of big money Conservative donors has been given direct access to Downing Street officials – and even the Prime Minister – by virtue of their patronage.

"It was implied that what we said would go straight up to the Prime Minister," one witness to the meetings said. "It was a two-way street. They [Downing Street] gave us information on what was going on. We gave our advice."[174]

These individuals – who include Lubov Chernukhin, the wife of Russia's former deputy finance minister – used their political access to lobby for 'pro-business' policies during the pandemic, according to the *Sunday Times*. In other words: to lobby for more relaxed COVID restrictions.

None of the meetings were logged in official records or were minuted. "According to sources, some donors started to use meetings to lobby for their own personal or business interests," the *Sunday Times* reporting adds.

Essentially, over the last decade, the Conservative Party has instituted a system in which access to the Government is sold to the highest bidder – and the effects of this can be witnessed through its actions in power.

Take the housing market. The Conservatives have made annual promises to solve Britain's housing crisis, with little success. In part, this is because the Government's solutions have concentrated on demand rather than supply. From 'Right to Buy' to 'Help to Buy', the Government has attempted to boost the spending power of buyers, failing to address the structural supply problems in the market.

Yet, fixing these structural issues – and reducing the overall cost of housing – would of course involve confronting the vested interests in the market, particularly big housebuilders and development companies whose profits would be eroded. Between 2010 and 2020, companies and individuals with a substantial interest in housing donated £60.8 million to the Conservatives – 20% of all funds given to the party during this period.[175]

Of the dozen or so donors who gave more than £500,000 to Liz Truss's Conservative leadership campaign, there featured at least three billionaires, two property developers, a hedge fund manager, two investment bankers, a mining company, Enoch Powell's former private secretary, a former Brexit Party politician, and three members of the House of Lords.[176] This was the corporate and political establishment feeding up their prize turkey.

A housing crisis precipitated by the financial sector triggered the global economic crisis of 2008, from which Britain has barely recovered. Even so, the Government has been a passive watchman, applying new regulations to ensure financial stability, but ultimately doing little to reduce individual economic dependence on the banks. Low interest rates over the last decade have been accompanied by stagnant wages and ever-growing property prices – meaning that household debt stood, even before the cost of living crisis, at roughly 130% of disposable income, which is only marginally lower than during the financial crash.[177]

And while bankers receive eye-popping bonuses – £1.9 billion at Barclays alone in 2021 – these institutions continue to commit repeated corporate violations. As the *Byline Times* team has calculated, the banking and finance sector was found guilty for 46% of the £9.8 billion in penalties handed down by government agencies for business misconduct during the last decade.[178] An estimated 40% of the Conservative Party's income comes from the financial sector.[179]

But this fundraising process is not entirely straightforward. Indeed, the Conservative Party must dance for its dinner. So, in June 2022, Tory politicians engaged in an act for which they have become renowned in recent times: partying.

The Conservative Party's annual summer soiree was hosted at London's prestigious Victoria and Albert Museum (V&A), where senior ministers mingled with those who could afford entry. Tables at the event were snapped up for anywhere between £12,500 and £20,000.

It's not known whether wine was spilled or karaoke machines deployed as many of the details from this event have been kept secret.

But, in time-honoured Tory tradition, various prizes were auctioned to the assembled guests – the highest-value item reportedly being a dinner with former Prime Minister Boris Johnson and his two predecessors, Theresa May and David Cameron, which sold for a neat £120,000.[180] The lucky donor should have been advised to sit May and Johnson at different ends of a very long table.

Auction prizes also included an African safari trip sold for £65,000, a shooting weekend for £37,000, and a wine tasting event for £30,000 – bought by Lubov Chernukhin.

There is no legal obligation for the donors or the party to declare the identity of the fortunate recipients of the auction prizes. Party donations worth more than £7,500 must be registered with the Electoral Commission – likewise for donations worth £1,500 to local bodies – but there is no obligation to declare what the money paid for. The details above only slipped out via canny reporters sniffing around the event.

So, the Conservative Party can sell its wares in the comfort that it can easily sidestep scrutiny.

The party was asked whether and how it vets the donors who purchase auction prizes at these fundraising events – in particular those who pay for meetings with senior ministers. The *Byline Times* team did not receive a response.

Chernukhin has regularly paid for events with party grandees. She parted with £135,000 for dinner with May when she was Prime Minister, and £160,000 for the chance to play tennis with Johnson and Cameron.[181] Since 2009, the Conservative Party has earned at least £3.4 million from individual auction items at fundraising events such as the one held at the V&A, with the figure likely to be much higher.

Chernukhin has been the subject of considerable media attention in recent months and years, due to the past proximity of her husband, Vladimir Chernukhin, to the Russian regime. He served as Russia's deputy finance minister from 2000 to 2002, after which he was appointed by Vladimir Putin as the chair of a state bank.

The Chernukhin family claims that it was forced to flee Russia to the UK in 2004 after Vladimir was dismissed from his position. Chernukhin has said that none of her Conservative donations – which have exceeded £2 million in recent years – have been funded by improper means, while she has condemned Russia's invasion of Ukraine, saying that: "Putin's despotic regime has degraded to Stalinesque persecution of the Russian people. It is truly horrifying to witness the situation unfolding in Ukraine and my heart goes out to the millions of innocent Ukrainians whose lives and freedoms are in danger and those who are forced to flee their homes."

In total, Russian-linked donors have given some £5 million to the Conservatives since 2012 but – once again – the party is evasive about how it vets these individuals.[182]

The Electoral Commission says that the political party in receipt of donations is responsible for conducting permissibility checks on potential contributions, based on vague guidelines set by the commission. Donations from purely foreign sources are not allowed, but donations are allowed from citizens or company owners based in multiple jurisdictions, as long as one of those jurisdictions is the UK.

There are no national security or conflict of interest guidelines applied by the Electoral Commission to political donors. It is unknown if the Conservative Party applies any further checks to donors beyond the basic requirements set by the Electoral Commission, or whether the party turns down funds accordingly.

Just as British democracy relies on 'good chaps' in power behaving virtuously, so too does our political fundraising system rely on self-regulation – with the parties themselves tasked with rooting out suspect donors. In an age of sophisticated foreign interference from all corners of the globe, this seems like a sub-optimal system, to say the least.

As Parliament's Intelligence and Security Committee wrote in its 2020 report into Russia political interference: "Several members of the Russian elite who are closely linked to Putin are identified as being involved with charitable and/or political organisations in the UK, having donated to political parties, with a public profile which positions them to assist Russian influence operations.

"It is notable that a number of Members of the

House of Lords have business interests linked to Russia, or work directly for major Russian companies linked to the Russian state – these relationships should be carefully scrutinised, given the potential for the Russian state to exploit them."[183]

There is no evidence that any of the individuals mentioned in this chapter are working against Britain's interests or are being exploited by Putin or any other hostile actor. However, their ties – past or current – to foreign regimes, and the flimsy nature of Britain's democratic safeguards, have given pause for concern.

Johnson quipped in 2016 at the opening of a gallery displaying the work of Downing Street photographer Andrew Parsons, perhaps semi-sarcastically:

> "His mean, moody, magnificent studies of... whatever... Dave and Ed Llewellyn preparing a speech on Europe or something like that. They're auctioned, aren't they? They are auctioned for tens of thousands of pounds at Conservative fundraising balls. And I ask you, what do they think, those oligarchs in Russia, when they reach into their pockets and they lash out for these?
>
> "Do they think that they're buying influence in the Tory party, my friends? No! [audible laughter] Do they think they're buying friends in high places? No!
>
> "What are they buying?... They're buying an original, 100% authentic Parsons, to hang with the Picasso... on the wall of their super yacht."[184]

This is a naïve interpretation of political auctions, and perhaps Johnson knew it. Indeed, the porous rules on who can give to political parties are not the only loopholes in our democratic machine.

The Conservative Party – that has seen its last two prime ministers elected by the party and not the country – does not require its members to be UK citizens, nor for members to be registered to vote in this country.

Under the 'frequently asked questions' on the Conservative website, the party states that "Overseas residents are invited to join Conservatives Abroad and will be entitled to all the benefits of party membership. Your membership will be administered by Cities of London and Westminster Conservative Association".[185]

On attempting to join the Cities of London and Westminster Conservative Association, its website states explicitly that: "You do not have to be eligible to vote in the UK to join the Conservative Party or Conservatives Abroad."

It only cites the fact that donors giving £500 or more to the party must be on the UK electoral register.

"As an overseas member, you are entitled to all the benefits of party membership, including participation in the Conservative Policy Forum, attendance at party conferences and a vote in the election of the party leader," the website adds.

The terms and conditions of membership state that: "Application for membership of the Conservative Party is subject to review by the party and its constituency associations before final approval."[186]

However, minimal information is requested from prospective members (just a name, address and bank details). Given the party's liberal rules on foreign membership it therefore seems unlikely that someone would see their membership rejected on the grounds of nationality (Russian nationality, for example) – and there are seemingly few ways for the party to detect influence from malign foreign actors, given the lack of information requested.

The *Byline Times* team approached the Conservative Party to ask what safeguards are in place to ensure that foreign actors are not able to join the party *en masse*, in an attempt to influence internal party processes – including a Conservative leadership election. We did not receive a response.

By contrast, Labour's membership rules state that you are only eligible to join if you "are a British citizen or have lived in the UK for a year or more."

It is worth stating that there is no material evidence of foreign interference in internal Conservative politics, though the party doesn't release a geographic breakdown of its 200,000-strong membership.

The Tories wouldn't be the only party to have built a questionable online funding system, however. In 2019, the Electoral Commission stated that the Brexit Party's online funding system left it open to "a high and ongoing risk" of impermissible donations – potentially from foreign sources.[187] The party's fundraising system was so weak that I was able to give money to the party under the name 'Vladimir Putin'.

One of the most notorious recent demonstrations of the gaps in our political system, is the case of Evgeny Lebedev.

Lebedev is, seemingly, a party boy with an interest in politics – as a '00s hotshot on the London dinner club circuit, Lebedev was listed by high society magazine *Tatler* as one of its most eligible bachelors.[188]

Bolstered by the riches of his father, Lebedev has integrated himself into British high society – cultivating an image as a Great Gatsby figure; a refined and enigmatic member of a globe-trotting elite, with a flair for a banquet.

Elton John and Hugh Grant are known to be close friends of the Moscow-born maverick – as is Boris Johnson. Their accord began more than a decade ago, in 2009, when Evgeny Lebedev and his father, Alexander, purchased the *London Evening Standard* and *The Independent* a year later – the first investment giving them a foothold in the affairs of the capital, at the time overseen by Johnson when he was London's Mayor.

It didn't take long for Evgeny and Johnson to strike up a friendship, both prominent members of London's high-society scene. Johnson visited the Lebedevs at their palazzo near Perugia in Umbria, Italy, for four consecutive years from 2012 to 2015. These trips were paid for by Evgeny, with a Freedom of Information request showing that the 2014 trip cost £2,625 for a two-night stay. Multiplied across the four years, this represents gifts worth more than £10,000.[189]

This wasn't a passing fling, however. Despite the

paper's generally progressive, anti-Brexit editorial stance, the *Evening Standard* came out firmly in favour of the Conservatives at the 2019 General Election, running the headline: 'Vote for Boris – Corbyn is unfit to lead Britain'.[190]

Returned to Parliament with an 80-seat majority in December 2019, Johnson celebrated his landslide victory by attending Alexander Lebedev's 60th birthday party at his £6 million mansion overlooking Regent's Park in central London, the day after the result. Guests included David and Samantha Cameron, former Chancellor George Osborne, Princess Eugenie, the actors Matt Smith and Rosamund Pike, and the model Lily Cole.[191]

Johnson's reverence of Evgeny was so great that less than a year after victory, in July 2020, the newspaper baron became a member of the House of Lords – nominated by Johnson and anointed under the title 'Baron Lebedev of Hampton and Siberia'.

But this is where the story gets messy.

Johnson reportedly pressured the UK security services to reverse their assessment of Lebedev's appointment, with the initial intelligence advice being that installing him in the Upper Chamber "could be a threat to national security".[192]

Based on this assessment, the House of Lords Appointments Commission – which vets peerages – wrote to Johnson in March 2020 advising him against granting Lebedev a peerage. Two days after this advice was sent, on 19 March, Johnson met with Lebedev for a "general discussion", according to Government records.

Johnson subsequently "took a personal interest in the case" after meeting with Lebedev, reported the *Sunday Times*. "A former advisor said [that Johnson] refused to accept the verdict of the security services and would not drop the issue," the paper reported.

The minutes of this discussion between Johnson and Lebedev were not recorded. Johnson denies that he overruled security advice but has said, "it's very, very, very important that we get the message over that we're not anti-Russian."

Despite this, the Government has so far refused to release information about the decision to make Lebedev a peer, having been instructed to produce this evidence by Parliament. Lebedev has denied being a threat to national security and has called for the information relating to his appointment to be released.

The concerns, it seems, relate to his father, Alexander – the source of the family's wealth – who was a KGB officer in London from 1988 to 1992.

Following his time as a spy, Lebedev senior moved into the financial sector, amassing vast personal wealth. He was listed as the 39th richest Russian by *Forbes* in 2008, with an estimated wealth of $3.1 billion. This fortune diminished significantly, but not entirely, after one of his Russian newspapers published an exposé about President Vladimir Putin and his alleged affair with a famed gymnast.[193]

It seems, to me at least, that the Lebedevs sought an insurance policy – a way to protect their wealth and insulate themselves from Putin's retribution – by assimilating into the London elite, and courting favour with influential politicians.

For a time, this was successful. Luke Harding, a respected *Observer* reporter on Putin's oligarchs, wrote a favourable profile of Alexander in 2009, noting both his altruistic endeavours – building a cancer hospital in St Petersburg – and his disdain for the Russian leader's cronies.[194]

"They don't read books. They don't go to exhibitions. They think the only way to impress anyone is to buy a yacht," Harding quotes Lebedev as saying about Putin's allies.

But as Putin's westward march has continued, culminating in his full-scale invasion of Ukraine in early 2022, questions have been raised about whether there is an enduring relationship between the Lebedevs and the Russian state. In other words: is there such a thing as a 'former' Russian spy?

The Canadian Government certainly appears to believe that Alexander is closer to Putin than he seems – sanctioning him for being among those who have "directly enabled Vladimir Putin's senseless war in Ukraine".[195]

Johnson's own conduct makes this tale even more worrying. When serving as Foreign Secretary, the Old Etonian flew directly from a high-level NATO summit in April 2018 to the Lebedev palazzo in Umbria. The NATO meeting focused on the West's response to the poisonings of a former Russian double agent and his daughter, Sergei and Yulia Skripal, in Salisbury.

Johnson seemingly abandoned his security team for this trip – a breach of government protocol – and was pictured at San Francesco d'Assisi airport looking dishevelled, clutching a book about war strategy.[196]

Alexander Lebedev attended this party and, according to an investigative podcast produced by *Tortoise*, offered to mediate between Johnson and Putin.[197]

Johnson claims that no Government business was discussed at the party – but, as former UK diplomat Alexandra Hall Hall has written for *Byline Times*, "I learned early on that, when you are a British diplomat, there is no such thing as 'private business' – you are on duty all the time... The bottom line is that, as Britain's top diplomat at the time, Johnson should not have been consorting with former KGB agents. He should not have been going to such events alone. And he should not have allowed himself to get so drunk that he cannot give a proper account of what took place there."[198]

Evidence of the continued links between the Lebedevs and the Russian state have also been provided by Evgeny. Indeed, documents show that Evgeny attempted to lobby Johnson to support his pet projects while the latter was London Mayor – including a Russian Arts Festival in the capital. Minutes from the meeting show that the festival was aimed at "transforming global perceptions" of Russia and that Lebedev claimed he would be able to "lead discussions in establishing further substantial support from the Russian Government."[199] Ultimately, Johnson provided no support and the event didn't materialise.

Evgeny's other alliances have also given cause for concern. The Lord has joined the board of a non-profit enterprise created by the Saudi Government, holding his position alongside Crown Prince and current Saudi Prime Minister Mohammed bin Salman.[200]

The Saudi enterprise is called Hevolution – founded to research the science of anti-ageing, which is a preoccupation of many wealthy 'philanthropists'.

"It's time to focus science and business on ageing as a treatable process, not just on its terminal symptoms," its website states.

Funded by the Saudi state, Hevolution reportedly has an annual $1 billion budget to fund the science of increasing the healthy human lifespan.

American intelligence agencies have alleged that bin Salman personally "approved an operation in Istanbul to capture or kill Saudi journalist Jamal Khashoggi" in October 2018 – a conclusion backed-up by UN special rapporteur Agnès Callamard, who accused the Saudi state of the "deliberate, premeditated execution" of Khashoggi.[201]

Khashoggi, a journalist for the *Washington Post*, was a critic of bin Salman's regime, having previously been an advisor to the Saudi Government. He fell out of favour and went into self-imposed exile in the US in 2017.

Bin Salman has denied any role in the murder and has said that the US intelligence report is "negative, false and unacceptable".

Bin Salman is the head of the Hevolution board of trustees, while its board includes Abdullah bin Bandar Al Saud (Minister of the Saudi National Guard), Yasir Al-Rumayyan (Governor of the Saudi Public Investment Fund), and Fahad Toonsi (advisor to the Saudi Royal Court).

Lebedev has seemingly been a close acquaintance of bin Salman for some time. Indeed, he hosted a dinner with bin Salman in 2018, during the latter's state visit to the UK. They were joined by Virgin co-founder Richard Branson, whose spokesperson confirmed bin Salman's attendance.[202]

Moreover, Lebedev Holdings – which owns the *Evening Standard* and *The Independent* – has been accused by the UK Government of being part-owned by the Saudi state, due to a series of "unconventional, complex and clandestine" deals involving a Saudi businessman that resulted in a 30% acquisition of the firm.

The Government initially sought to investigate the deal, voicing concern that the Saudi Government could potentially exert editorial influence over the publications. However, a tribunal ruled in 2019 that the Government had missed the deadline to force a full investigation.[203]

"Editorial independence and freedom of expression have always been, and continue to be, critical to our publications," a spokesperson for the media outlets said after the ruling.

Yet, there are reasons to doubt this statement. The two publications accepted an undisclosed sum of money from Saudi Arabia to publish dozens of positive environmental stories about the country before, during, and after the COP26 UN Climate Change Conference in Glasgow in 2021.[204]

These links are particularly concerning given the Saudi Government's repression of individual freedoms. The Kingdom reportedly executed 81 people just days before Boris Johnson's trip to Riyadh in March 2022, and three on the day he arrived.[205]

"Saudi authorities in 2021 routinely repressed dissidents, human rights activists and independent clerics," according to the monitoring organisation Human Rights Watch. "Detainees, including children, commonly face systematic violations of due process and fair trial rights, including arbitrary arrest."[206]

The actions of Alexander and Evgeny suggest that the pair have sought to become members of the British establishment, in an attempt to dilute their reliance on Putin's capricious regime. This could be achieved, for one, by penetrating Britain's largely unregulated political system and courting an old aristocracy desperate to regain its relevance in the modern world.

What we know for sure is that aristocratic institutions are increasingly populated by new money interests that just happen to be closely associated – financially or otherwise – with the governing party.

Indeed, the crimson robes of House of Lords members have been donned by most major Conservative donors. More than a quarter of those who have given £100,000 or more to the party in recent years have been awarded a peerage or an honour, increasing to 55% among those who have given more than £1.5 million to the party.[207]

It is not illegal to make a political donation in the hope or expectation of receiving an honour – the law is only broken when it can be proven that a formal agreement has been made.

The large proportion of donors who have received honours or peerages soon after, or immediately before, gifting large sums of money to the Conservative Party does however raise questions about the ethics surrounding political donations, access to power, and the honours system itself.

A more recent trend has been a concerted attempt to appoint Conservative-leaning figures to public bodies. One former Government official told the *Financial Times* that "there has been a lot of placement of political cronies" and that "Number 10 has taken a close interest in it".[208]

It has been calculated that at least 16 Conservative Party allies have been given supposedly 'independent' roles as non-executive directors of government departments.[209]

Byline Times revealed, for example, that Jacob Rees-Mogg's business partner, Dominic Johnson – also a former Conservative Party Vice-Chair – had been appointed as a non-executive director of the Department for International Trade. He was appointed alongside Douglas Carswell, a former Conservative MP and a senior figure in the Vote Leave EU Referendum campaign.[210] Dominic Johnson was subsequently installed to the House of Lords and was appointed as a minister in the Cabinet Office and the Department for International Trade during Truss's short time in Downing Street.

One of Matt Hancock's former university friends, Gina Colangelo, was infamously appointed as a non-executive director of the Department of Health and Social Care, with a £15,000-a-year taxpayer-funded salary. Hancock was forced to resign from the department for being caught in an embrace with Colangelo during a period of COVID restrictions.

Other Government non-executive directors have included Ben Goldsmith, Conservative donor and brother of minister Lord Zac Goldsmith; Gisela Stuart, co-chair of the Vote Leave campaign; and Nick Timothy, a former joint Chief of Staff to Prime Minister May and a *Telegraph* columnist. Stuart has more recently been appointed as the first civil service commissioner – a role (some might say ironically) designed to ensure that appointments to the civil service are made openly and on merit.[211]

From the waterfall of private cash that pours into Parliament on an annual basis, to the barely-veiled appointment of political allies to public positions, democracy is not treated by the elite as inalienable and incorruptible, but rather as something that can be bent in favour of those in power – a tool for the preservation of the privileged, rather than an expression of collective will.

Politics is a plaything for the rich, rather than a mass participation event. In the early 1950s, three million people were Conservative Party members, while more than a million belonged to the Labour Party. Now, the two main parties can count barely 600,000 members on their books combined.

And the privatisation of politics can be seen most clearly in the outside employment of MPs.

An investigation in late 2021 by the then Parliamentary Commissioner for Standards, Kathryn Stone, judged that Conservative MP Owen

Paterson had "repeatedly" used his position as an MP to benefit two firms – Randox and Lynn's Country Foods – that employed him as a consultant to the tune of more than £110,000 a-year (on top of his £80,000 MP's salary).

Parliament's Committee on Standards said that Paterson broke multiple rules when he lobbied the Government on behalf of the two firms. "No previous case of paid advocacy has seen so many breaches or such a clear pattern of behaviour in failing to separate private and public interests," the committee said.[212]

It was recommended that Paterson should face a 30-day suspension from the House of Commons. That was until Conservative MPs rowed behind one of their own – 59 Conservative MPs signed an amendment, proposed by former Business Secretary Andrea Leadsom, that would have blocked the suspension of Paterson while a new committee was established to consider the evidence against him.

This amendment was initially backed by the Government before ministers realised – with the help of an outraged general public – that it was a political and ethical disaster to support an MP who had used his democratically elected position to benefit private companies.

Paterson, for his part, maintained that he was not guilty and that "a fair process would exonerate" him. He also described the inquiry as "a major contributory factor" to the death of his wife, Rose, who committed suicide in 2020.[213]

The scandal, however, triggered an avalanche of fury about the outside earnings of our elected representatives. *Byline Times* found that the 59 MPs who backed Leadsom's amendment had second jobs that cumulatively provided more than £1 million in additional income every year.[214]

Top of the list of profit-making parliamentarians is Sir Geoffrey Cox – the former Attorney General who mesmerised the privately-educated commentariat with his verbose sermons in Parliament during the May years. From 2019 to 2022, Cox earned a staggering £2 million from his outside legal work, including advising the British Virgin Islands (BVI) in an inquiry launched by the UK Government into alleged corruption in the tax haven. During lockdown, Cox even cast parliamentary votes remotely from the Caribbean.[215]

Defending his actions, Cox said that he had received approval from then Attorney General Suella Braverman before taking on the work. He claimed that his role was to advise the BVI Government "in a public inquiry into whether corruption, abuse of office or other serious dishonesty may have taken place in recent years" in the territory and to "to carry out a review of its systems of government in preparation for that inquiry."[216]

"This is not to 'defend' a tax haven," he said – adding that his local constituents would be able to decide "whether or not they vote for someone who is a senior and distinguished professional in his field and who still practises that profession."

Of the £17 million earned by MPs from private-sector jobs from 2019 to 2022, Tory MPs benefitted to the tune of £15.2 million.

And while parliamentarians have been boosting their bank accounts, ordinary people haven't been quite so fortunate. On average, there has been a 20.4% increase in child poverty within the 10 constituencies represented by the highest-earning MPs.

These MPs – all of whom are Conservatives – cumulatively earned £6.7 million in second jobs from the start of the 2014/15 financial year to the end of the 2019/20 financial year. Meanwhile, the number of children in poverty in their constituencies increased by 4,526.[217]

One of the highest earners during this period was John Redwood, the pro-Brexit, Conservative MP for Wokingham. Redwood earned more than £1 million from supplementary employment from 2014/15 to 2019/20, largely in the investment banking sector. During the same period, child poverty in Wokingham increased by 35.8%. Records show that Redwood has earned more than £200,000 a year for various roles at private equity and investment companies. One of the roles requires Redwood to work for 50 hours a month. If Redwood was working an average week, this role would have occupied a third of his time.

Another top earner during the period was Fiona Bruce, the MP for Congleton, who earned more than £1 million in supplementary income – exclusively from legal consultancy work. Meanwhile, child poverty increased in Bruce's constituency by 24.5%.

Sometimes these MPs are continuing their pre-politics occupations. Given that they have stood to be a representative of the people, accompanied by a healthy salary, it's perfectly reasonable for voters to be angry that their MP is not devoting their full attention to the job.

There are other MPs, however, who seem to be receiving new opportunities for money making by virtue of their status in Westminster.

Take Ruth Edwards, the Conservative MP for Rushcliffe, who became a director and shareholder of Mongoose Bridges Limited – a firm co-owned by her husband – on 1 May 2021.

On the same day, the MPs' register of interests showed, Mongoose Bridges began a seven-month-long, £5,000-a-month contract with MHR International – a software company that specialises in payroll and human resources.[218] Mongoose Bridges provided 16 hours of advisory work on "public sector, technology strategy and cybersecurity" for MHR every month. A month after this contract concluded, Edwards ceased to be a director and shareholder of Mongoose Bridges.

The register of interests stated that Edwards was an 'unpaid' director of Mongoose Bridges, though it is unclear whether she drew dividends from the company. Her office did not respond to multiple questions on the matter. It is also unclear whether and how her husband is or was remunerated by the firm.

The contract with MHR started just six weeks after Edwards held a constituency meeting with the company. On her official MP website, Edwards publicised a summit with the company's founder, John Mills, on 18 March. This page on her website has now been deleted.

"I met with founder John Mills who talked me through how MHR software is helping to support people and businesses with its software and outsourcing services for HR, talent management, payroll and business intelligence," the website read. "MHR currently employs 700 people – most based at their main sites in Ruddington [a village in Edwards' constituency], but also others in Nottingham, Ireland, the USA and Singapore!"[219]

There is no evidence that Edwards and MHR discussed private business opportunities at this meeting or as a result of this meeting – this was another question posed to the MP that remained unanswered.

Prior to becoming an MP, Edwards worked in cybersecurity policy and was head of commercial strategy and public policy for British Telecom. She was elected to the constituency formerly held by long-serving MP Ken Clarke at the 2019 General Election.

Edwards did not disclose how much time she personally devoted to working for MHR every month. She previously told *The Guardian* that her caseload as an MP had increased threefold due to the COVID pandemic.[220]

The furore around MPs' second jobs was a strange moment in British politics. These facts had been known about for years – the financial interests of MPs listed publicly, updated monthly, and periodically reported by the press. More than anything, the Paterson affair and its aftermath showed the inadequacy of existing political reporting, which focused on new stories and quick 'hits' over and above systemic and structural problems. The accumulation of outside jobs had occurred at such a gradual rate – and was such a normalised feature of Westminster – that few reporters stood back and thought about the sheer scale of this industry, and whether voters were aware of it, or how they would feel about it.

This was similarly the case with a series of lobbying scandals that broke in 2021 – largely surrounding former Prime Minister Cameron. Indeed, while lobbying is an engrained feature of the Westminster system, the attention of the press and public grew after it was revealed that Cameron had lobbied senior officials and Cabinet ministers, including the Chancellor, on behalf of the financial services firm Greensill, which collapsed in mid-2021.

Cameron was attempting to secure greater involvement for Greensill in the Government's emergency COVID loans scheme. Ultimately, officials rejected Greensill's proposals despite Cameron's persistent lobbying, with the firm filing for insolvency protection on 8 March 2021, after its insurer walked away.

It was later revealed that Lex Greensill, its owner, had worked for the Cabinet Office as an unpaid 'advisor' from 2012 to 2015, during Cameron's time in office.[221] Greensill had also been commissioned by the Government to introduce an early payment facility for health workers and a working capital programme for pharmacies.

The *Financial Times* reported on 12 July that

Cameron was paid more than $1 million a year – equivalent to $40,000 a day – by Greensill.[222]

The current system acts primarily to the benefit of backbench MPs; serving ministers are banned from retaining second jobs. However, financial advantages also accrue to the high-fliers of yesteryear, when they leave the top government jobs, and in particular former prime ministers.

After leaving office, former Prime Minister Tony Blair became one of highest-paid public speakers in the world, regularly charging £200,000 a speech and reportedly making up to £1 million-a-month.[223] Goldman Sachs even paid him an extraordinary £300,000 for one such event back in 2008. Even Theresa May, lacking the charisma of both Blair and Johnson, has earned more than £2 million from speeches in recent years.[224]

Similarly, Cameron earned millions as a commercial speaker after resigning in the wake of the Brexit vote. His limited company reported profits of £1.6 million from 2017 to 2019. In April 2019, however, he took the unusual move of re-registering the firm as an unlimited company. Shareholders therefore have unlimited liability, but Cameron doesn't have to file public accounts.

Another particularly lucrative opportunity for former prime ministers are book deals.

Johnson has already penned 11 books, including a biography of Winston Churchill and a novel about a tousled-haired, bicycle-riding MP who foils a terror attack to distract from scandals about his personal life. HarperCollins has stumped up £510,000 as an initial advance for Johnson's memoir, with the total book deal predicted to make the former Prime Minister more than £6 million.[225]

Blair, meanwhile, sold the advances to his bestselling *A Journey* for £4.6 million, although later pledged to donate all profits to the Royal Legion. Cameron, who was reportedly asked to cut 100,000 words from his initial manuscript, sold the rights to his memoirs for £800,000.[226]

Despite the opportunities for money-making, leaving high office and the public limelight can be difficult for outgoing prime ministers. After departing Downing Street, Margaret Thatcher seemingly didn't know how to dial a phone and resorted to placing calls on a police line from her garage with the help of her Special Branch protection team.

Taking pity on his predecessor, John Major introduced the Public Duty Cost Allowance, which provides an annual entitlement of up to £115,000 to be spent on office and secretarial costs. Since 2009, it has cost the taxpayer £6 million. Nick Clegg, despite never having served as prime minister, has claimed £444,775 since 2015.[227]

Indeed, only Gordon Brown bucks the trend of former prime ministers leveraging their status and connections to accumulate personal wealth. He earned millions on the speaker's circuit after leaving office yet did not personally receive a penny of it. Instead, it was all either donated to charity or the Office of Gordon and Sarah Brown to fund their public service and charity work, from which he derives no income.[228]

It seems unlikely that Johnson will adopt such an

approach. His money struggles are well documented, as is the fact that he has already accumulated millions in the few short months after leaving Downing Street.[229]

These skewed priorities of our current and former leaders – oriented more towards money and power than public service – is a by-product of the way in which MPs are recruited and hardwired.

As described by Isabel Hardman in *Why We Get the Wrong Politicians*, prospective MPs are often drawn from higher social classes, due to the financial commitment demanded from prospective candidates – their suitability for the role primarily assessed on their devotion to the party or its dominant faction.

"The cost of standing for Parliament is absurd," Hardman writes. "It is an embarrassment to Westminster, not just because requiring people to shell out a sum of money comparable to a deposit on a house naturally filters out good candidates who cannot afford this, but also because few of those in the [Westminster] bubble acknowledge just what a problem it is."[230]

This dearth of talent is noted by Johnson's former chief aide Dominic Cummings, who says that "Most people in politics are recruited based on whether they can stand up and speak," rather than whether they are capable of leading a government or formulating sound public policy. This bias towards inflated oratory is also naturally an impediment to working-class candidates who may be less skilled in such hollow charisma.

"Rolling news and social media encourages more

of the narcissists to get involved as a sort of low-grade alternative to being a celebrity," Cummings adds.[231]

And once this conveyor belt starts whirring – once the highly egoed see similar people running the country – it is difficult to stop. Especially given that the economy is now propelled by middle class 'knowledge' professions, while industrial and manufacturing jobs have been gutted.

Indeed, this can be mapped in the composition of the House of Commons. In 1979, 21 MPs had previously worked in politics before entering Parliament; by 1997, the figure had jumped to 60, rising to 90 by 2010. This was even a trend in the Labour Party, previously a vehicle for the trade union movement and the industrial working classes, which became more managerial during the New Labour years. Some 34% of newly elected Labour MPs in 2010 had previously worked in politics.[232]

Commensurately, MPs with an employment history in education fell from 17% in 1997 to 5% in 2010, and whereas 15.8% of MPs in 1979 had previously been manual workers, the figure stood at just 4% by 2010.

Cabinet ministers are likewise selected almost exclusively based on their loyalty to the occupant of 10 Downing Street. Not a single member of Truss's first Cabinet had served in the executive prior to 2019, and there was a measurable lack of experience compared to historical standards.

"What is the common theme running through these appointments? Loyalty," *The Spectator*'s Katy Balls wrote, the day after Truss appointed her Cabinet.[233]

MPs are selected not primarily on their intelligence, nor spirit of public service, but their devotion to the party-political cause (influenced heavily by the factional interests of an incumbent leader). Ministers are then selected on a similar basis, their willingness to absorb blows on behalf of their leader being far more important to political success than their competence or experience. And throughout this entire process, the beneficiaries of a shamelessly anti-meritocratic system are allowed to feather their nests with private-sector cash.

While politics is supposed to function in the public interest, Westminster runs on private finance. Companies donate tens of millions to the political parties (mainly now the Conservative Party), employ their MPs – both during and after their time in Parliament – and benefit from billions in government contracts, as well as a neoliberal economic consensus. The line between the ideological convictions and financial self-interest of Conservative MPs is entirely blurred.

In October 2010, Chancellor George Osborne said that those with the "broadest shoulders should bear the greatest burden" of the Government's austerity in the wake of the global financial crash. "We're all in this together" was a slogan deployed by the Conservative Party during the election campaign earlier that year – promising that our collective health and prosperity would be ensured if we all paid our fair share.

The last few years, however, have unravelled this myth – showing that, in reality, those with political and economic power do not play by the same rules as everyone else. In fact, it appears as though they are playing a different sport entirely.

Take the fact that current Prime Minister Rishi Sunak's wife, Akshata Murthy, previously held non-domiciled tax status, ensuring that she did not have to pay UK tax on income earned abroad. Sunak himself held a US 'green card' until October 2020 – he was appointed as UK Chancellor in February 2020 – meaning that he paid taxes in the US.[234]

Former Conservative Deputy Chair Lord Michael Ashcroft, and *Daily Mail* proprietor Lord Rothermere are both also famous exponents of non-dom tax rules – though the newspaper insists that Rothermere derives "zero tax advantage" from the arrangement.[235]

MPs and ministers – and seemingly their spouses – do not operate in the everyday economy. Their individual experiences are divorced from the nurses, bus drivers and teachers who they claim to represent.

Instead, those in power are firmly entrenched in the plutocracy. Their knowledge and connections allow them to locate the income opportunities, and the loopholes, excluded to most ordinary people. Sunak and Murthy are reported to be worth more than £700 million, ranked 222nd on the 2022 *Sunday Times* Rich List of the wealthiest families in the UK.[236]

Sunak's predecessor in the Treasury, Sajid Javid, earned more than £750,000 from 2019 to 2022 through second jobs. And his successor, Nadhim Zahawi, has reportedly amassed a property empire worth more than £100 million.[237]

This is common among the Conservative Party, with its backbenches populated by the property-owning elite. A quarter of Tory MPs earn money from private properties, many of whom still claim relief from the taxpayer for the homes they rent in London.[238]

Meanwhile, ministers are seen as collector's items by wealthy benefactors. Lord David Brownlow, who funded Johnson's extravagant Downing Street flat refurbishment – worth £208,104 – has a history of underwriting prime ministers, having donated £104,000 to Theresa May's local party from 2016 to 2020.[239] Lord Brownlow also reportedly offered funding for a £150,000 treehouse for Johnson's son to be built at Chequers – the country retreat that can be used by prime ministers.[240]

All of these issues demonstrate the contempt held by the ruling elite towards the laws and the moral standards governing the rest of the country – perhaps because those in power exist in a different economic and social stratosphere to most people. They are friends with playboys and oligarchs – breeding an air of impunity; a perception, grounded in lived reality, that they are above the law.

These are the values now embedded at the top of government, with our rulers drawn from and beholden to a rich, self-serving elite. And they formed the basis of Johnson's downfall. Indeed, prior to the 'Partygate' affair, Johnson was stubbornly popular – former industrial heartlands in particular believing that he had been sent to liberate the people from their poverty, poor health and political marginalisation. His promise was to destroy the 'old politics' – plagued by the perceived greed of elected fraudsters – and to create a better country.

Johnson was elected as a political wrecking ball – an image he aptly embodied through his brash, impertinent style of politics. He was sent to trash the existing system, including previous iterations of his own party.

Johnson's violation of his own lockdown rules and – worse – his repeated attempts to deceive the public about these 'work events' was therefore a transgression of the moral code on which he was elected.

Disillusioned voters knew that Johnson was a bit rogue – a philanderer and an ego-maniac – but their pact with him involved an understanding that they would never be on the wrong end of these toxic traits. When this pact was broken, it reanimated the same feelings of resentment and betrayal that provoked the Brexit vote in the first place, only – this time – Johnson was no longer the beneficiary.

6 THE GAME

Politics is fought in a village, between a long-standing cast of characters, dramatised by the media. It's not an open, level playing field for the most talented and altruistic to serve their country. Exactly the opposite.

Westminster is not merely a place but a culture – one that is alienating to outsiders, requiring years of practice to navigate its ancient nooks and crannies. As academic Aeron Davis writes in *Reckless Opportunists*: "Whether entering Parliament, the Square Mile or a big corporate headquarters in the West End, there is a diverse and alien culture to experience. Such spaces are intense, insular and self-referencing."[241]

In effect, the people ruling these domains create their own moral codes that are often distant from the views of the majority, he writes. "The higher a leader goes the more removed they become. The constant danger is that those at the top come to believe that *their* world experience is *the* world experience.

"They then act on those misplaced views. Corrupt, self-serving practices become unquestioned."

This is exactly what has occurred in Westminster, with prospective leaders conditioned in loyalty over competence as the ministerial production line inexorably transports them to a pot of gold on retirement, regardless of their performance. The institution of government has become estranged from its people, with repeated, fatal consequences.

Take Brexit, for example. The Government released an official report in February 2022 into the benefits of Brexit, written by civil servants and paid for by the taxpayer. As Chris Grey has observed, the Government's report was not an objective, mathematical cost-benefit analysis – given that not a single downside of Brexit was mentioned in its 100 pages. Rather, it was a word salad of half-truths, exaggerations and policies that could have been implemented even despite Brexit. It was a party-political broadcast, packaged as official, impartial, objective fact.[242]

In this way, the apparatus of democracy has gradually been warped away from rational decision-making – instead favouring those who best 'play the game'.

Jacob Rees-Mogg, for example, was appointed as 'Brexit Opportunities Minister' in the same month that the 'benefits of Brexit' paper was released. And he is not the only current or former Cabinet member whose title has been derived from a Conservative Party slogan. A Secretary of State for Levelling Up was created in September 2021 – using a political phrase coined and deployed by Johnson during the 2019 General Election campaign. This suggests an administration motivated by projection over substance, with the roles of ministers derived from a party manifesto rather than the concerns of the nation.

Ultimately, Johnson's Government was a product of the Instagram age – it recognised that clever branding (and a carefree attitude to controversy) is the recipe for viral popularity, diminishing the need for competence, substance and detail. The advisors tasked with cultivating Johnson's image were brought from the Conservative campaign trail into Government – let loose on the machinery of the state.

The meme merchants Sean Topham and Ben Guerin – reportedly responsible for the Conservative Party's notorious 'Fact Check UK' Twitter stunt during the 2019 election campaign, when they rebranded the Conservative HQ account to seem as though it was an impartial fact-checking service – were hired by the Government to advise on COVID communications. Chloe Westley, who has run social media for various libertarian campaigns, was a Downing Street special advisor throughout Johnson's premiership.[243]

On 29 May 2019, Guerin appeared as a special guest at the Friedman Conference, a right-wing event hosted by the Australian Libertarian Society

(ALS) and the Australian Taxpayers' Alliance (ATA).

A week before, his bootstrap firm had played a major role in propelling the right-wing Liberal Party, headed by Scott Morrison, to victory in the Federal Election.

Reflecting on the social media strategy he deployed during the election, Guerin described a campaign of highly repetitive messaging – what he called "water dripping on a stone" – to convince voters that the opposition Labor Party would hike-up taxes. Guerin boasted that an especially high-performing piece of content was an image of a dog accompanied by the message "tax is bad".[244]

In this spirit, the social media spin doctor went on to explain how "crude", poorly-produced memes attracted more engagement than slick, formulaic graphics.

"You've got to surprise people. You've got to shock people. Unlock and arouse an emotion in people," he recommended.

"The particular emotions we've got to unlock are arousal emotions," he continued – echoing the ideas expressed by Cambridge Analytica executives in the wake of Donald Trump's 2016 victory. "We're talking: anger, excitement, pride, fear. Your content should be relating to one of these emotions."

Emotive content was pumped out by the Morrison campaign, said Guerin, and the professionalism of that content didn't seem to matter.

"That's how you get what we call the 'boomer memes'. Because you have to crank stuff out quickly," he said. "You couldn't spend too long doing an artisanally perfect graphic. You're going to slap some Calibri font on a shitty, reused meme and you're going to publish it, and then get on to the next one. And you know what: that content is going to do better than the thing your poor graphic designer spent a week on."

This tactic, Guerin claims, resulted in Morrison and the Liberal Party receiving twice as much engagement on social media than their Labor opponents.

"And when most of that is concentrated in marginal seats, that's how you win an election that no-one thinks you're going to win," he said.

The 2019 Australian election wasn't the first taste of political campaigning for Guerin and his partner Sean Topham, nor the last. The pair had cut their teeth on a contest two years earlier, drafted in by the centre-right New Zealand National Party to hold back the tide of support for Labour Leader Jacinda Ardern.

Gaining notoriety in right-wing circles, the Kiwi meme manipulators entered the patronage of Sir Lynton Crosby, the world-renowned conservative campaigner. It's claimed that the pair helped Crosby to run Facebook pages that "sidestepped Facebook's rules on transparent political campaigning" on behalf of clients including major polluters, the Saudi Arabian Government, anti-cycling groups, and various foreign political campaigns. All parties have previously pointed out that they operated entirely within the law.[245]

It was during this period, from 2017 to summer

2019, that Topham and Guerin crossed paths with the man who would propel them into the maelstrom of a UK general election campaign.

Having worked for Crosby out in Washington DC, Australian political strategist Isaac Levido was rushed back to his native country to help with Morrison's 2019 election bid. Operating as the deputy director of the campaign, Levido – dubbed "the new Lynton" – was evidently impressed by the work of the two Kiwi upstarts. And so, when Levido was commissioned to run the Conservative Party's 2019 General Election bid, he brought Topham and Guerin in his suitcase.

Under the wing of Levido, the pair unleashed meme warfare on the British public. Following the model of the Australian election, 'Topham Guerin' deployed all of its expertise in shitty fonts – notably posting a graphic on the Conservative Party's official social media channels using Comic Sans.

This meme generated so much attention that 'Comic Sans' trended on Twitter and the internet flooded with news articles from click-hungry media outlets. This undoubtedly – as Guerin foretold – spread the Tory message to millions more people than if they would have posted a predictable, corporate illustration.

Yet, as with much on the internet, Johnson's fame was only fleeting.

As Daniel Finkelstein observed in *The Times*, Johnson has in the past been the beneficiary of cascading popular opinion – his following was built on an infectious sense that he is funny and likeable. However, without any policy substance to underpin this support – and with his tendency to avoid media interviews that could have cemented his virtues and therefore his popularity – public opinion rapidly shifted away from Johnson, evaporating into the ether.[246]

Johnson's popularity was premised on good vibes, and once those good vibes disappeared as a result of the 'Partygate' scandal, he didn't have much else to fall back on.

What remains, however, is the widespread adoption of Johnson's techniques among his former Cabinet acolytes, who have manipulated the machinery of the state to buttress their own PR efforts.

When serving as Chancellor, Rishi Sunak was mocked even within the Conservative Party for using every policy announcement as a self-promotion opportunity. Flashy graphics were frequently deployed by the Treasury on social media with the Chancellor's signature, usually accompanied by his beaming, airbrushed headshot.

Indeed, the trend of style-over-substance vaulted from Number 10 to Number 11 – epitomised by Sunak's 'Eat Out to Help Out' scheme, which gave discounts to diners in the summer of 2020, when lockdown restrictions had been eased. The scheme incubated new COVID infection clusters, and barely improved hospitality trade, but it allowed the Chancellor – a millionaire privately educated former banker – to swagger through Wagamama with a katsu curry, captured by the nation's cameramen, his image as a regular guy seemingly reinforced.[247]

Under Sunak, the Treasury's communications budget increased by 62% in two years, standing at almost £3.4 million by the time he left.[248] Sunak was accused by Labour's Deputy Leader Angela Rayner of spending taxpayers' money on "a vanity exercise" after it was revealed that he had handed more than £500,000 to run focus groups and an online poll in an attempt to "repair his image".[249]

Truss followed this fad, accused of being so obsessed with social media that her colleagues at the Department of International Trade reportedly quipped that it would be better named the 'Department for Instagramming Truss'.[250] Her impersonation of Margaret Thatcher, posing on a tank in Estonia, seemed to prove their point.

This deployment of state resources in the name of political posturing may seem trivial to some, but it has established a precedent with more serious implications: namely, if senior Cabinet ministers believe that the organs of the state are tools to further their own ambitions, then democracy itself can be subsumed to the interests of one person or political party.

This has been evident in the case of the Government's voter ID reforms, whereby people will be required to produce a photo ID when they vote. Such a policy will hit marginalised people the hardest – particularly immigrants – who are comparatively less likely to vote for the Conservatives.[251]

Gerrymandering has been a feature of the American political system in recent decades, through which Republican legislators have manipulated the boundaries of democracy to boost their chances of victory. Under Donald Trump, this approach reached its logical end-point, with the Republican President claiming that he alone had the right to govern, despite comfortably losing the 2020 election to Joe Biden.

Ultimately, if you believe that you have an unalienable right to govern – combined with a sense that democracy is a game without basic rules – you are entirely unwilling to consider that it sometimes involves you losing.

As mentioned earlier, the fallibility of British democracy – its exposure to the whims of political schemers – has been described by Peter Hennessy as the 'good chaps' theory. Indeed, the prime minister and to some extent the wider Cabinet is self-regulating, exempt from formal codes of conduct and accompanying punishments, risking moral decline and even autocracy if our leaders do not uphold high virtues in office.

Those who wield power are not bound by formal rules of engagement or the law but are rather guided by often perverse political incentives. Rather than remunerating intellect, decency and independent thought, our current system rewards the greedy, sycophantic and image-obsessed – witnessed once again during the 2022 Conservative leadership race.

When Johnson was selected for the top job in 2019, there was a sense that the party was going through the motions. It almost seemed an inevitability that Johnson, a longstanding darling of the Conservative grassroots, would eventually storm the contest.

His predecessor Theresa May had an even easier ride – anointed by Conservative MPs after a Johnson-Gove firefight knocked out Vote Leave's two big-hitters.

In contrast, there was no clear winner at the start of the 2022 contest, no obvious leader-in-waiting – and so, in order to climb above the rest, the candidates were forced to resort to old-fashioned political skulduggery.

Indeed, as the candidates put the finishing touches to their campaigns, the *Sunday Times* reported that "at least two rival leadership campaign teams have passed the Labour Party a digital dossier containing a series of lurid allegations about their potential opponents."[252] Apparently included in the dossier was evidence of affairs, penchants for BDSM, and explicit photos that could be used as *kompromat* – compromising information that could be used as blackmail.

A lot of this is gossip; fodder for the tabloid press.

However, the dirty dossiers matter on a more fundamental level, because of how they can be used to compromise MPs beyond these leadership contests, polluting our democracy.

There's only one reason why such a dossier exists: to influence political outcomes.

In this case, candidates hoped that by making it known that they had salacious details about illicit activities, their rivals would have been forced to step aside, assisting the dossier-holder. The dossier is designed to neuter its targets.

Undoubtedly, this process of blackmail isn't the

way in which most voters want the Prime Minister to be selected, and the wider implications are profound. If embarrassing materials exist and are being used to put pressure on senior MPs to quit a leadership race, they can also be used in the normal process of politics – forcing ministers to adopt certain policies, or MPs to vote against their conscience.

Holding politicians to account for their personal behaviour is not about pearl clutching or trying to impose a moral code. It's a positive thing that society is more tolerant and accepting of certain facts of life – relationships break down, affairs happen, people have a range of legal sexual preferences.

But when private issues become a source of embarrassment, or something an MP is keen to hide, they can become a weapon of blackmail.

This is also a threat to national security – not least when hostile states are more than willing to use kompromat to achieve their geopolitical ambitions.

When unproven allegations emerged that there was a tape of former US President Donald Trump with sex workers in a Moscow hotel, intelligence officials expressed concern that such compromising materials could be wielded by Russian intelligence agents to manipulate the former Commander-in-Chief.[253]

As for Britain, Boris Johnson provoked security concerns for his lazy attitude to phone security, with his personal phone number having been displayed publicly online for 15 years, including when he was Foreign Secretary, and later Prime Minister.[254]

This is particularly important during a time

of Russian interference in British politics, when geopolitical conflicts are intensifying and new superpowers emerging. Can we trust ministers to make the right decisions for the country and the world, if they are always looking over their shoulders, hoping that a secret doesn't come out?

As well as a threat to national security, the use and abuse of kompromat makes for a weakened political system.

When Gavin Williamson was the Government's chief whip, it was well-known that careers could be shaped by his little black book of secrets. Williamson was pictured with a whip on his desk, while serving as Education Secretary, after announcing an embarrassing U-turn on the grading of students during the pandemic. This was thought to be a veiled threat to those who had been critical of his decision; a warning to those who sought to remove him.

And the media is complicit in this process – avidly lapping up the spoils of political warfare while publicising Machiavellian plotting above effective policymaking. To some extent, reporters simply haven't been prepared for the economic and political convulsions of the last 12 years. The '90s and '00s, which heralded the expansion of the democratic world and the supposed end of 'boom and bust' economies, was soon followed by a global economic crash and the resurgence of nationalist populism across the globe. It has been difficult to adjust from an era of relative political stability and consensus – when politics did seem relatively stable – to the current high-stakes era.

However, the newspaper industry in particular

has excessively and intentionally trivialised politics, partly to distract from any meaningful reform of the system and partly to rinse as many clicks as possible from the banalities of Westminster.

Political wrongdoing is therefore either actively rewarded, or there is a minimal chance of any serious consequences. Johnson, a fountain of immortality, was written-up by the media as a lovable rogue; his depravity became, for a short time, his political strength. And while the single-parent in a minimum wage job has seen their income shrink, the state blaming them for existing on the bread line, the Conservative MPs who filed into the voting lobbies to approve austerity measures have faced virtually no harm to their political careers or personal circumstances.

Of course, it's not true to say that accountability has been entirely absent in the domino-ring of scandals that have engulfed British politics in recent times. Rather, those who have fallen on their sword have a generally similar profile: influential but not at the top of the hierarchy; directly responsible for an offence but not for the institutional culture that allowed it to occur, nor for the cover up.

It feels as though the drug runners have been convicted while the mob bosses remain at large. Even Johnson, who used the architecture of the British political system to hide from the repercussions of his actions, is seemingly mulling a political 'comeback' mere months after he was unceremoniously dumped out of Downing Street.

In essence, the prime minister is self-regulating,

beholden only to their conscience, the mood of their political party, and the outcomes of occasional general elections. Even the Cabinet does not have the direct power to topple a prime minister – despite the inhabitant of Downing Street ostensibly being the first among equals.

Johnson's survival for so long – as in the mafia complex – was assisted by an absence of viable rivals for his turf. The closer that Cabinet ministers clung to Johnson, in the hope of absorbing some of his aura, the more they were protected by his constitutional power. In the moral maelstrom created by their leader, they increasingly sought refuge inside this protective bubble – ironically limiting their ability to dethrone the king.

On resigning from Cabinet – the act that precipitated Johnson's eventual downfall – Sunak and the former Health and Social Care Secretary Sajid Javid cited the "standards" that Johnson had failed to uphold in office. If they were so concerned about standards, the question remains as to why they didn't resign sooner, when Johnson deceived Parliament about parties held in Downing Street during lockdown, or when his Government awarded billions in contracts to Conservative donors, or when his policies were reversed by the Supreme Court.[255]

The resignations of Sunak, Javid and eventually a host of other Cabinet ministers had close to nothing to do with morality or political standards. It was because the Conservatives were trailing in the polls, with angry voters repeatedly referencing Johnson's lockdown lies.

And Johnson's survival throughout was facilitated by the flimsy rules of political engagement described by Hennessy.

The Ministerial Code, for example, is supposed to be the moral handbook for prime ministers, underpinned by the Nolan Principles of Public Life: selflessness, integrity, objectivity, accountability, openness, honesty, and leadership.

However, breaches of the code are adjudicated by the prime minister – with Johnson rewriting the code to remove all references in the foreword to honesty, integrity, transparency and accountability, and removing the clause stipulating that a breach of the code should prompt the resignation of the culpable minister.[256]

The prime minister's application and behaviour under the code is typically overseen by an ethics advisor. This position was held until 15 June 2022 by Lord Christopher Geidt, who resigned by saying that he "could not be a party to advising on any potential law-breaking". Johnson was issued with a fixed penalty notice by the Metropolitan Police on 12 April 2022 for breaching COVID lockdown rules, and Lord Geidt said that it was "reasonable" to suggest that Johnson may have violated the Ministerial Code.[257]

Lord Geidt had taken over the role from Alex Allan, who resigned in November 2020 after Johnson refused to sack the then Home Secretary Priti Patel, despite an official investigation concluding that she had bullied civil servants.[258]

While the ethics advisor may resign at a time of their choosing, this appears to be the limit of their independence. They can only initiate investigations with the consent of the prime minister, and – as witnessed in the case of Patel – their advice is not binding.

Ergo, the agents of democracy installed to uphold morality, probity and transparency are often fig-leaves. They are individuals appointed by the administration, whose loyalty is primarily to the party and the government, not the democratic system.

Take the Government's former 'anti-corruption champion', Conservative MP John Penrose, who defended the way in which public money was distributed during the pandemic.

"What we discovered is that our government procurement and buying, while it had all sorts of in-built transparency measures, is too slow when you're trying to work in COVID time and when you're trying to get fast procurement for things like protective equipment," Penrose said.[259]

In other words: anti-corruption measures were relegated due to the need to procure supplies quickly. And the man tasked with monitoring state corruption seemingly thought this was entirely reasonable.

Penrose's unwillingness to address corruption concerns about the Government's actions during the pandemic, despite his title, constituted a failure of the political system. It showed how the guardians of British democracy are often hollow name-plates with little scope to either reform the system or criticise those in power.

"The anti-corruption champion's role is clear and

should not include commenting on or investigating individual cases, but to support and challenge the government's broader anti-corruption efforts," Penrose told *Byline Times* previously. "As part of this, I have commented both privately and publicly on how to improve the overall system."

The anti-corruption champion is directly appointed by the prime minister and serves at his pleasure. In effect, the government is marking its own homework.

This is likewise the case for the Cabinet Secretary, the most senior civil servant in the UK, whose authority is drawn from the prime minister. Incumbent Simon Case was asked by MPs whether there would be an investigation into reports that Johnson attempted to install his then-girlfriend, now-wife Carrie Symonds into a £100,000-a-year role when he was Foreign Secretary, to which Case responded that, "any investigation under the Ministerial Code can only be authorised by the PM."[260] In other words: there won't be an investigation.

In this same sitting, Case revealed for the first time that both he and the Prime Minister's spokesperson were facing disciplinary proceedings for their role in the 'Partygate' scandal – the latter for misleading political journalists by claiming that no parties occurred in Downing Street and that all the rules were followed.

Fortunately for the spokesperson, misleading the media "is not automatically a breach of the civil service code", according to Case.

But this vacuum of accountability hasn't just been

created by a toothless Ministerial Code. There are several other ways in which British democracy offers platitudes – warm sentiments and good intentions – where strong constitutional safeguards should exist.

Case's confessional also included the detail that former Department of Health and Social Care non-executive director Gina Coladangelo had failed to declare her personal links to Matt Hancock when she was appointed to her £15,000-a-year role in his department.

There are virtually no repercussions for those in power who accidentally or intentionally suppress financial or personal conflicts of interest. The widespread cronyism of the COVID pandemic led to no punishments or resignations, even despite billions of pounds ending up in the pockets of Conservative associates and donors. In fact, there is a lack of transparency by design: government contracts contain no information on conflicts of interest when they are released to the public.

In similar fashion, our system actively allows ministers to shield their financial interests from public view by allowing the use of a 'blind trust' arrangement, whereby the minister holds shares in a company but is removed from the management of their investments. This is a mechanism that has been deployed by Sunak – whose family fortune stretches beyond £700 million – to prevent his investments from being seen by the wider public.[261]

Meanwhile, ministers are able to use private companies as an additional buffer from scrutiny – with Zahawi able to conceal £1.3 million in payments from an oil company by processing the payments through his self-titled consultancy firm 'Zahawi & Zahawi'.[262]

So, while ministers periodically declare their financial and personal interests – giving the appearance of transparency and probity – there are ways in which potentially damaging information can be kept off the books.

This applies also to official correspondence. The law firms Foxglove and the Good Law Project, alongside the campaigning outfit The Citizens, have challenged the Government over its "rampant" use of WhatsApp messages for official business – a practice that circumvents the standard ways in which official decisions are recorded.

If officials conduct government business on WhatsApp, and these messages are not retained, there exists a gap in the institutional memory of our highest authorities – that in turn cannot be accessed by journalists, researchers or the public. Indeed, when Johnson changed his phone in April 2021, none of his past WhatsApp messages were retained.[263]

Next, there is Freedom of Information (FOI) legislation, which is supposed to ensure access to official records – for example, internal government documents and correspondence – the release of which would be within the public interest.

However, in recent years, and particularly since Johnson came to power in July 2019, this journalistic avenue has been stymied. Journalists at *Byline Times* have been denied access to information related to Johnson's meetings with Cambridge Analytica in

2016, and to information about his meetings with 'business leaders' and right-wing newspaper barons at the outset of the pandemic.[264]

All of the available evidence suggests that this is a concerted effort among the institutions of power to limit public access to information, not just that it's an unhappy accident. As *openDemocracy* has exposed: a secretive 'clearing house' previously existed in the Cabinet Office that effectively blocked FOI releases to selected reporters and campaigners – while tens of thousands of pounds was spent in an attempt to shield the clearing house from scrutiny.[265]

Meanwhile, the epicentre of this democratic reputation-laundering is Parliament itself – where, in the House of Commons, a prime minister can lie with impunity while those who accuse them of deceit are ejected from the chamber – as Labour MP Dawn Butler was in July 2021.[266]

Parliament's elaborate system of committees, debates and procedures projects the illusion of democracy – sustaining the 'Mother of all Parliaments' myth. In reality, though, our rigged First Past the Post voting system emaciates opposition parties and delivers lopsided majorities that allow those in power to ignore dissenting opinion – while the executive dominates the legislative agenda.

Harsh words are the only constraint on executive power in Parliament, and even those are tempered by the conventions of parliamentary decorum.

This has been fully exploited by the Brexit era. The very politicians who promised to "take back control" of power from Brussels have instead hoarded power in Westminster, attempting to skirt democratic conventions whenever possible. Despite their claims to the contrary, Brexiters do not instinctively object to 'red tape' imposed by unelected bureaucrats. After all, our post-Brexit trade relationship with the EU and the world – which has seen Britain's trade performance fall to its worst level since 1955 – was negotiated by unelected House of Lords member David Frost.[267]

In other words, we now import far more than we export – because of the bureaucracy faced by firms seeking to trade internationally.

A customs clearance manager at Dover, for example, told me that 95% of problems at the port are caused by "the red tape which is now necessary because we left the EU".

"The jobs that were taking five minutes can now take over an hour to do," he said.[268]

Rather than objecting on principle to red tape, our Bullingdon Club elites (Frost was educated at a private school co-founded by King Henry VIII) merely object to rules and regulations that are out of their control.

Instructively, the avoidance of democratic accountability by those in Westminster in recent times has been matched by the lack of penalties imposed after the financial crash of 2008, when a financial elite tanked the global economy with its risky housing bets. Up to 1.3 million people were made redundant between 2007 and 2010 in the UK, and real wages still haven't recovered. Yet, as of 2017, only 28 people had been charged by UK authorities for their role in the crash, and five had been convicted.[269]

In both high politics and big business, there are incentives to break the rules. The sound functioning of democracy and capitalism requires constraints of the sort that are entirely missing from our toothless regulators.

Yes, this story is about people and their individual choices; people whose experiences in life produce a warped sense of personal entitlement. Martin Hammond, one of Johnson's masters at Eton, wrote to his father in 1982 to explain that "Boris seems affronted when confronted with what amounts to a gross failure of responsibility... I think he honestly believes that it is churlish of us not to regard him as an exception, one who should be free of the network of obligation that binds everyone else."[270]

But, while it's important to understand the backgrounds and the motives of these people, of equal significance are the weak safeguards that allow democracy to be appropriated and exploited by the power-hungry.

After all that I have described, you may wonder why there hasn't been a major public revolt in the UK over the last 15 years. This is because the Bullingdon Club elite is so accomplished at distracting its subjects and trivialising any accusation of wrongdoing.

In fact, this has been Johnson's strategy from the start – revealed by the man himself in a 2006 interview with the BBC.

"I've got a brilliant new strategy," he said, "which is to make so many gaffes, that no one knows what to concentrate on... You pepper the media with so many gaffes that they are confused."[271]

Steve Bannon put it another way: "The way to deal with [the media] is to flood the zone with shit."[272]

This strategy has borne fruit on both sides of the Atlantic – the media firmly embedded within the Bullingdon Club elite, turning the fringe, radical philosophies of Tufton Street into tabloid talking-points.

7 THE PROTECTION RACKET

The British media is a formidable institution. The BBC is the largest news site in the world, recording 1.2 billion monthly visits – comfortably more than the second largest platform, MSN (800 million).[273]

There are many things wrong with the BBC's output, not least its misplaced obsession with 'balance', but the UK on the whole benefits from its stabilising presence. We only have to look across the pond to see the political culture that has been created by commercial, partisan news. For millions of Americans, the conspiracy theories of Donald Trump and the Republican Party – channelled through supportive TV networks and amplified by their professional outriders – are the only 'news' they receive on a daily basis.

Meanwhile, in the UK, Ofcom's 2021/22 BBC

Annual Report found that 73% of UK adults use a BBC service every week for news.[274] Given the broadcaster's commitment to accuracy and impartiality, the BBC therefore anchors political debate – generally (although not always) acting as an antidote to wild exaggerations and outright conspiracy theories.

However, the BBC has in recent years given precedence to debate over fact. On Cambridge Analytica, Vote Leave lawbreaking, the deception of Brexit, Russian electoral interference, Boris Johnson's attempts to undermine democracy and so on, the broadcaster has awarded a platform to both sides, instead of relentlessly and shamelessly pursuing the truth.

In essence, the BBC has been too timid; not brave enough to clamp down on Trumpian deceit. To stop the migration of America's zombie democracy to the UK, the BBC must be bolder. Defunding the corporation, removing it from the ecosystem entirely, is not the solution.

And the BBC is not the only bastion of sanity in the British media. There are scores of decent, tenacious reporters working at broadcasters and newspapers that preach good values. Indeed, throughout the 'Partygate' scandal, this wing of the media proved itself to be one of the few barely functioning pillars of British democracy. Johnson's law-breaking would not have been exposed had it not been for a few determined reporters, notably at ITV News and *The Mirror*.

Parliament cannot meaningfully hold the prime

minister to account without the active participation of the governing party – nor can the Ministerial Code, which is ultimately enforced by the prime minister. The judiciary has proven on multiple occasions that the Government has acted unlawfully – by proroguing Parliament and awarding 'VIP' contracts – yet this has not changed the way in which the Conservative Party has governed.

This is why we need a principled, honest media – to hold those in power to account, which should surely be the mission of anyone in this profession.

Yet, a large part of the British media works primarily in the interests of its rich, ideological benefactors, rather than in the interests of the people.

This ideological alliance was no more evident than during the Johnson years – when a man spewed up by Fleet Street made the leap to Downing Street.

Sacked from his graduate traineeship at *The Times* for inventing quotes, Johnson managed to wangle his way into a job at *The Telegraph* through its then-editor Max Hastings, whom Johnson had met at an Oxford Union debate – Johnson's colourful journalism eventually carrying him to the editor's job at *The Spectator*.

Johnson was a product of the press – an old boy's club that favoured (and still favours) flair over fine-print. And, when he took his seat at the navel of the Cabinet table, Johnson made sure to reward those who had delivered this prize.

Dominic Cummings, who sat at Johnson's side for much of his time in office, later claimed that the ex-Prime Minister received "direct repeated calls" from press proprietors and editors, who told him that working from home norms were "killing" the newspaper industry. They urged him, Cummings claimed, to "get commuters back".[275]

Asked if he came across any examples of private lobbying leading to lockdown rule changes during the pandemic, Cummings said that: "Newspapers negotiated direct bungs [payments] to themselves with him [Boris Johnson]".

There were "no officials on [the calls]", he added, and Johnson "told officials to send the [money] dressed up as COVID relief".

The mechanism used to deploy this financial help was a Government-sponsored advertising campaign, ostensibly designed to publicise its COVID-19 policies. Content for these articles was seemingly spoon-fed to the newspapers by the Government, with the same interviews and the same quotes appearing across several titles. The stories often involved praise for measures taken by the Government, some of it barely relevant to the pandemic.

The Cabinet Office has failed to provide the receipts for this spending – merely referring journalists to its opaque monthly spending records, that agglomerate all advertising output.

What we know, however, is that this special subsidy arrangement began in April 2020 and was called 'All In, All Together'. Budgeted at £35 million for the first three months, it was seemingly still operating two years later – *The Guardian* published a story under its banner in March 2022.

The chief beneficiaries of this state largesse were seemingly the big, wealthy news providers: the Mail group, the Murdoch group, the Telegraph group and the Mirror group – and they could hardly have deserved it less. The Mail is owned through trusts based in Jersey and the Bahamas and its proprietor is the billionaire Lord Rothermere. The Telegraph is owned by Sir Frederick Barclay, who lives on Brecqhou, a private island in the Channel Islands.[276] Rupert Murdoch is of course an Australian-American media tycoon worth some $19 billion.

If this scheme had continued at its initial rate for 24 months, its total spending would have been well in excess of £200 million.

And while Johnson lent his Government's financial support to the newspaper giants, he also – as we well know – heeded their call to relax lockdown measures in the autumn of 2020.

But the media's influence on Johnson's Government didn't stop there. This pressure carried on even when Johnson's COVID missteps were exposed.

On 20 November 2020, the *Mail Online* – the *Daily Mail*'s online edition – published a story lambasting the Government's medical and scientific advisors for warning the nation about an incoming second wave of COVID.

Emails between Cabinet Office staff and the Department of Health and Social Care (DHSC) – revealed through Freedom of Information (FOI) requests – show that official concerns were raised about the article on the morning of 21 November.[277]

An email seemingly from the Government's 'rapid response unit', which aims to combat online misinformation, flagged "growing engagement" with the *Mail Online* story – noting that "the article has now been picked up by several high profile lockdown sceptics such as Simon Dolan and Adam Brooks." The unit recommended that someone from the DHSC should contact the *Daily Mail* press office and offer a comment from the Government to be included in the article.

Later that same day, it was noted that the *Mail Online*'s story was achieving "fast growth" – prompting the unit to recommend that the DHSC should post a tweet, rebutting the article.

"I'd suggest responding to the *Daily Mail*'s post, rather than to the lockdown sceptics," the unit noted.

This advice was adopted and the DHSC posted a tweet in response to the *Daily Mail*, stating: "This article is misleading. This is a global pandemic – national restrictions have been introduced to keep people safe and save lives. It is vital people follow the rules and continue to stay at home so we can bring the transmission rates back down and get back to normality."

By 22 November, however, the Government had backtracked – and the DHSC had deleted its tweet. A further FOI request revealed that the decision to delete the tweet was taken after the *Daily Mail* leant on the Government.

An email from an individual working in the DHSC press office on the morning of 22 November read: "I understand REDACTED have been speaking to the

Mail Online about this rebuttal tweet. REDACTED wants us to delete for relationship management purposes and replace with the below: 'The measures introduced by the Government to keep people safe have saved lives. The July protection cited in the article did not account for possible measures to stop the spread of the virus.'"[278]

In other words, individuals from the *Mail Online* spoke to the Government about the tweet – a conversation that presumably led officials to believe that, unless it was deleted, relations could sour between the newspaper and the administration. For whatever reason, the Government was sufficiently worried about this outcome to remove its Twitter post.

The participants in the conversation between the *Daily Mail* and the Government are unknown.

However, while the Government decided to let the issue lie, the *Mail* didn't. On 23 November, it published an article with the following headline: "Department of Health in climbdown after online swipe at the *Mail*'s analysis of COVID-19 facts and figures".[279]

This second article defiantly quoted several lockdown-sceptic Conservative MPs supporting the newspaper over the Government.

Professor Carl Heneghan of the University of Oxford, who advised the Government against imposing the circuit-breaker restrictions in September 2020, even went so far as to accuse the DHSC of "censorship through social media".

Yet, the Government was right. The original

Mail Online article criticised by the Government contained a number of assertions that, in hindsight, were mistaken.

The article was premised on a press briefing delivered by England's Chief Scientific Advisor Sir Patrick Vallance and Chief Medical Officer Professor Chris Whitty on 31 October 2020. During that briefing, they presented four models from different academic institutions, estimating the potential daily deaths from COVID, if further restrictions were not imposed by the Government.

The *Mail Online* accused Sir Patrick and Professor Whitty of trying to "scare the Government into implementing a lockdown", saying that "the second peak seems to have passed".

"Its warnings simply don't bear any relation to reality," the *Mail* added.

Yet, two of the models cited by Sir Patrick and Professor Whitty anticipated that the number of daily COVID deaths would hit roughly 1,500 during the winter peak – if the Government did not implement new restrictions. Daily deaths in reality reached 1,300 in the second wave, even with local tier restrictions gradually ramped-up from mid-October onwards.

The models suggested that daily deaths could peak at some time from mid-December to mid-January – which indeed they did, on 19 January. The *Mail* chided Sir Patrick for suggesting in mid-September that daily COVID cases could reach 50,000 by mid-October. "We have never got near that figure," the article stated.

Yet, from the publication date of the article

on 20 November to 29 December, daily cases rose precipitously from 16,858 to 81,569.

"I couldn't be more concerned about the repeated failures of modelling we've experienced," Conservative MP Steve Baker was quoted as saying by the *Mail*, as the newspaper celebrated the Government's removal of its Twitter rebuttal.

Despite the clout of the *Mail* and Johnson's recent history of employment with both *The Telegraph* and *The Spectator*, another media giant has arguably the greatest influence on British politics: Rupert Murdoch's News Corp.

As the owner of *The Times*, *The Sun*, talkRadio, Talk TV and the publisher HarperCollins, Murdoch has cast his net across the UK's media landscape – setting the pulse of political debate.

Indeed, the political fortunes of prime ministers have often been reliant on the stance taken by Murdoch-owned titles. After the surprise election victory of John Major's Conservative Party in 1992, Murdoch's tabloid title emblazoned a headline that stuck in the British media membrane: "It's The Sun Wot Won It".

Consequently, when Tony Blair became leader of the Labour Party, a key facet of his 'modernisation' project was to curry favour with Murdoch and his newspapers – to the annoyance of left-wing activists.

This is a state of affairs to which Murdoch has become accustomed in his three primary domains: the UK, the US, and his native Australia.

Murdoch owns *Fox News*, the US broadcaster that acted as a mouthpiece for Trump during his time in the White House, while Murdoch-owned newspaper titles account for up to 60% of circulation in Australia – in 2011 ranking as the third most concentrated in the world, behind only China and Egypt.[280]

A nonagenarian (currently 91 years old), the billionaire media mogul is hardly a recluse. Government records show that Murdoch and his right-hand woman, Rebekah Brooks, held seven private meetings with five senior ministers – Boris Johnson, Rishi Sunak, Michael Gove, Jacob Rees-Mogg and Priti Patel – over a seven-week period in August and September 2020.[281]

Gove, who used to work at *The Times*, has maintained an ongoing friendship with his old boss during his political career – Murdoch joining Gove for an interview conducted with President Trump for the newspaper in 2017.[282] After exiting the Cabinet under Liz Truss, Gove was set to be hired by *Times Radio*, forced to decline the offer when Sunak reversed Truss's decision. Records show that Gove also had a tipple with *Daily Mail* owner Lord Rothermere on 15 August.

Despite being logged as official meetings, the content of these discussions are entirely hidden from public view.

For her part, Brooks is firmly embedded in the Murdoch machine. She was the editor of the now defunct *News of the World* from 2000 to 2003, editor of *The Sun* from 2003 to 2009, and CEO of *News International* from 2009 to 2011. Brooks was a prominent figure in the phone-hacking scandal, when it was revealed that a *News of the World* story published during her tenure allegedly involved illegal phone-hacking. She was cleared of charges in 2014 and has since been appointed as the CEO of News UK.

This all points to a few dominant newspaper owners and editors with a disproportionate influence over Conservative politicians, many of whom are former colleagues and course mates.

But while the lobbying of ministers by media proprietors is an important and under-appreciated part of Bullingdon Club Britain, perhaps even more significant is how these outlets lobby the nation.

As mentioned, while several tenacious journalists have exposed the political scandals of recent years, a legion of reporters has seemingly been tasked with covering them up. *The Sun*, for example, Murdoch's flagship tabloid, stoically refused to give prominent coverage to the 'Partygate' affair – for which 124 fines were issued – while the *Daily Mail* dedicated a dozen front pages to 'Beergate', a lockdown 'scandal' involving Labour Leader Keir Starmer, for which he was investigated and not fined.

From mid-January 2022 to the end of May – during the most intense months of the 'Partygate' affair – 90% of the *Daily Mail*'s front page coverage of the scandal was positive towards the Government, including one infamous splash, "Don't they know there's a war on", which attempted to use Russia's invasion of Ukraine as political cover for Johnson.

Of the eight leading UK newspapers, only three (*The Guardian*, *The Mirror* and the *Daily Star*) ran front pages on 'Partygate' that framed the Government in a negative light the majority of the time, according to an analysis by the *Press Gazette*.[283]

Exemplifying the cosy relationship between Downing Street and Fleet Street, the Number 10 director of communications between January and March 2021, James Slack, left Johnson's administration to become deputy editor of *The Sun*.

Slack's leaving party was infamously held the day before the funeral of Prince Philip, which perhaps indicates why *The Sun* gave such scant coverage to Downing Street's boozy antics.

Despite the political preferences of these titles having been known for decades, there is strong evidence to suggest that there is now a more intimate relationship between these media outlets and politicians, with the objectives of Conservative ministers and right-wing newspapers running in parallel.

Certainly, it's difficult to see the Murdoch empire supporting the Labour Party in the current political climate, even if the party reincarnated the Blairite spirit.

This sentiment is reflected by those who executed Blair's pact with Murdoch, claiming that the right-wing papers have ditched any previous residual commitment to objectivity. "Something very strange has happened to our political-media ecosystem," former Downing Street Director of Communications Alastair Campbell told me in a *Byline TV* interview in April 2021.[284]

"Lies aren't called out, scandals are not seen as scandals," he said. "For all the new media stuff that's around, the old media – the kind of oligarchical, right-wing owned media – they want a right-wing government, they want a right-wing prime minister."

Campbell is perhaps benefitting from his detachment from the political maelstrom. He is now an external political observer of an administration that he dislikes, rather than someone seeking to win and preserve power.

However, it is undoubtedly true that objectivity – the measured and fair assessment of known facts – is an increasingly antiquated concept in the media.

"Compliance" from journalists towards those in power "is part of a pattern", writes veteran Westminster reporter Peter Oborne – one of the few insiders to call out the incestuous relationship between political insiders and the press. "Political editors are so pleased to be given 'insider' or 'exclusive' information that they report it without challenge or question."[285]

Oborne himself served under Johnson at *The Spectator*, and resigned as chief political commentator of *The Telegraph* in 2015 after claiming that the newspaper deliberately suppressed stories about HSBC in order to keep its valuable advertising account with the banking giant. He said one former *Telegraph* executive told him HSBC was "the advertiser you literally cannot afford to offend".[286]

Indeed, the Westminster system incubates a closeness between politicians and journalists that has a tendency to suffocate the truth. The clique of political reporters is called the 'Lobby' – in reference to the quarters in the Palace of Westminster where these journalists are allowed to lurk, hoping to pick up scraps of gossip. The success of the political reporter is therefore largely derived from their exclusive access to power, rather than their unique grasp of policies or international affairs, for example. Fearing that they will be cut off from this occupational lifeline if they get on the wrong side of power, reporters are conditioned to tread lightly.

In the Westminster Village, journalists are scared of calling out lies and wrongdoing in unequivocal terms for fear of having their access to power revoked. The pursuit of the truth has therefore been eschewed in favour of a reality show populated by political 'personalities'.

Read the opinion section of most major newspapers or tune into any political TV or radio programme and you'll soon realise that topical debate has been raided by self-serving actors who use the space not to express the best version of the truth, sustained by sound reasoning and pertinent facts, but as a means of buttressing their personal brand.

These media personalities range from tabloid journalists to failed politicians, to young commentators seeking their moment in the spotlight.

These people are media savvy – knowing the pressure points of political debate that are likely to cause most fury; strategically stirring in statistics or anecdotes that, without wider context, seem to form the basis of 'common sense' opinions.

Twitter is an intrinsic factor in the rise of these political personalities. An internal study by Twitter even found that the algorithmic bias of the platform favours right-wing figures.[287] And so, they have been given a head-start on a platform that encourages the speedy and the sensational over the calm and the judicious, allowing previously little-known loudmouths to gain inflated levels of public notoriety.

Old Harrovian Laurence Fox, for example, is a former actor and unsuccessful 2021 London Mayoral candidate who told *The Times* in 2019 that he had been "totally radicalised" against 'woke culture' and 'political correctness' by watching YouTube videos.[288]

Since then, his standing as a political figure has mushroomed, triggered by an appearance on BBC *Question Time* in January 2020, helping him to gain hundreds of thousands of politically-engaged Twitter followers.

Fox is now something of a regular on the media, spouting his hard-right agenda across the airwaves. A vaccine sceptic, Fox was pictured on Twitter wearing a T-shirt with the words, "No vaccine needed, I have an immune system". Four days later, he reported having contracted the virus.[289]

Fox epitomises what journalist Otto English has described as 'politainment' – the rise of "ridiculous diversions into colourful stories about bells and fireworks overshadowing the real issues of the day."[290]

Entertainment factor – what is described commonly in newsrooms as "good TV" – now dwarfs the pursuit of accuracy, with this bizarre Punch and Judy act justified by broadcasters on the basis that it provides political 'balance'.

Of course, the truth is not the midpoint between a fact and a lie, and so the consecration of 'balance' as the guiding commandment of broadcasting – and in particular BBC broadcasting – has therefore served up rational political opinions alongside those of the right's well-funded misinformation apparatus, presenting them as equally valid.

As a result, political debate has become commodified and a lack of seriousness pervades modern British politics, from Downing Street to the dimly-lit studios of *GB News*.

One spill over effect has been the creation of destructive narratives in political discourse – helping those on the right who seek to atomise society and weaken our collective bonds through contrived culture wars. It is easier to tear something to pieces than to offer solutions, and the absence of substance in the media encourages this feeding-frenzy.

From environmental activism to racial equality campaigns, sensationalist commentators undermine the enduring progressive coalition in the UK in an effort to neuter these social causes. Thus, those belonging to Extinction Rebellion, the environmental movement that has drawn the world's attention to the imminent threat posed by climate change, are described as "eco-zealots" by the *Daily Mail*.[291]

This punditocracy is largely free from expertise; it therefore destroys rather than creates – contributing to the glaring absence of public policy knowledge in frontline politics.

Yet, while the BBC has contributed to the worsening of political debate, it is one of the few institutions capable of holding back the tide of rampant populism and misinformation that is surging on both sides of the Atlantic. The BBC shouldn't be defunded; it should be improved. It should recognise that its public service lies in the pursuit of objectivity and truth, not 'balance'. For, if we lose the BBC as an arbiter of our national conversation, we will be swept up by the same forces that have corrupted the printing press.

GB News, for example, has so far raised £120 million for its expedition into British broadcasting – giving a platform to an assortment of fanatical right-wing politicians and commentators, most prominently Nigel Farage, with a light dusting of lefties sprinkled in to satisfy the anaemic impartiality rules set by Ofcom, the broadcasting regulator.[292]

GB News has relied on the usual populist tropes during its time on air so far, claiming that it is 'anti-establishment' – despite two of its shareholders being Conservative peers – and raging against the supposed relentless march of poisonous 'woke' values in Western society.[293]

Andrew Neil, who was briefly the channel's chief presenter, launched *GB News* by promising to "puncture the pomposity of the Westminster elites", to curtail the "metropolitan mindset" supposedly infecting the established broadcasters, and to tackle the "threat to free speech" posed by "cancel culture". Neil initially denied that the platform had been designed as a UK equivalent of *Fox News* but, on quitting the show a couple of months later, he appeared to suggest that it had turned into exactly that.[294]

As for the BBC, one of its big problems – as with many other democratic bodies – is that the government retains significant control over the selection of its management team. This occurs in two ways: through the government's right to appoint five non-executive members to the BBC board (out of 10 non-executives overall), and indirectly through the BBC's negotiation of its charter (its governing principles) with the government, which typically takes place every 10 years. Appointing executives who are seen as allies by the government is therefore in some ways a savvy strategic move by the corporation.

Ergo, Robbie Gibb is currently on the BBC board. Gibb is a self-professed Thatcherite and a former director of communications for Prime Minister Theresa May who helped to set up *GB News* and has called Boris Johnson "a Prime Minister who has all too often been misunderstood and maligned... a man who wants to unite not divide.[295]

Gibb – labelled as an "active agent of the Conservative Party" by former BBC Newsnight presenter Emily Maitlis – is joined on the board by chairman Richard Sharp, who has in the past donated more than £400,000 to the Conservative Party, and director-general Tim Davie, who stood as a council candidate for the Conservatives in 1993 and 1994, and was deputy chairman of the Hammersmith and Fulham Conservatives in the 1990s.[296]

The life of an investigative journalist in Britain is also hampered by our country's draconian libel laws – which favour those with deep pockets and rich grievances – turning London into a courtroom for brassed-off oligarchs.

HarperCollins was forced to settle a libel suit brought by former Chelsea Football Club owner Roman Abramovich over the book *Putin's People*, authored by journalist Catherine Belton. Had the libel trial gone ahead in the High Court, the legal bill was likely to have exceeded £10 million.[297] Fellow British journalist Tom Burgis, meanwhile, was faced with a libel suit from a Kazakhstan-based mining company over his book *Kleptopia* – a claim that was ultimately dismissed by the High Court.[298]

Despite neither having lost their cases, both Belton and Burgis have described the personal toll of spending hundreds of hours defending their journalism, faced with endless threatening legal letters from their opponents. "In my experience [these letters] are often written in a tone of righteous indignation where the journalist is said to have behaved appallingly," Burgis told a committee of MPs – naming the law firms that assist oligarchs in their cases against journalists.[299]

Other reporters, who aren't protected financially by their publishers, face the prospect of going bankrupt – losing their savings and possessions – if they are defeated by their wealthy opponents.

The pursuit of the truth can break someone both financially and emotionally, if you get on the wrong side of a powerful opponent.

"Cases are just too expensive to defend", regardless of the quality of the journalism involved, Belton told the same committee of MPs, "and the system is stacked in favour of deep-pocketed litigants from the outset."

This is an issue faced by all reporters seeking to expose the truth about the rich and powerful – not just those taking on oligarchs. *Byline Times*, for example, has faced legal threats from PPE Medpro – a company that won more than £200 million in Government contracts during the pandemic.[300]

The *Byline Times* team contacted PPE Medpro in 2020 to find out whether the firm had any connection to Conservative peer Baroness Michelle Mone or her husband, Douglas Barrowman. The first reply from PPE Medpro stated: "Thanks for your email. Your email has been sent onto our legal lawyer as your comments are defamatory! We are putting you on notice and you will hear from us by tomorrow."

The following day, PPE Medpro's principal director, Anthony Page, emailed to state: "We trust that there will be no inaccurate or misleading statements within your article. If that were to be the case then we will instruct our lawyers immediately."

Page told *Byline Times* that "Baroness Mone is neither an investor, director or in any way associated with PPE Medpro. She has never had any role or function in PPE Medpro, nor in the process by which contracts were awarded to PPE Medpro. Similarly, Mr Barrowman is not an investor, director or shareholder in PPE Medpro. He has also never had any role or function in PPE Medpro, nor in the process by which contracts were awarded to PPE Medpro."

It is now known that some of Page's claims were not true – though it is unclear whether Page knew this at the time. He may have believed that threatening legal proceedings was a proportionate response.

In fact, Page has strong links to Baroness Mone, and both Baroness Mone and Barrowman have financial ties to PPE Medpro. As reported by the *Financial Times*, Page was "the registered secretary of MGM Media – the company that manages Mone's personal brand, according to the House of Lords register of financial interests, until he quit the role on the same day that PPE Medpro was set up."[301]

In November 2021, it was further revealed – by the Government – that Baroness Mone was indeed the person who referred PPE Medpro to the Government's 'VIP' procurement lane.[302]

After these facts were revealed, *Byline Times* contacted Page again, asking if he still maintained his previous assertion that Baroness Mone was in no way involved with the company. It received no reply.

Then, in March 2022, private emails between Baroness Mone and Lord Theodore Agnew – at the time a Cabinet Office minister responsible for procurement – were released, showing that Baroness Mone had used a private email address to correspond with the minister.

The Guardian described Baroness Mone's emails as a "sales pitch" for the procurement of PPE from Hong Kong. Baroness Mone copied senior Cabinet minister Michael Gove into the email, telling Lord Agnew that Gove had asked her to "urgently" contact him. At the time, PPE Medpro had not been incorporated as a company.[303]

Finally, in May 2022, according to the *Sunday Times*, Baroness Mone's husband Barrowman admitted that he did have a financial interest in PPE Medpro. "Sources close to the Glasgow-born businessman said he had declared this 'at the outset' to the Cabinet Office," the newspaper reported – contradicting the previous testimony of Page.[304] *The Guardian* has since reported that Baroness Mone and her adult children received £29 million originating from the profits of PPE Medpro.[305]

It is unclear whether Page was aware of these facts or not when he emailed us threatening legal action. It is also not known if some of the profits from the £200-million taxpayer contracts have been used to pay PPE Medpro's legal team.

UK law, as in politics and economics, is designed to instinctively protect the privileged and wealthy. Since Putin's invasion of Ukraine and the focus on the actions of his oligarchs, the Government has pledged to clamp down on Strategic Lawsuits Against Public Participation (SLAPPs). These lawsuits are typically launched by high-profile individuals or corporations against journalists or publications to "financially and psychologically exhaust" them and "evade scrutiny in the public interest", according to the Government's definition.[306]

Yet, the current legal system has not only been exploited by the super-rich. *Byline Times* reporters have received legal threats from two former Cabinet ministers, warning that they would consider launching proceedings, if we published information about them. Our stories were in the public interest, thoroughly researched, and much of the information had been published before by other media outlets.

A similar approach was taken by former Chancellor Nadhim Zahawi when his past tax affairs were questioned by the blogger Dan Neidle, a former head of tax at the law firm Clifford Chance. Neidle says that he received a series of "threatening" legal letters asking him to withdraw his allegations and recommending that he seek advice from a libel lawyer.[307] Zahawi later stumped up nearly £5 million in previously unpaid taxes, including a penalty charge, precipitating his sacking as Conservative Party Chair.[308] He said the error was "careless and not deliberate".

Ultimately, it is highly unlikely that an MP or a Cabinet minister – present or former – would launch legal proceedings against a media outlet or a journalist. However, the threat alone – which raises the spectre, however distant, of millions of pounds in legal fees – has a chilling effect on free speech and freedom of the press.

Unfortunately, we only seem to be travelling in one direction: the regression of our right as journalists and citizens to know what those in power are doing in our name, and with our money.

8 THE CULTURE WAR

So, a privileged elite has assumed power and exploited a flimsy political system to entrench its wealth and power – assisted by a compliant media.

However, getting away with it has required an equally pervasive and sophisticated distraction campaign; the creation of an alternate worldview in which the ruling elite is actually the saviour of the working class.

This worldview is the culture war – a key political tool for conservatives on both sides of the Atlantic, designed to break working-class solidarity through the invention of conflicts between social liberals and social conservatives.

So, rather than Boris Johnson being an enemy of the working class, because he's an Old Etonian Bullingdon boy, he has been portrayed instead as a champion of the 'left behind' – due to his supposed antipathy towards a distant, liberal, metropolitan elite (embodied by his support for Brexit).

The culture war has turned Johnson into a cultural ally of the working class, even despite his own privileged background and his pursuit of elitist politics.

While this has been a conservative ploy for decades – former Conservative Leader Michael Howard ran an anti-immigration campaign back in 2005 that included the policy of introducing an 'Australian-style' points system, later supported by Nigel Farage and adopted by Johnson's Government – the understanding of this phenomenon has crystallised in recent times through the culture war.

Typically, 'culture war' is used to describe a battle of ideas between two divergent groups. On the one hand are older and less well-educated people who are socially conservative (likely to be more hostile to immigration, LGBTQ+ rights, and permissive social mores) and typically rooted in small towns and rural areas. On the other are younger graduates based in cities, who are generally more accepting of immigration and fluid identity values.

As Maria Sobolewska and Rob Ford write in *Brexitland*: "Many of those who grew up in a more ethnically homogeneous, socially conservative Britain have a profoundly different view of what Britain is and ought to be than members of the youngest generations, who have grown up in a much more ethnically diverse and socially liberal country."[309]

However, the right-wing media suggests that

this war is being fought equally aggressively by both groups; a form of social Darwinian warfare that has spawned from a natural ideological divide, with no clear provocateur.

This is patently not the case. Although there is a small band of hyper-liberals who are attempting to rapidly and combatively erode 'traditional' ideas regarding borders, the family nucleus and gender identity – on occasion shutting down those who disagree – there is a much wider liberal consensus in Britain that is not so forthright nor so antagonistic about these values divides.

In an effort to turn moderate conservatives against from this body of sane liberal opinion, however, right-wing culture warriors exaggerate the influence of hyper-liberals – portraying the latter as the dominant progressive faction.

This distortion of reality is aided by the isolated information bubble inhabited by social conservatives – many of whom are older and therefore more reliant on right-wing newspapers and susceptible to online fabrications. Those over the age of 65 share nearly seven times as many articles on Facebook from 'fake news' domains as those aged between 18 and 29, according to a study by the journal Science.[310] Nigel Farage also instructively claimed that Brexit and Trump would not have happened without Facebook.[311]

These separate information spheres are mirrored in the physical geography of liberals and conservatives, with the two groups increasingly clustering in different parts of the country.

"White voters with low education levels move

less often, and are becoming concentrated in more ethnically homogeneous and less economically successful rural and small-town areas," write Sobolewska and Ford in *Brexitland*. "These trends magnify identity conflicts by increasing social segregation and reducing the level of contact and common experience between people on either side of the identity politics divide."[312]

Therefore, the 'culture war' more accurately describes a political conflict manufactured by the right to distort and exploit the largely unsubstantiated fears of social conservatives towards hyper-liberalism.

As social class researcher Ellie Mae O'Hagan has written: "The hard right is successfully pushing a narrative that the division in this country is between the white working class and the 'woke mob'."

This is despite a plurality of people subscribing to basic, progressive opinions. People widely believe, for example, that people of colour face greater barriers to success than white people. There is also popular support for policies such as gay marriage, access to safe abortions and a low salary threshold for immigrants seeking to enter the UK.

In 2000, just 25% of those who responded to the British Social Attitudes Survey – a socially and politically weighted survey of 6,000 people – said that equal opportunities for black and Asian people had not gone far enough. At the latest count, this figure had risen to 45%. The 'woke mob' is the growing plurality of people in the UK.[313]

Reflecting the tempo of modern politics, the

culture war is trans-Atlantic – waged by the likes of Ted Cruz, a multimillionaire Republican who spends his time lamenting "west coast liberals" – distracting from the corporate greed of America's actual elites who fund his brand of libertarian politics.

As author Tom Nichols writes in *The Atlantic* about the culture war frenzy stoked by 'MAGA – Make America Great Again' (in other words, pro-Trump) Republicans: "They will tell you that they are for 'liberty' and 'freedom', but these are merely code words for personal grudges, racial and class resentments.

"What makes this situation worse is that there is no remedy for it. When people are driven by fantasies, by resentment, by an internalised sense of inferiority, there is no redemption in anything."[314]

This is also the approach of the Bullingdon Club elite. There can be no victory for ordinary social conservatives who have been captured by the culture war – no final victory against the supposed liberal enemy – only a never-ending Ferris wheel of intensifying grievances built to serve successive reactionary political campaigns.

Take the 2022 Conservative Political Action Conference (CPAC) in Texas, which offered a bingo card of the issues currently enraging the right.

Far from focusing on the cost of living crisis, Russia's invasion of Ukraine or the climate emergency, instead talk centred on transgender people, educational indoctrination, and how – as Nigel Farage termed it – "madrasas [schools] of Marxism" are supposedly teaching white children to hate their race.[315]

When the big global crises were mentioned, it was with a tone of dismissal. Farage told his audience that far more dangerous than Vladimir Putin's aggression is the "fifth column" – a group of people supposedly working with our enemies – in English-speaking countries infecting children with the virus of 'wokeness'.

Farage and his fellow travellers are waging a 'revolution' against imagined enemies, rather than concerning themselves with real-life issues of the economy and national security – a big departure from conservatives of yesteryear.

In attendance at CPAC was Steve Bannon, formerly Trump's right-hand-man and one of the ideological forefathers of the culture war.

As journalist Joshua Green writes in *Devil's Bargain* – the story of how Bannon rose to prominence at *Breitbart* and under Trump – at an early age, Bannon was taken with the idea that "Western civilisation had to be constantly and vigilantly defended against shadowy, shape-shifting enemies."[316]

This prominence of this idea, of a civilisational conflict between a supposed liberal elite and working-class conservatives, was apparent in 2018 when Bannon told the *New York Times* that he wanted to "build a vast network of European populists to demolish the continent's political establishment." Farage had discussed fronting a new movement set up by Bannon during this period.[317]

Indeed, Farage is a disciple of the Trump-Bannon school of culture war populism. He was the first foreign leader to meet Trump following his shock 2016 victory, he campaigned for Trump again in 2020 and has continued to support the disgraced former President despite Trump's false claims of electoral fraud and mounting federal investigations into his conduct.

Now, Farage acts as the cultural bridge between the populist-right in America and Britain – absorbing the talking points that emanate from *Fox News* and unloading them on domestic airwaves through *GB News*. And Farage's relationship with American populism is symbiotic. The politician-turned-broadcaster is credited with educating MAGA Republicans about the culture war through Brexit, which targeted social conservatives with anti-immigration and anti-establishment sentiments. "Brexit and the Trump election are inextricably linked," Bannon has said.[318]

This populist alliance is now almost a decade old, and Farage is readily importing political tools back from his students in America. Like the manufacturing of a car, Farage provided the raw materials and is now taking shipment of the finished product.

And so, during his CPAC speech, Farage wielded one of the new scapegoats created by Republican politics: critical race theory – an academic discipline that explores how institutionalised racism operates in society.

"This terrible virus, worse than anywhere else in the world," Farage bellowed, "this is a Marxist attempt to break Western civilization! A Marxist attempt to destroy everything we are."

Reverberations of this debate have been felt in the UK, with the right caught in a state of frenzy about attempts in some academic institutions to examine the negative impacts of the British empire, and to teach a form of history that accommodates more non-white viewpoints.

The UK's so-called 'strictest headmistress', Katharine Birbalsingh, who was recently the short-lived head of the Social Mobility Commission, used *GB News* to suggest that Shakespeare may be 'cancelled' in UK schools for being a "dead white man".[319]

This is a trend observed by public policy expert Sam Freedman, who says that when culture war protagonists "run out of real culture war issues," they instead "just imagine ones that might exist in the future and fight them."

The Times followed Birbalsingh's lead in August 2022, lamenting the supposed mass censorship of classical texts by universities – the newspaper claiming that lecturers fear that these books may offend students. This story was given front-page coverage by the Murdoch-owned publication, despite it finding only two examples of books having been removed from university courses in the UK.[320]

This idea – that educational institutions are turning into havens for 'snowflakes' (a derogatory term used to describe people who are concerned with social equality and justice issues) – has even been echoed by Liz Truss. In 2020, she delivered a speech in which she claimed that, during her education at a comprehensive school in Leeds in the 1980s, she was "taught about racism and sexism" while "there was too little time spent making sure everyone could read and write."

Several former pupils of the same school have pointed out that it was far better administered under Labour than under the Conservatives. "We were not 'taught about racism and sexism' to the exclusion of the basics," said one of Truss's former peers. "We were taught the national curriculum."[321]

This epitomises the culture war strategy: exaggerate well-meaning liberal reforms – or cherry-pick an isolated example of liberal overreach – to argue that the country is being infected with crazed, gender-fluid (Labour voting) woke warriors, and can only be saved by sensible (Conservative voting) traditionalists.

As right-wing culture warrior Toby Young has claimed: there is "nothing liberal about" the progressive movement. "Instead, it has far more in common with the hysterical witch-hunting of the Middle Ages."[322]

This hyperbole is defended with the nebulous threat of 'what next?' – implying that legitimate reforms benefiting minority groups should be snuffed out as they may fuel vague, future incursions into individual 'freedoms'.

On their own, these culture war debates sound trivial – particularly compared to the economic turmoil that Britain is currently experiencing. However, the culture war has over recent years been attached to the campaign to leave the EU – increasing its political potency.

Indeed, through years of parliamentary prevarications and media debate, Brexit has become a worldview. The Brexit mission is the crystallisation of the right-wing culture war, almost entirely divorced from the boring administrative practicalities of the UK's real-world relationship with the EU.

To be a 'Brexiter' is to be anti-woke, anti-metropolitan and anti-expert, with an active hostility to social justice campaigns. As O'Hagan says: "The use of the 'wokemob' concept is clever, because it does not paint people of colour as the enemy. Instead, it names advocates of racial justice as a threat to the white working class. This allows the proponents of this narrative to sidestep accusations of racism."

To be a Brexiter is also to be overly concerned with statues and a triumphant (white-centric) version of British history. It also means being constantly under attack; the plucky outsider fighting for democracy and common sense against a corrupt establishment.

Truss articulated these values assertively after the 2016 referendum – despite supporting Remain – and so was seen as a more authentic Brexiter than her 2022 leadership opponent, Rishi Sunak, who voted Leave.

As I have mentioned already, before selecting his camp for the referendum, Boris Johnson wrote two columns for *The Telegraph* – one in favour of Remain and one in favour of Leave. In his book, *The Age of the Strongman*, Gideon Rachman recalls meeting Johnson in 2002 when both were reporting from Brussels. Rachman remembers prodding Johnson by saying that a lot of Johnson's friends thought that he was secretly in favour of the EU. "Johnson looked back at me, with a faintly hurt expression. 'Of course,

I'm in favour of the EU,' he exclaimed. 'How could you not be?'"[323]

Brexit is not just simply about membership of the EU; it is the embodiment of the culture war and a mythical populist project which seeks to 'make Britain great again' through neo-imperial rule.

Outside of the UK, however, Rachman writes, "Brexit was understood for what it was: a serious blow to the power and coherence of the West and the liberal democratic values that the Western alliance has traditionally upheld."

A focal point of culture war is the demonisation of expertise and those who carry information to the public at large. This plays into the legitimate and widely felt anger towards a distant intelligentsia who have failed to grasp the concerns and the suffering of 'little people' over recent decades.

However, rather than attempting to improve the flow of public discourse, culture warriors exploit this anti-establishment fervour to question the very basis of established facts. These individuals then use the vacuum created by this mistrust of expertise to manufacture a new reality in which rampant woke warriors are tearing down statues and hurling non-binary pronouns at baffled grannies.

Indeed, a MAGA worldview has been created by Trump – absorbed by those who marched on the Capitol on 6 January 2021 – with the former US President positioned as a superhero figure, saving America from seditious liberal-communist forces. The convictions and the language that support this worldview are so absolute, and so aggressive, that its advocates were conditioned to support a violent attack on American democracy. Up to 75% of Republican supporters have said that Joe Biden's victory in the 2020 Presidential Election was not legitimate, while journalists howl into the wind – unable to convince these cult followers of basic facts.[324]

At CPAC, Farage hurled pejoratives at the media during his speech – "You're fake news! Fake news!" – echoing Trump's own campaign to demean and discredit those scrutinising his actions.

Britain has been more successful at resisting these trends. Farage's anti-media fist waving has been largely confined to his jaunts stateside – perhaps due to the recent elevation of former journalists to high power, particularly Johnson and Michael Gove, who instinctively flinch away from punching their former colleagues (also wary of their future work prospects, one suspects).

However, in the post-Johnson era, this may change. In a 2022 Conservative leadership hustings event hosted by Talk TV, frontrunner Truss slammed the media, suggesting that journalists were to blame for the ousting of Johnson. She even claimed that the host, Tom Newton Dunn, was parroting left-wing talking points when he asked why she was ruling out extra Government help for people during the cost of living crisis. "I believe in Britain, unlike some of the media who choose to talk our country down," she said.[325] Truss later implemented a major package of state spending to restrict the cost of energy – exposing the hollowness of her remarks at the hustings.

However, anti-expertise hyperbole isn't always empty bluster – as shown during the COVID crisis. In *Failures of State*, George Arbuthnott and Jonathan Calvert quote a Downing Street advisor who said that, "Brexiters at the top of government instilled a culture in which the views of scientists were often dismissed out of hand, a practice developed during the Brexit referendum."

The advisor is quoted as saying that, "Whereas the government used to stop play and listen to the scientists, now they had lost the ability to hear expertise... They demeaned people who sat in front of them and said this [COVID] is a risk. They had lost the ability to hear scientists."[326]

This inability to sort fact from fiction is particularly evident on the topic of 'free speech' – a primary preoccupation of those engaged in culture-war politics, who claim that dissenting voices are subject to McCarthy-style censorship from students and the left.

The Conservative Government has even admitted that its beliefs about university free speech – supposedly under threat from gangs of bespeckled Marxists – is based on virtually no real-world evidence.[327]

The Department for Education (DfE) announced in February 2021 that it would be appointing a free speech 'champion' with the power to fine universities or students' unions that, in its view, wrongly restrict free speech. This individual would also have the power to order action if staff are sacked or disciplined for their opinions.

At the time, the DfE was criticised for failing to provide any tangible examples to justify its approach. As a result, Liberal Democrat peer Baroness Jenny Randerson lodged a written parliamentary question, asking how the Government is ensuring "that policies on higher education and freedom of speech are based on (1) accurate research, and (2) evidence which reflects a balance of information."

In response, the Government confessed that there have only been "a small number of high-profile reported incidents in which staff or students have been threatened with negative consequences" for their political viewpoints, "including loss of privileges or dismissal, sometimes successfully".

The limited evidence highlighted by the Government included studies by King's College London (KCL), the University and College Union (UCU), the right-wing Policy Exchange think tank, and the Joint Committee on Human Rights.

Ironically, the KCL study opens with the observation that academic free speech has been "politicised" by the Conservative Party and figures on the right of politics.[328]

"Irrespective of whether this is factually correct or not, the long-term political strategy seems to be to force universities to acknowledge that there is an issue and, through that, create (one could argue, ironically, a 'safe') space for more open discussion on issues on the right of the political spectrum and, through that, secure long-term political support for right-leaning parties," the study reads.

A few paragraphs later, it states that free speech

incidents – in which "you could legitimately critique [KCL] for not upholding its commitment to freedom of expression" – are "rare", with just six events out of 30,000 falling into this category between 2015 and 2020. This is equivalent to just 0.002% of events held at KCL during this time period.

As for the so-called "chilling effect" that has been cited by the Government, whereby a general left-wing climate dissuades right-wing individuals from expressing their opinions, the evidence is also flimsy. Only 12% of students surveyed by KCL said that they hear about free speech incidents at university fairly or very often, with just a-quarter saying that they were anxious about expressing their views openly.

"Our survey showed that students consider freedom of expression to be a highly salient issue, but few have had any direct experience of freedom of expression being inhibited in their own institution," the report concluded.

If a Conservative MP had actually been to a university campus in the last 10 years, they would have realised that most students care infinitely more about shagging and drinking than political debate (unfortunately for politics, and for women, our Bullingdon Club elite pursued both).

What's more, students themselves are broadly in support of selective censorship. The overwhelming majority – 63% – of students surveyed by KCL said that university officials should have the right to ban people with extreme views from speaking on campus.

Finally – and tellingly – the study states that:

"there is already a strong policy framework" on free speech at university and that "further regulation in the UK is unlikely to make any difference to the issue and thus will be wholly symbolic."

Even more bizarre is the Government's reference to the UCU, given that the body trashed the Government's free speech champions policy when it was first announced.

"It is extraordinary that in the midst of a global pandemic the Government appears more interested in fighting phantom threats to free speech than taking action to contain the real and present danger which the virus poses to staff and students," its general secretary Jo Grady said.

In fact, if there is any threat to academic freedoms, it comes from the Government itself, the UCU says. "In reality the biggest threats to academic freedom and free speech come not from staff and students, or from so-called 'cancel culture', but from ministers' own attempts to police what can and cannot be said on campus, and a failure to get to grips with endemic job insecurity," Grady added.

Not only is the right's 'free speech' obsession devoid of fact, it's also hypocritical. For, if there is a crisis, it has been created by the Conservative Party through its attempts to limit the freedom to protest, its policy of banning individuals from Whitehall events who have previously been critical of the Government, and its anathema to basic transparency.[329] The death of the Queen, and the subsequent rage at anyone debating the merits of republicanism, also aptly illustrated this point – as did the years-long efforts of Brexiters to shut down those calling for a second referendum.

However, this has not stopped the Conservatives – and, even more aggressively, its allies in the press – from fighting the mythical 'woke' scourge that plagues university campuses.

It's true that some right-wing speakers have faced protests on campus and have been sidelined by the media. The former *Breitbart* editor and alt-right icon Milo Yiannopoulos, for example, is now a pariah – banned from Twitter and broadly unwelcome on campuses on both sides of the Atlantic. Likewise, former *The Sun* and *Daily Mail* columnist Katie Hopkins has been cancelled by the British political establishment.

Yet it can hardly be argued, from a free speech perspective, that Hopkins and Yiannopoulos have been treated poorly. Their views are so incendiary that, when given a platform, they actively obstruct the freedoms of others. Hopkins, for example, wrote that she would "use gunships" against migrants crossing the channel to Dover,[330] while Yiannopoulos once asked the question to his followers: 'Would you rather your child had feminism or cancer?'[331]

Cauterising them from the mainstream public conversation resulted in few negative side-effects. And, indeed, the decision not to consume someone's content is a manifestation of free expression.

Others who claim to have been 'cancelled' – such as Toby Young, who lost a Government job in 2018 after concerned members of the public protested against some of his past unsavoury comments – have not really been cancelled in any meaningful way.[332] Young has a sizable Twitter following, is an associate editor of *The Spectator* and has set up a 'trade union' to ostensibly defend free speech, whose trustees include a number of high-profile journalists and academics.

To a large extent, as Young's case demonstrates, the participants in this debate about woke censorship are simply (and successfully) attempting to increase their own profile – knowing that it will attract the attention and jubilation of the right-wing media. The cancel culture conversation does not thrive within a free market; it is subsidised and promoted by big-money media moguls who seek to perpetuate a political agenda.

If 'cancel culture' does exist, it does so beyond the studio fights of pampered media personalities. The reality is that to be cancelled, you have to hold a position of influence; positions that are invariably and predominantly held by people from privileged backgrounds.

The upper reaches of academia, journalism and publishing, politics, entertainment and business are all dominated by white, privately-educated men from the south-east. Most people outside this system, who are unfamiliar with the gowns of Eton and the spires of Oxford, are effectively pre-cancelled. Their opinions can't be shut down, because they are simply not heard in the first place.

As a reminder: 29% of MPs were educated at private school, compared to 7% in the population as a whole; 74% of Liz Truss's Cabinet were privately educated; 50% of Boris Johnson's 2020 Cabinet went to either Oxford or Cambridge; 65% of senior UK judges went to a fee-paying school; 33% of newspaper columnists attended both an independent school and Oxbridge; at the turn of the century only 18% of MPs were women; less than 10% of MPs are from an ethnic minority background; in February 2019 it was reported there are more FTSE 100 CEOs called Steve than there are CEOs from ethnic minority backgrounds.[333]

Britain's elite is a tightly knit cabal of former private school kids and heirs to wealth and influence. These elites pontificate over 'cancel culture' while monopolising the airwaves and shutting out those not belonging to this privileged tribe.

Yet, it's clear why the likes of Young worry about being 'cancelled'. Reaping the benefits of an elite education and the patronage of their families, they have always been heard; always provided with a platform. At the slightest sign of this elevated position being threatened, they have gone on the offensive. Unfortunately, however, the rest of us are forced to listen to their identity crisis, whether we like it or not.

The British establishment has always been infatuated with its own image. That's why the top private schools, universities and their debauched drinking societies wear silly gowns and engage in pompous rituals. It is a projection; a way to make noise and to be seen. The members of this club therefore think they have an innate right to be heard, which is why they are so worried about being 'cancelled'.

Funnily, the Bullingdon Club elite has used subtle strategies to limit the speech of opposition groups for centuries – namely by claiming that they alone are sensible, rational moderate actors, and that progressive ideas demonstrate a silly misunderstanding of the world we live in.

Here, too, the culture of the elite comes in useful for its members – allowing them to coat their regressive ideas in the veneer of intellectualism derived from ornate language. As the late political theorist Tom Nairn has written: "What the contemporary Anglo-British idiom does is to fuse literacy with aristocracy."

In other words: the ideas expressed by the upper classes, because they are ordered, composed and presented in a way that is believed to be superior, are in turn assumed to be correct and grounded in well-evidenced, measured thought.

A pig in a top hat, however, is still a pig.

Former US President Barack Obama has long been a proponent of the 'arc of history' – that the slow evolution of humankind always bends towards a more just, progressive and liberal world. In present-day Britain, it is difficult to hold faith in this philosophy.

A crisis of national identity has sprung forth a resurgence of flag-draped nationalism, in turn empowering authoritarian-shaped leaders who are interested in consolidating power by exploiting the UK's flimsy democratic conventions. Meanwhile, the dominant parts of the press act as the vanguard and narrator of this reactionary moment.

The prorogation and steady marginalisation of Parliament; the demonisation of asylum seekers; pointless provocations of the EU; endless antics over statues and national symbols; the erosion of the freedom to protest and even to vote.[334] This all signals an arc that seems to be veering sharply away from progress.

The foot-soldiers of this movement, it is claimed by right-wing culture warriors, are the 'left behind' – the people in small, former industrial towns who have been caught in the updraft of rapid globalisation and its associated liberal, cosmopolitan values. These are the people who voted for Brexit in 2016 and knocked holes in Labour's 'Red Wall' three years later.

There is a disjuncture, however, between colourful representations of left-behind areas and mundane reality. These places have been appropriated by a radical conservative clique and their 1950s tribute act – individuals like Farage and Johnson who have donned the clothes of the left behind and used them as a cloak for their own barely veiled prejudices.

On the launch night of *GB News*, for example, Farage complained that Brexit voters have been smeared as "knuckle-dragging racists". But it is Farage himself who has created this caricature; using the left-behind masses to bestow his brand of nativism with a badge of popular authenticity.

Yet Farage has never summoned mass appeal and has never been elected to Parliament, despite seven attempts. As David Goodhart points out in *The Road to Somewhere*, most Brexit-inclined voters are in fact moderate – "decent populists", as he calls them, who "have reservations about the drift of modern liberalism but are not, in the main, illiberal."[335]

The latest British Social Attitudes survey notes, for example, that a majority of people in the north and the midlands (57% and 56%, respectively) have either have 'liberal' values or sit somewhere between liberal and authoritarian. The percentage in the south is only marginally higher, at 61%.[336]

Theirs is a centre-ground agenda, whereby corruption and racism are deplored, public services should be properly funded, and family-orientated community life is respected. This is a fundamentally different form of politics to that created by the populists running our country, promoted by their allies in the media, which has involved the fattening of cronies, the demonisation of experts, and the departure of decency from our democracy.

Perhaps the most uncomfortable fact for these reactionary forces is that Britain's liberal base has barely germinated. Even in the areas of the country that delivered Johnson's overwhelming 2019 majority, individuals belonging to the next generation are far more liberal, outward-looking and progressive than their parents.

As I was growing up in the outskirts of a former mill town in West Yorkshire – the Conservative Party's new stomping ground – my peers had the same tolerant values that supposedly belong to the London-based 'woke' elite.

As observed by academic Michael McQuarrie in his London School of Economics paper on the 2016

US Presidential election, Hillary Clinton swung three groups of people decisively behind the Democrats: well-off communities; university towns; and areas dominated by the 'political class'.[337] Due to the US electoral system, only one of these shifts made an impact on the result. In contrast, Trump's harvesting of votes in the Midwest – the 'Rust Belt' of America – flipped key states and secured the White House.

Trump's victory didn't mean that America was becoming less liberal and less diverse – demographic changes mean that even Texas, a Republican fortress, came close to flipping blue four years later. Rather, election results can obscure the real cultural shifts in a nation, by handing a microphone to small groups of people who swayed the result while depriving attention from everyone else.

This equally seems to be the case in the UK, where nuance has been entirely absent from the debate. Despite the political chaos of recent years, Britain is in fact tolerant and liberal. Our supposed disunity is largely a figment of Conservative imagination – concocted by those who seek to divide and rule.

9 ETONOMICS

Yet, while the culture war seeks to erode class solidarity, our present economic circumstances may help to bind disparate social groups together against the Bullingdon Club elite.

Since 2010, Britain has been experiencing multiple, augmenting economic crises – encouraged by the ideological convictions of several Conservative governments.

The public sector has been knee-capped, on the basis that a smaller state is fiscally responsible and that it encourages more productive private enterprise. Yet the economy has stagnated for the vast majority of people; in eight out of the 14 years since 2009, real wages have fallen.[338]

From 2007 to 2022, wages are expected to have risen by just 9% (the worst rate on record) – or basically nothing, if inflation is taken into account. During the previous 15 years, wages rose by 50%.

The UK also logged "dreadful productivity performance" from 2008 to 2018, according to the Institute for Fiscal Studies. Over that period, productivity per hour grew by just 0.3% a-year against a historical trend of 2%. As a result, productivity is now 30% lower than it otherwise would have been if recent trends (since 1971) had been matched.[339]

If the second half of the 20th Century represented the age of affluence in Britain and America, the period since the financial crisis of 2008 has been marked by stagnation, austerity and inequality. In the UK, real wages have flatlined while state spending has been retrenched. Unlike the post-war period, when economic growth heralded an era of mass prosperity – of enduring abundance – growth is slow and unevenly distributed.

Though inequality is nothing new, people are now paying closer attention to the concentration and imbalances of wealth, both in terms of social class and region. Indeed, if everyone is getting richer, the differences in wealth between the rich and the poor do not seem so significant.

This was exposed through the Brexit referendum, with people in 'left-behind' areas of the country protesting against their relative deprivation – in terms of education, infrastructure and industry – compared to the UK's thriving metropolitan hubs.

The architects of Brexit were scorned for predicting that the 'dividends' of the project would not be seen for decades, but there is a reason that these gloomy forecasts didn't repel voters in the 'Red Wall': people thought that short-term pain was necessary to re-orientate an economy that didn't serve their interests.

As mentioned earlier, the wealthiest 10% of households hold 43% of all the wealth in Britain, according to the Office for National Statistics (ONS), while the bottom 50% hold only 9%. From April 2018 to March 2020, median household wealth was highest in the south east of England at £503,400, having risen in real terms by 43% since 2006, while wealth was lowest in the north east at £168,500, having fallen by 17%.[340]

And while London and the south-east produced 4.1 million Brexit voters, compared to a marginally higher 4.3 million in the north of England, it was the surprise movement of traditional Labour areas to the cause that tipped the referendum result.[341]

Inequality is also typically underestimated, failing to consider the decline of the shared public 'commons' – like free libraries or the NHS – from which people, in particular poorer people, derive intangible benefits. The money stowed away offshore by the super-rich is also not recorded, as it's purposefully shielded from public view. It has been estimated that financial assets stashed away in tax havens could amount to 10% of global GDP, while financial fraud costs £137 billion-a-year in the UK.[342] Yet, while fraud makes up 40% of all crime in the UK, only 2% of police budgets go to fighting it.[343]

Inequality in the UK is likely therefore to be even worse than most estimates suggest.

Essentially, the current neoliberal system allows the market to run riot, policed only by light-touch regulations, with the state left to prop up those who suffer from the worst excesses of the system.

Ironically, the world – and the UK – is moving towards a more preventative healthcare system, whereby regular health testing (alongside genetic mapping) allows illnesses to be spotted early and treated before they become dangerous (and expensive). In terms of economics, however, we are moving in the opposite direction – intervening only after people have been pushed into unemployment and poverty.

From 2009/10 to 2015/16, under David Cameron's Coalition Government, local government spending was cut by a staggering 60% in real terms, while the Department for Work and Pensions budget – which administers benefits on behalf of some of society's poorest – fell by marginally less than 60%.[344] The UK's child poverty rate (the proportion of kids in relative poverty) consequently soared in the years after these decisions, from 15.5% in 2016/17 to 19.3% in 2019/20, an increase of 24.5%.[345]

The suicide rate in England and Wales, meanwhile, increased from 9.3 to 11 per 100,000 from 2010 to 2019 – with many poorer parts of the country experiencing a suicide epidemic. In 2021, the suicide rate in the north-east was 14.1, compared to 6.6 in London.[346]

Austerity didn't encourage private firms to replace the state, nor did it boost corporate investment. Rather, the state's role as the protector of citizens and incubator of entrepreneurship was weakened – in turn diminishing the prospects of companies and their workers. As former Greek finance minister Yanis Varoufakis writes: "by choosing to suppress real wages and welfare benefits via spending cuts, the government signals to businesses that they would be reckless to spend money building up the capacity to produce stuff that consumers out there won't have the money to buy."[347]

In the UK context, it's worth noting that 40% of benefits (Universal Credit) claimants are actually in work.[348] By limiting benefits, the Government has therefore punished the 'hard working families' that it has repeatedly pledged to support.

The UK economy has been largely propped up by financial services and a buoyant property market – the golden geese – both of which concentrate wealth among certain regions and socio-economic groups. Some 20% of landlords have rental property portfolios worth more than £1 million, while renters struggle to reach the bottom rung of the housing ladder.[349]

Average advertised rents in Greater London – the nerve centre of the British economy – increased by 16.1% from October 2021 to 2022, and ever-growing numbers of people are forced into this cycle of insecurity through their inability to ever buy a property.[350]

The proportion of Londoners in social housing has fallen from a high point of 35% in 1981 to just 20% today – the least typical avenue for Londoners, thanks largely to Margaret Thatcher's housing reforms. The private rented sector, meanwhile, has boomed – its share increasing from roughly 10% in the late 1980s to nearly 30% today.[351]

At the beginning of 2005, the average house price in London stood at £232,000 – roughly twice as much as the average house price in the north-east (£111,000). In the 17 years since, the average house price in London has more than doubled, to comfortably more than £500,000, cleaving the capital away from the rest of the country. House prices at the start of 2022 stood at £151,000 in the north-east – roughly the same as the average *deposit* for a first-time buyer in London.[352]

In other words: wages and growth have stagnated while house prices and rents have increased, particularly in urban centres, and state support has been curtailed. This has created a 'precariat' – those working in poorly-paid, insecure jobs, whose living circumstances are reliant on the benevolence of their landlord. To put it differently, the UK has been reviving the concept of feudalism, whereby a vassal provides labour and taxes in exchange for military protection, and the 'right' to live on (but not own) land possessed by a nobleman.

Upon the succession of King Charles III to the throne in September 2022, an image went viral on social media – a venn diagram, with one circle labelled '13th Century social media' and the other labelled '21 Century social media'. In the overlap between the two circles were the words: "My landlord is cruel, I dislike the new king, and I fear I will freeze to death in my hovel this winter."

This economic imbalance is further fuelled by Britain's relationship with tax havens – a hangover of our extractive empire – that operate thanks to the legal assurances offered by the British state. Journalist Oliver Bullough notes in *Butler to the World* that the British Virgin Islands (BVI) and other Caribbean tax havens are "backed ultimately by British courts" – the UK Privy Court being the island's final court of appeal – "which helps soothe investors' fears that their money might be at risk from capricious politicians in developing nations."[353]

Meanwhile, the British Government has tended to ignore the potential for tax evasion and money laundering in these jurisdictions. Bullough quotes former Conservative MP David Shaw as saying that, "Too many tax havens have traditional relationships with the United Kingdom. That is no excuse for allowing their economies to develop around fraud."

This relationship between the corporate and political elite is self-fulfilling – the former profiting from the policies of the latter, and the latter receiving donations from the former. Inequality is therefore baked into the system, with the political and economic elite all benefiting from the continued success of high-earners.

What's more, neither the state – which is orientated around five-year election cycles – nor the private sector is currently occupied with making the long-term investments needed to improve productivity, equality and growth. The private and the public sector are mutually focused on scoring a few easy points without being too concerned with how the scorecard looks in 10- or 20-years' time.

For all the justified criticisms of Dominic Cummings's Brexit fascination, he is right that there is a rot within the British political establishment; both that it has run out of ideas, and capable people to implement them. Financial short-termism is now predominant, with the state incapacitated.

"The processes for selecting, educating, and training those at the apex of politics are between inadequate and disastrous, and political institutions suffer problems that are very well known but are very hard to fix – there are entangled vicious circles that cause repeated predictable failure," Cummings wrote in 2014.[354]

"Whatever the outcome of the next election, the big problems will remain, Number 10 will continue to hurtle from crisis to crisis with no priorities and no understanding of how to get things done, the civil service will fail repeatedly and waste billions, the media will continue obsessing on the new rather than the important, and the public will continue to fume with rage."

Of course, Brexit has contributed to these problems – something that Cummings attributes to the fact that a post-Brexit revolution did not take place in Whitehall – but his essential diagnosis of the state of British politics is correct.

However, like most neoliberals, Cummings exaggerates the sanity of the free market – arguing that "markets have developed institutional mechanisms for error-correction that allow the building of reliable knowledge and some control over complexity."

Such optimism is tempered by Aeron Davis in *Reckless Opportunists*, who quotes a financial expert describing the behaviour of UK financial markets after Thatcher deregulated the sector.

"Regulation worked. Why? Because they knew that if they didn't self-control somebody else would come along and kick them a lot harder," the financier told Davis. "Once you have self-regulation, which is what we now have in the City, to all intents and purposes, then everything goes by the board. You get the lunatics running the asylum quite frankly... Collectively, they behave like dogs that will pull down the structures around them and can, and will, rip them to pieces. It happens on a weekly basis that they will tear down a company or take over a company and then destroy it."[355]

The UK, formerly the engine of the industrial revolution, has now remade itself as a stock exchange and money laundering den. Thatcher's banking reforms of the 1980s, which the Conservatives are now promising to replicate, allowed the flight of capital down to London's glorified betting shops – to the hedge funds and investment banks that gamble on firms and assets, particularly the property market, and accrue largely unearned income from the subletting and speculative inflation of these resources.

"In 2017, financial assets held by financial corporations, including derivatives, totalled 1,056% of UK nominal GDP... Since so much of the money at the disposal of banks and financial institutions is in speculative finance, one could say that most economic growth in the 21st Century has been fictitious," writes economist Guy Standing in *The Corruption of Capitalism*.[356]

"The primacy of finance has corroded a fundamental claim of advocates of capitalism, that a system of private property rights encourages long-term accumulation and investment. In fact it does the opposite. It encourages short-termism because both managers and shareholders gain by moves to push up share prices," he adds.

Yet a consensus has percolated from Tufton Street think tanks into the media and through to the Conservative Party, that regulation is bad. That, rather than allowing capitalism to function more effectively and productively, by guarding against monopolies and encouraging greater competition, regulation almost always stifles the 'free market' and inhibits growth.

When Liz Truss sought to introduce 'supply side' reforms in September 2022, she drew on this philosophy – proposing the loosening of regulatory constraints allegedly hampering the market. Truss pledged a new era of deregulation in the financial sector – promising to "unshackle" the City of London to fuel growth. One of her early moves in Number 10 was to promise an end to the cap on bankers' bonuses – the same bankers who bet against her economic plans and caused her to fold after just 45 days in the job.

Rishi Sunak, a former banker, took over from

Truss in Downing Street – with 20% of his Cabinet ministers sharing his background in the industry. Of the 94 individuals who currently hold Cabinet positions and non-executive roles at ministerial departments, 82 have exclusively worked in finance, law, consulting, politics or business.[357]

Unsurprisingly, Sunak's Government has promised to carry on Truss's financial deregulation agenda, and to retain her decision to lift the cap on bankers' bonuses.

This signifies the free market fundamentalism that has currently captured the Conservative Party, from root to branch.

However, as economist Ha-Joon Chang says, "the free market doesn't exist". In reality, "every market has some rules and boundaries that restrict freedom of choice. A market looks free only because we so unconditionally accept its underlying restrictions that we fail to see them."[358]

The market is therefore not a natural organism, as suggested by Cummings, but the real-world culmination of a series of political choices – for example, to institute paid annual leave and sick pay for employees, as well as environmental safeguards and food standards.

These regulations ensure that firms, which have an inherent interest in maximising profits, are not allowed to do so at the expense of their workers, consumers and the environment. Take the deposit protection scheme, for example, introduced in 2007 by the Labour Government. The scheme essentially acts as an impartial mediator between a tenant and landlord, ensuring that claims against a deposit (for damage to a property) are settled fairly. The scheme protects both tenants – who are protected from spurious claims from landlords – and property owners, who see their claims handled by a professional body.

Deregulation, by contrast, is a key component of the Brexit project – led by Cummings and avidly (albeit belatedly) supported by Truss – under the false belief that a free market is both possible and desirable.

While the political project – how Vote Leave sold Brexit to the public – was economically interventionist, promising greater state investment in key public services, its ideological masterminds were libertarian.

The motif of Brexit, in free market circles, was the creation of a 'Singapore-on-Thames' – slashing red tape and taxes to boost corporate investment, ostensibly emulating the South-East Asian nation. "If we are to thrive, our post-Brexit model should exactly be Singapore, a tiny country devoid of natural resources, but with a booming economy," wrote Brexiter Owen Paterson in November 2017.[359]

Not only is Singapore a very different country to the UK – with a much less comprehensive social safety net and less than a-tenth of the population – its relative economic success has been ensured in part through Government intervention in innovation and industrial development.[360]

However, to the extent that there has ever been a coherent ideology among its most ardent advocates, it has been anti-establishment, anti-academic, anti-expert, and anti-regulation. Therefore, it has been destructive; devoted to unclipping the social and economic harness offered by the Government, to further concentrate wealth and power among a narrow elite – as is the Bullingdon Club mentality.

While the Remain campaign was criticised for failing to offer a positive vision for Britain's membership of the EU, the Brexit campaign promised a bonfire; something revolutionary and destabilising.

This revolution was sold to ordinary people on the basis that it was a realisation of the discontent felt towards the established political and economic order, yet it was a Trojan Horse – an elite project cloaked in the language of the proletariat.

Take the fishing industry, for example, which came to symbolise the economic logic of the project. Brexiters promised to negotiate a better settlement for British fishermen, in theory allowing them to keep a greater proportion of the catch farmed in UK waters.

Yet, at the eleventh hour, the UK crumbled, agreeing to only gradually reduce fishing rights for the EU's fleet in British waters over a five-year period – something that was seen as a betrayal of the declining coastal communities that Brexit had vowed to protect.

"The flags flying over our vessels for the last couple of years had a slogan which was 'no sell out' and that really spelt out our fears. Those flags now seem both politically astute and prescient because that's what has happened," said Barrie Deas, chief executive of the National Federation of Fishermen's Organisations, after the agreement had been reached.[361]

What's more, the Government has made no real effort to fracture the vested interests in the fishing industry that loom over Britain's small fleets. More than two-thirds of UK fishing quotas are awarded to just 25 dominant firms, while 76,000 small fishing companies have been handed 6% of the market, despite making up 79% of the domestic fishing fleet.[362]

Ultimately, Brexit will involve the lowering of standards, less funding for public services and likely an even greater regional concentration of economic growth in London among an already disturbingly affluent elite.

A portent of the future is the largely unregulated tech space, which in little over a decade has spawned a new iteration of capitalism – 'platform capitalism' – whereby giants like Facebook, Google and Amazon have gained monopolies through the mass accumulation of data and users. These platforms have increased inequality – concentrating vast wealth in the hands of a few titans of tech, the likes of Mark Zuckerberg, Jeff Bezos and Elon Musk, while many of their workers toil under insecure contracts.

For those who voted for Brexit, the presence of vast wealth inequalities is intolerable in an era of mass economic stagnation. However, for those who have led the campaign, both during and after the referendum, inequalities are seen as necessary – and even desirable.

The aforementioned book, *Britannia Unchained*, co-authored by Liz Truss, Kwasi Kwarteng, Dominic Raab, Priti Patel and Chris Skidmore, makes the case for a new era of national vitality based on deregulation, the lowering of taxes, and the dismantling of workers' rights. It proposes eroding Britain's social safety net as a way of encouraging greater economic dynamism – arguing that the state is cossetting too many people. Truss and her allies believe that efforts to ensure greater equality reduce the impetus to succeed.

Successive economic crises – COVID and inflation – have forced the Government to use the financial clout of the state to protect the poorest, and there is little current evidence, as I have previously stated, that free market economics measurably boosts economic growth.

Yet, the Conservative Party is sinking ever-further into the free market fallacy.

Boris Johnson captured a massive majority in 2019 by pledging to build 40 new hospitals and hire 20,000 new police officers – his flagship policy being to 'level up' the left-behind areas of the UK. "Even before the pandemic began, the UK had and has a more unbalanced economy than almost all our immediate biggest competitors in Europe and more unbalanced than pretty much every major developed country," Johnson said in July 2021. "And when I say unbalanced, I mean that for too many people geography turns out to be destiny."[363]

As *The Guardian*'s John Harris has argued, levelling up under Johnson was simply the process through which "flags and badges are pinned to things, but almost nothing actually changes."[364] Its focus on small infrastructure projects and heritage assets is at the expense of crumbling public services, systematically deprived of funding over the last decade.

However, rhetorically at least, and to some extent in practice, Johnson was socially conservative and economically progressive, the embodiment of the Vote Leave's political project.

This attitude is now being eschewed in favour of the 'trickle-down' economics favoured by neoliberals during the 1980s and by most Brexit protagonists aside from Johnson, whereby market freedom is prioritised, even if the gap between rich and poor widens.

"To look at everything through the lens of redistribution, I believe, is wrong," Truss said, immediately after becoming Prime Minister. "Because what I'm about is growing the economy. And growing the economy benefits everybody."

As Torsten Bell, CEO of the Resolution Foundation, notes, Truss "doesn't think people staying where they were born is the top priority and says it's a problem [that] workers don't change jobs [or] place often enough."

In other words, if your local area is struggling, you should buy a map and move somewhere with more opportunities, rather than waiting for the Government to intervene. Her approach echoed the infamous words of Norman Tebbit, a Cabinet minister during the Thatcher years, who said: "I grew up in the 30s with our unemployed father. He did not riot, he got on his bike and looked for work."

In the past, this theory has suffered a harsh meeting with reality. The Thatcher era spurred economic growth in the metropolitan fiefdoms of the new service-led economy – gutting industrial areas in the process. In the space of just six years, from 1984 to 1990, the GDP of London soared from £38 billion to £71 billion, while household income in the north lagged behind the capital by 25% by the end of the decade.[365]

As the Government restricted support for Britain's declining industries and resisted the urge to incubate new forms of skilled employment in these areas, unemployment sat above 10% for six of Thatcher's 11 years in office. Workers generally didn't move to new places to find work – they just dropped off the labour market.

Former industrial heartlands were collateral damage in Thatcher's 'survival of the fittest' economy – stoking regional resentments that were unleashed during the 2016 EU Referendum, which Johnson pledged to remedy.

"If the UK had the average income and inequality levels" seen in the likes of France, Germany and the Netherlands, Bell says, "typical household incomes would be a third higher – that's a massive £8,800 per household. Economic failure has a high price."[366]

The Tufton Street playbook sees economic policy as a spreadsheet – an attempt to maximise profit – rather than something involving people and lives. This blinkered pursuit of economic freedom, thereby stoking inequalities, is morally callous – as shown through the prism of healthcare.

The pandemic "further exposed" health inequalities in Britain and "amplified them", according to one of the country's leading public health experts, Sir Michael Marmot, who has tracked differences in health outcomes between the richest and poorest regions and individuals for more than a decade.[367]

Sir Michael released a report in 2020, evaluating how the past decade of Conservative rule had impacted health inequalities. According to Sir Michael, since 2010, Government spending on the key social determinants of health had fallen, and the funding was allocated in a less equitable way.

In particular, Marmot ascribed declining health outcomes to the Government's austerity programme. "From rising child poverty and the closure of children's centres to declines in education funding, an increase in precarious work and zero hours contracts, to a housing affordability crisis and a rise in homelessness, to people with insufficient money to lead a healthy life and resorting to food banks in large numbers, to ignored communities with poor conditions and little reason for hope... Austerity will cast a long shadow over the lives of the children born and growing up under its effects," he wrote.[368]

As a result, the healthy life expectancy – the length of time you are expected to live in good health – fell in 80% of 'Red Wall' areas for either men or women from 2009 to 2011 to 2017 to 2019.[369] Prior to the pandemic, Blackpool logged an average life expectancy for women that was last seen nationwide in 1994.[370]

The number of food parcels delivered in England, meanwhile, increased from 867,000 in 2014/15 to 1.5 million in 2019/20 – an increase of 71.7%.[371]

"Put simply, if health has stopped improving it is a sign that society has stopped improving," Marmot has written.

New Labour continued Thatcher's neoliberalism, with successive left-wing administrations actively encouraging the excesses of the financial sector – using it as the primary conduit for economic growth. This approach crashed the economy in 2008, while David Cameron's austerity agenda stalled its recovery, inflicting a decade-long cost of living crisis on those least able to cope.

The British economy is now defined by a shrinking welfare state, precarious 'gig' employment, the persistent desperation of key workers, with intergenerational and regional wealth inequalities sustained by an inflated housing market. In middle England – for nurses, cleaners, bakers, and all of those not cocooned within the financial and professional sectors, living in this country is a test of physical and financial endurance.

Conservative politicians tell seafarer's myths about the greatness of the British Empire, our industrial heritage, and the cultural example that we continue to set for the world. So, when small-town Brits wander down the high street and see not parades and poppies, but boarded-up shops, police cordons and glum faces, they are bound to rebel –

even if their anger was misdirected by self-serving populists like Johnson and Farage.

Perceptively, Donald Trump's former right-hand-man Steve Bannon told *The Guardian* in 2019 that, in the American economy, "We have oligarchs and serfs. That system is not going to survive."[372]

He didn't tell the newspaper's readers, however, that these same oligarchs have funded his political endeavours – namely the Mercer family, whose members bankrolled Cambridge Analytica and the 2016 Trump campaign.

Trump is a pluto-populist; a plutocrat (someone who has political power because of their wealth), who has stolen the clothes of the working class to serve his political aims – and Bannon is his butler. After claiming that his 2016 opponent Hillary Clinton was a "defender of the corrupt and rigged status quo", allegedly using her power to "line her own pockets and taking care of donors instead of the American people," Trump used his time in office to empower the super-rich and frustrate the democratic will of the US electorate.

Pluto-populism has boomed because these agents of anger have articulated a vague yet pervasive sense of working-class disillusionment with the existing economic order – adopting a form of "pantomime radicalism", as described by *The Economist* in the context of Truss.[373]

Part of this disillusionment stems from the erosion of community spaces and services that previously sustained bonds of mutual reliance and support in working-class areas. This has been supplanted by predatory capitalism, epitomised by private equity firms buying up businesses that are either gutted, merged with a larger (soulless) enterprise, or sold off for scraps.

Take the foster care system, which (one would hope) would be a beacon of charity and compassion – run in the interests of the vulnerable people who pass through this system, and those who are tasked with helping them. Alas, no. The social-care system (for both adults and children) is now dominated by private equity firms and hedge funds. Eight of the 10 largest providers of children's social care now have some kind of private equity involvement. These 10 firms made profits of £300 million in 2021.[374]

In total, private equity firms in the UK now own more than 3,400 companies and employ 800,000 people.[375]

Community capitalism – a network of small firms that are integrated into the social fabric of a place – has been upended by corporate monoliths that have flattened the spirit and identity of deprived areas to maximise profit.

Indeed, economic logic would indicate that public services like water and rail should be kept in public hands. After all, genuine competition in these markets is impossible (you can't have two rail companies offering exactly the same service from London to Leeds, for example, as there isn't space on the track for both of them).

However, successive Conservative governments have insisted on an elaborate, privatised system through which operators – often owned by foreign states – have extracted tens of millions in profits. Research in 2017 found that of the 28 private rail operators in the UK, 20 (70%) were partially or wholly owned by foreign states or their railways.[376]

Many of these operators have behaved poorly – either requiring a government bailout after getting into financial trouble, or providing blatantly rubbish services (or both).

As Laurie MacFarlane has pointed out for the New Economics Foundation, these rail companies have profited "not by creating new wealth or adding any real value, but by exploiting a position of monopoly privilege to extract existing wealth from others."[377]

Privatisation, deregulation, tax cuts and austerity are not a path to growth for the majority. Rather, they are an attempt to guarantee growth for the elite – and perhaps also a recognition that Britain, in its entirety, cannot grow at the same rate as previous eras. Therefore, those at the top of the pyramid are taking emergency measures to ensure that, at the very least, they continue to prosper.

Britain – a declining nation – is being asset-stripped by the Bullingdon Club elite. This is happening in conjunction with an international oligarchy, with the UK kowtowing to despots, funding their wars, and allowing its national resources, this green and pleasant land, to be owned by a small, serving-sustaining establishment.

10 THE NEW ARISTOCRACY

Liz Truss and Boris Johnson have exposed the moral and economic bankruptcy of the ruling class. However, recent evidence has shown the capacity of the elite to recoup, restructure and regenerate – perennially propped up by billionaire backers.

The Conservative Party and the domestic aristocracy have well understood the modern evolution of capitalism – tapping into a fountain of oligarchic, international finance in order to sustain their elevated social and political position.

Take Ben Elliot, who was the co-chair of the Conservative Party from July 2019 until September 2022, during this time operating as a key figure in the party's fundraising operation. In both his personal and political dealings, Elliot traverses the boundaries between the old aristocracy and the new oligarchy.

Elliot's father was a landowner in Dorset, while his maternal aunt is Camilla Rosemary Shand, in more recent times referred to as Camilla, Queen Consort. Elliot was educated at Eton and is the co-founder of Quintessentially, a concierge company for the super-rich, offering everything from travel advice to real estate consultancy, to personal shopping. The firm has 40 offices across the globe and drew criticism for operating an offshoot in Russia after Putin launched his Ukraine invasion in February 2022.[378]

And Elliot's unique skills appear to have benefitted the royal family also. A Conservative donor said that Elliot arranged access to King Charles III, before he assumed the throne, in exchange for sizable donations to the King's charities. Elliot has refused to answer questions about these claims when approached by journalists.[379]

Separately, it has been alleged that an aide to Charles offered to help a Saudi billionaire obtain a knighthood and British citizenship in exchange for "generous" cash donations to the Prince's Foundation.[380] Clarence House, Charles's former office, said that Charles had no knowledge of offers made on the condition or basis that donations were made to his charitable projects.

Charles also reportedly accepted a suitcase containing £1 million in cash from a former Qatari prime minister. This was one of three payments totalling £3 million that Charles personally received from Sheikh Hamad bin Jassim bin Jaber Al Thani between 2011 and 2015, according to the *Sunday Times*.[381]

A spokesperson for Charles at the time said that

the funds "were passed immediately to one of the Prince's charities who carried out the appropriate governance and have assured us that all the correct processes were followed."

These are examples of a mutually sustaining partnership between two elite crowds, each helping the other to achieve its goals.

The first, the old British aristocracy, saw its wealth and political position jeopardised during the 1970s, 1980s and 1990s, threatened by the rise of a middle-class meritocracy and the ever-looming spectre of labour unrest and high inflation.

The aristocracy has therefore appropriated Thatcherism, as shown by the bourgeois makeup of Truss's short-lived Government, using it as a tool to concentrate money and power among the already embarrassingly wealthy. And, in some ways, this aristocracy has corrupted Thatcher's basic ideals.

"This concentration of power in a few companies is the opposite of what she would have wanted for the free market," says Maurice Saatchi, who helped to run the Conservative Party's marketing campaigns during Thatcher's time in office.

"She thought that from competition would come better quality and more variety. But it hasn't worked out: most industries are now global cartels. Customers have become irrelevant. Big companies like Facebook and Google are worse than big government. They have no accountability. It's so disappointing."[382]

So, while Thatcher may have abandoned the free market if she could have seen the concentrations of power that it has created, the beneficiaries of her policies – the landed, financial elites – have now become the most ardent advocates of Thatcherism.

The frightening prospect of their prospective decline also led the aristocracy to search for new alliances abroad – welcoming the spoils of oligarchy into their businesses and their political parties, and setting up new ventures acting as butlers to dirty money.

In exchange, these international oligarchs are coated with the veneer of respectability that comes with such an intimate relationship with the world's most cultivated and cunning aristocracy. Their reputations are fortified in the private members' clubs of Mayfair, while their money is sanitised in the high-rises of Canary Wharf and safely stored in London's luxury property market.

Britain is the fixer: using the tools that it evolved during the colonial era to hide illicit wealth, both offshore and onshore, and in return taking a cut of the proceeds.

There is no more brazen example of how Britain has been flogged to an international elite than the government's approach to visas. While politicians within and on the fringes of the far-right have lamented a supposed 'invasion' of asylum seekers and immigrants into Britain, the UK has allowed oligarchs to buy access to our country with minimal security checks.

Established in the 1990s – following the break-up of the Soviet Union – and expanded after 2008, the Government operated a 'golden' visa scheme for people promising to invest millions in the UK.

If granted an investor visa, the individual in question was allowed to live and work in the UK for roughly three years. From 2010 to 2020, 12,000 individuals were offered entry clearance visas on this basis.

According to the immigration specialists Richmond Chambers, participation in the golden visa scheme typically led to these individuals being eligible for the right to permanently settle in the UK after five years.

However, in exchange for investing more money, individuals were allowed to speed up their permanent settlement applications – becoming eligible after three years in exchange for at least £5 million in investment, or two years for at least £10 million.

From 2010 to 2020, 2,823 of these investors were granted permanent settlement status in the UK – with 2,117 coming from the Government's list of 31 countries "where we are particularly concerned about human rights issues", including 1,067 from China.[383]

There is no suggestion that these individuals have been directly involved in the human rights violations committed in these countries. However, in repressive states, it is often the case that wealthy individuals are only afforded their wealth at the behest of the state.

This is very much the case in China and Russia, with former Russian investor Bill Browder telling the news and analysis website *Tortoise* that Russian President Vladimir Putin can eliminate someone's wealth "in a fraction of a second with the flick of an administrative decision."[384]

Yet, the UK Government has applied minimal scrutiny to these 'investors', leading to concerns that the golden visa scheme has facilitated money laundering and the influx of oligarchs into the UK.

Estimates suggest that more than £3.1 billion entered the UK through the scheme from 2008 to 2015, with 97% of investors subject to minimal 'blind faith' checks from UK financial institutions.[385]

Essentially, the Government approved golden visas before due diligence checks had been undertaken by domestic banks. However, these financial institutions "used the fact that an individual had been awarded an investor visa as qualifying evidence to overcome due diligence concerns when assessing the applicant's legitimacy", according to Transparency International.

So, "not only would the corrupt have been attracted to an investor visa in order to achieve UK residency status, but it would have also been attractive to help circumvent a bank's due diligence checks," the organisation says.

The Government subsequently announced measures to strengthen the golden visa programme in 2015 and 2019 – closing it down entirely when Russia launched its invasion of Ukraine.

Following the Salisbury poisonings of former Russian double-agent Sergei Skripal and his daughter Yulia by the Russian Government in 2018, the UK launched a review into the investors awarded visas between 2008 and 2015, when due diligence checks were at their weakest. However, at the time of writing, the Government still hasn't officially published its review, instead issuing a short statement from Home Secretary Suella Braverman, who confirmed that 10 oligarchs on the UK's sanctions list had obtained a golden visa.[386]

A total of 2,300 Russians were granted golden visas and 750 of these individuals were awarded permanent settlement in the UK. Meanwhile, only 30 Ukrainians were granted asylum by the Government from the beginning of Putin's hostilities in the east of the country in 2014, until his full invasion in February 2022.[387]

Britain's marriage with illicit finance is long-standing – especially in its capital, London, described in the 2020 report by Parliament's Security and Intelligence Committee as "Londongrad" – a place in which "PR firms, charities, political interests, academia and cultural institutions [are] all willing beneficiaries of Russian money."[388]

Wealthy Russians have used London for a reason – the capital has provided a dumping ground for the spoils of oligarchy, often stowed away in the luxury property market. There are 138,000 offshore-owned properties in England and Wales, according to academic research by academic Rex McKenzie. Some 95,000 of these properties are registered as residential, with almost half located in London. The average value of an offshore home in London is £1.3 million – meaning they are worth £56 billion cumulatively.[389]

London's capture by oligarchs from across the

globe can therefore be seen in the very architecture of the capital, with estimates suggesting that anywhere between 20% and 60% of 'prime' London real estate is purchased by overseas buyers.[390]

To a large extent, Britain no longer owns the landmarks so closely associated with its capital. Battersea Power Station is now one of London's largest new property developments – converted into more than 4,000 flats, with most of the luxury homes sold 'off-plan' long before they were completed. The power station was sold to the Malaysian sovereign wealth fund and the Employees Provident Fund of Malaysia for £1.6 billion in 2019 – a form of foreign ownership that reflects many neighbouring developments in the Nine Elms area of south-west London.[391]

The Shard, the tallest freestanding structure in the city and the second tallest in the country, is owned by the Gulf state of Qatar, now the 10th largest landowner in the UK.[392] The Gherkin is owned by a Brazilian conglomerate and the 'Walkie Talkie' is owned by a Hong Kong company best known for its Chinese-style food sauces. City Hall and its promenade is entirely owned by Kuwait.

In 2017, up to 160 UK properties worth more than £4 billion were identified as being purchased by high corruption-risk individuals, and Transparency International has identified at least £1.5 billion worth of UK property owned by Russians accused of financial crime or with links to the Kremlin – most of which is owned by offshore companies.[393]

This process is called 'capital flight' – domestic

instability causing wealthy individuals to move their money overseas. It has been estimated that Russians hold some £1 trillion in wealth abroad, with capital flight increasing to record levels in 2015 – a year after Russia invaded eastern Ukraine and annexed Crimea – with £131 billion leaving the country. Since 2008, £100 billion of London property has been bought by companies based in offshore jurisdictions that both minimise the tax liabilities of investors and have historically protected their identities.[394]

This state of affairs has been facilitated by the UK Government – if only due to its consistent lack of action. In 2016, then Prime Minister David Cameron announced that the Government would introduce a public register of the owners of overseas companies that have procured UK land titles – in effect pulling back the curtain on those individuals owning high-value properties.

This policy has only recently been enforced, in the clamour for action triggered by the Ukraine. The offshore operatives were given considerable advance warning, however, allowing them to sell their assets or to find a new ownership arrangement. The BBC has estimated that some 18,000 offshore companies – which between them hold more than 50,000 properties in England and Wales – have either ignored the register altogether or have filed their information in such a way that it remains impossible for the public to find out who ultimately owns and benefits from them.[395]

Former Justice Minister Lord Edward Faulks even claims that he was "leant on" in 2017 and 2018 to drop parliamentary amendments that would have forced the introduction of this public register. "I can only think a deluded desire to protect the City of London has led to all these delays," Faulks told *The Guardian*.[396]

And while some action has been taken in the UK to curb money laundering over the last decade, it hasn't exactly been bulletproofed. The *Criminal Finances Act 2017*, for example, introduced Unexplained Wealth Orders (UWOs), allowing law enforcement agencies to apply for a court order requiring someone to explain their interest in a property and how they obtained it. If that person failed to comply, a court could confiscate the property. Available from January 2018, the use of UWOs has been limited, however, having only been obtained in four cases as of September 2021.[397]

"The British services economy is so dependent on Russia – from educating their kids, to providing litigation and British courts for disputes among Russian business leaders, to processing investments," says Paul Stephan, a Professor of Law at the University of Virginia who previously served in the US Department of Defense.[398]

Proving this fact, on 15 February 2022, just nine days before Putin ordered his troops to advance westwards, the UK Government's export guide for Russia was still online.

Russia is an "attractive export destination for UK companies looking at new markets," the webpage said, offering guidance to firms considering trading in Russia. It added that: "[Russia] has abundant natural resources, well-developed infrastructure, high-tech production and a diverse range of industries supplemented by state-supported business incentives."[399]

There were opportunities for domestic firms ranging from infrastructure to healthcare, the export guide said – offering to put company owners in touch with "lawyers and distributors" who could facilitate their expansion into Russia. The page highlighted the sanctions imposed by the US and EU on the country – a reaction to its 2014 annexation of Crimea – but said that, even despite this, "there are plenty of opportunities across a wide range of sectors" in Russia.

This webpage no longer exists – deleted by the Government as Russian troops marched into Ukraine, launching an invasion that Johnson called a "hideous and barbaric venture".

The Government provides online advice for companies seeking to trade with nations across the globe – Russia is not exceptional in this regard. However, the tone of the Government's commercial advice in relation to Russia was particularly jarring, given Putin's long-standing expansionist ambitions.

As far back as 2011, US intelligence services forecast that the Russian President intended to use Ukraine as a launchpad to conquer and control – either directly or indirectly – vast swathes of former Soviet space.

"Russia has successfully launched a series of moves since approximately 2005 in which to reverse Western influence in the former Soviet states," one of the forecasting documents said. "This will lead to an escalation of hostilities between US and Russia – playing out in the Baltic region, central Europe and the Caucasus."[400]

True to form, following its support of separatist forces in Georgia in 2008, Russia instigated a war in eastern Ukraine in 2014 – annexing the peninsula of Crimea and retaining a military presence in the Donbas.

In other words: we have known about Putin's ambitions for a long time – for decades – and he has matched these ambitions with acts of war.

During this time, however, the UK Government has actively promoted Russia as a good place to do business.

The thawing of commercial relations with Russia can be traced back to Cameron – who took the unusual step of delivering a speech in Moscow in 2011, urging Britain and Russia to forge a new partnership.

"I accept that Britain and Russia have had a difficult relationship for some time and that we should be candid in areas where we still disagree, but I want to make the case this morning for a new approach based on co-operation," Cameron said – adding: "We want to do everything we can now to build on this and take our trade and our investment to a new level."

A day before Cameron's speech, four former foreign secretaries had written to the *Sunday Times*, urging him to treat Russia with caution – noting that corruption was still rife in the country.[401]

However, these warnings went largely unheeded, and Cameron's Government pushed for closer economic links between the UK and Russia. In March 2014, a British delegation composed of diplomats and entrepreneurs attended an aerospace conference in Moscow, hosted by the Russian state-owned defence conglomerate Rostec – a firm that has now been sanctioned by the UK Government.

Between 2010 and 2014, £54.9 million of UK military export licences were approved to Russia – £37.9 million more than to Ukraine.[402]

This summit followed a UK Trade and Investment visit to Ekaterinburg in September 2013, for the opening of a new JCB plant on the outskirts of the city, and preceded a visit to Kazan by trade representatives in December 2014. The participants discussed opportunities to "pursue joint research co-operation in the future".

And this was a two-way street. While UK businesses pursued greater export opportunities in Russia, Cameron opened domestic markets to Russian oligarchs through the golden visa scheme.

As Parliament's Intelligence and Security Committee said in its Russia report: "Russian influence in the UK is 'the new normal', and there are a lot of Russians with very close links to Putin who are well integrated into the UK business and social scene, and accepted because of their wealth. This level of integration – in 'Londongrad' in particular – means that any measures now being taken by the Government are not preventative but rather constitute damage limitation."[403]

The inflow of roubles bolstered the Conservative Party's war chest under Cameron, with at least £1.1

million donated to the party by Russian sources between 2010 and 2014.[404]

So, even after Russia invaded Ukraine in 2014 and annexed Crimea, the UK was both directly and indirectly fuelling Putin's war effort. Short-term economic self-interest trumped human rights and geopolitical concerns – the consequences of which are now being felt by Ukrainians fighting in and suffering from the war, and through higher energy prices across Europe.

And, though the commercial relationship between the UK and Russia chilled following the latter's annexation of Ukraine, the frost was only temporary. The total value of UK-Russia trade fell from £15.4 billion in 2011 to £10.1 billion in 2015 before bouncing back to £14.1 billion in 2019.

Russian officials, including former Russian Ambassador to the UK Alexander Yakovenko, met several times with senior figures of the Leave.EU campaign, evidently seeing Brexit as a diplomatic opportunity for Russia.[405]

The logic from Russia and its proxies was simple: to fracture Europe's liberal democracies, creating a climate of suspicion and resentment that would weaken the bloc's response to Putin's aggression. Regardless of whether Russia itself directly interfered in Brexit – and we simply don't know the answer to that question, because the security services have never been asked to investigate – the project benefitted Russia's interests.

Russia's trade representative in the UK, Boris Abramov, predicted as much in September 2019.

"After the UK's suspended membership of the EU's Customs Union, duties will again be levied on European goods," he said. "The prices on them will be higher and this will make Russian goods more competitive on the British market. So, Russian companies could strengthen their positions in such spheres as agriculture, metallurgy, chemicals, hi-tech and medicine."[406]

Prior to Putin's invasion, it seems he may have been right.

According to journalist Luke Harding, Yakovenko told a fellow diplomat: "We have crushed the British to the ground. They are on their knees, and they will not rise for a very long time."[407]

Of course, Russian officials are prone to both exaggeration and delusion, and this statement almost certainly contains both. But there's no doubt that Russia took advantage of the UK's commercial and geopolitical naivety.

Cameron's landmark 2011 speech in Moscow, heralding a new era of economic collaboration, came just three years before Russia annexed Crimea. Putin's direction of travel was already evident from his actions in Georgia and the forecasts of the international intelligence community. The warnings were clear, but we put all this aside and offered our cities and our political parties as safehouses for the loot of Putin's oligarchs.

The physical battle with Russia may be fought thousands of miles away, but it has been undermined by the actions that have taken on our doorstep for years.

Yet, this geopolitical naivety is not just reserved to

Russia. Rather than using the example of the Ukraine war to ensure that Britain isn't compromised by any other malign influences, the British establishment appears to have decided that our Russian overtures were an isolated failure. Under this warped logic, the UK has compensated for an economic freeze with Russia by relying more heavily on other oligarchies.

For example, since 2010, the UK Government has approved £33 billion worth of export licences for military goods to countries on its own 'human rights watch list'. This constitutes two thirds of the £50 billion in total military export licences granted by the UK during this period.[408]

Notably, a staggering £11 billion in military export licences has been approved to Saudi Arabia over this period. This is comfortably the largest total of any country in the world, with the second-placed USA standing at £6.3 billion, ahead of France at £4.6 billion.

In other words, Saudi Arabia represents more than a fifth of the military export licences granted by the UK since 2010, in terms of overall value, and a third of the military export licences granted to countries on the UK's human rights watchlist.

In relation to Saudi Arabia, the Government's human rights report says that, "Reports of enforced disappearances, arbitrary detention, torture and mistreatment in detention and lack of access to adequate legal representation [remain]. Freedom of expression and media freedom [are] very restricted."

Of the licences granted for military exports to Saudi Arabia by the UK, £6.2 billion was for 'aircraft, helicopters, drones' and £4.3 billion was for 'grenades, bombs, missiles, countermeasures'.

Up to £7 billion of the £11 billion Saudi total has been approved since 2015, when the Saudi-backed coalition began its war in neighbouring Yemen – a conflict which continues to this day. The UN has estimated that the war in Yemen had killed 377,000 people by the end of 2021.[409] More than 150,000 of these deaths were the direct result of the armed conflict, with the rest due to the hunger and disease caused by the war. Other estimates suggest that the conflict has pushed 5 million people to the brink of famine and 16 million towards starvation.[410]

Almost 11,000 civilian casualties have been caused by the Saudi-led coalition's use of explosive weapons in Yemen since 2015, with 9,881 civilian deaths and injuries caused by airstrikes.[411]

In June 2019, the Court of Appeal concluded that the Government's decision-making process for granting export licences to Saudi Arabia was "irrational" and therefore "unlawful". However, the Government announced a year later that it was resuming sales to the country.

In a briefing paper obtained by *Byline Times*, relating to an October 2020 meeting between the Saudi Minister of Commerce, Majid bin Abdullah Al-Qasabi, and the UK's Minister for Investment, Lord Gerry Grimstone, officials emphasised the commercial opportunities for Saudi Arabian firms looking to invest in the UK. This was portrayed, by the UK officials, as a means of fulfilling the Government's 'levelling up' agenda.[412]

One of the top objectives of the meeting was

to "promote the levelling-up agenda and the opportunities in the regions, including for the top Saudi companies their Government wants to see go global," the briefing paper stated.

"There are significant opportunities, including as part of the levelling-up agenda, for star names like Saudi Aramco, SABIC, Saudi Telecoms, ACWA Power and others to come and invest in and grow... in the UK," it went on to say – noting that a positive outcome would be to secure a "regional investment visit" from the Saudi administration "in support of the levelling up agenda".

It was revealed in March 2022 that the Saudi firm Alfanar Group would be investing £1 billion into Teesside to produce sustainable aviation fuel. This followed the announcement that Saudi chemical company SABIC would be injecting £850 million into a Teeside chemical plant. The UK Government has also reportedly approached Saudi investors about the possibility of pumping money into the proposed Sizewell C nuclear plant in Suffolk.[413]

This policy was taken up by the Government's long-awaited levelling up white paper – setting out the scope of its regional investment project. It was released in February 2022, and emphasised the merits of foreign direct investment (FDI) into left-behind areas.

"The UK Government's goal is to maximise the opportunities of its independent trade agenda for UK business," it said. "Internationally mobile companies are among the most productive, innovative and high investing firms in the UK."

The logic behind this was epitomised by former Northern Powerhouse Minister Jake Berry, who told BBC *Newsnight*: "The key to unlocking levelling up is to bring foreign direct investment into the north of England, so taxpayers in the garden of England [Kent] or anywhere else in this country do not have to pay for all of it."[414]

Likewise, Department for International Trade records show that the Government has held a series of meetings with sovereign wealth funds and foreign investment companies, about directing their resources to the UK.

Official records for the final quarter of 2021, for example, show that ministers met with the Saudi National Bank, the Kuwait Investment Authority and the Qatar Investment Authority to discuss 'investment opportunities' in the UK. All of these institutions are majority owned by their respective governments.[415]

In March 2021, the UK's Office for Investment and Abu Dhabi's Mubadala Investment Company – owned by the Gulf state – signed the UAE-UK Sovereign Investment Partnership, with the UAE pledging to invest £10 billion in technology, infrastructure, healthcare, life sciences, and renewable energy in the UK.

This mirrors the Strategic Investment Partnership signed with Qatar – the absolute monarchy pledging to invest up to £10 billion over the next five years in the UK economy, including fintech, zero emissions vehicles, life sciences and cyber security.

FDI is clearly important to the economic growth

of a country. It is a dangerous myth – one perpetuated by former US President Donald Trump and some Brexiters – that a nation is able to be prosperous and entirely self-sufficient.

However, Putin's war in Ukraine has shown the need to align our economic and geopolitical interests more closely – not allowing our country to be bought and compromised by the actors of hostile states.

Politicians have attempted to justify the UK's recent economic reliance on autocracies on the basis that liberal capitalism will calm the worst excesses of these regimes. However, in practice, integration has not led to moderation.

While Foreign Secretary in 2017, Johnson said that "we want to encourage Saudi Arabia down the path of reform and modernisation." Yet, as previously mentioned, this did not stop the Kingdom from murdering *Washington Post* journalist Jamal Khashoggi at its consulate in Istanbul less than a year later – allegedly at the behest of Crown Prince Mohammed bin Salman – though the Crown Prince denies any role in the killing.

Qatar doesn't have a clean slate either on this front. More than 24,000 workers suffered from human rights abuses on the projects devoted to the 2022 FIFA World Cup, while *The Guardian* has reported that 6,500 migrant workers died during the course of construction.[416] As we witnessed during the tournament itself, Qatar is a hostile place for LGBTQ+ people, with same-sex sexual activities criminalised in the country. Qatar's Preventive Security Department forces have reportedly arbitrarily arrested lesbian, gay, bisexual, and transgender people and subjected them to ill-treatment in detention – with this practice continuing to occur months before the World Cup.[417]

Meanwhile, Human Rights Watch claimed in its 2022 report on Kuwait that authorities continue to restrict free speech and prosecute dissidents. This includes criminalising speech deemed insulting to the Emir, its ruling monarch.[418]

These new alliances, spurred by our need to pivot away from Russian energy sources, have been forged with archetypal oligarchies, with state power and wealth amassed among a narrow band of influential families.

Inviting investment from bodies attached to these families is fundamentally different to encouraging the construction of a new factory by a Japanese car company or a German pharmaceutical giant. Unlike the German and Japanese firms, the sovereign wealth funds of Qatar, Kuwait and Saudi Arabia have political interests as well as economic ones.

The question is whether we want our infrastructure and our economy to be reliant on countries that do not share our core values – states that are perpetuating human rights abuses today, regardless of the crimes that they may commit in the future.

It's not as though they are reliable partners, either. In October 2022, the OPEC Plus cartel of the world's largest oil producers agreed to cut its output by two million barrels, in an attempt to raise prices. It's understood that the decision was agreed between Russia and Saudi Arabia, acting as leaders of the group. The cartel said that the decision to cut production was made "in light of the uncertainty that surrounds the global economic and oil market outlooks".[419]

In effect, through this decision, Saudi Arabia was helping to fuel Russia's war effort.

The moral suitability of our international partners is an issue agitating the Conservative Party – but largely focused on the case of China. There was a Conservative rebellion after the Government decided to allow a role for the Chinese tech company Huawei in the construction of the UK's 5G network – a backlash that forced a Government U-turn.

However, perhaps due to financial self-interest, given that the Conservative Party has raised substantial amounts of cash from foreign oligarchs in recent years, it hasn't lifted its gaze beyond the corrupting influence of investment linked to the Chinese state.

As a result, the Government is actively incubating new versions of Londongrad – creating silos of foreign states in the former industrial midlands and the north. Following the lead of London, these areas are becoming safe havens for the wealth of oligarchs and an insurance policy for foreign governments seeking geopolitical leverage against Britain and the West as a whole.

This subservience to extreme wealth – both new and old – has likewise been buttressed by the claim that high-value individuals would simply leave the UK if we hiked taxes.

In fact, as we have seen in recent times with the example of Russian oligarchs, our problem is that we struggle to force these people to leave. They are stubbornly lodged in British society, embedded in our institutions – political, cultural and corporate – through which they store their money and clean their reputations.

In his book, *The Myth of Millionaire Tax Flight*, Stanford Professor Cristobal Young suggests that "The corporate services complex – made up of the top firms in law, accounting, management consulting, and investment banking – is overwhelmingly concentrated in the major cities of wealthy countries."[420]

As a result, "globalisation has not meant that elite professionals and the executive class can now live wherever they wish. On the contrary, place is more important than ever, and top income earners are more and more concentrated in major cities."

In other words: super wealthy individuals, although they are likely to trade over continents, are still bound to certain countries and cities due to the nature of the modern economy. "When you achieve success in a place, it becomes harder to leave," Young adds.

After purchasing Chelsea and winning the Premier League, Russian billionaire Roman Abramovich wouldn't have sold the club and bought Real Madrid if economic conditions in the UK had become more hostile to the super wealthy. The time and resources involved in moving clubs would have cost more than any hostile measures put in place by the UK Government. But Abramovich doesn't have any special emotional attachment to the UK, and of course owns assets across the globe, as is the nature of the international elite.

So, the new and old elite have merged, leaving little respect for British values or tradition (or really anything aside from the robotic expansion of assets). The old elite is acting through desperate self-preservation, while the new elite is happy to exploit a country that acts as a safe haven for its cash, governed by a legal system that persecutes journalists for saying mean things about the wealthy, with long-established links to offshore tax havens, and a real estate market heavily biased in favour of luxury landlords.

This is the makeup of the Bullingdon Club elite. It is not the quaint, benevolent leadership of *Jeeves and Wooster* aristocrats, but a calculated alliance of old and new money, dedicated ruthlessly towards extending its own life opportunities.

How do we get out of this mess? Well, it's not going to be easy. The hyper-concentration of economic resources and political power has been taking place in Britain for four decades, justified by leaders with an ever-distant relationship with the truth. Anger and disillusionment are now woven into our political fabric and – as the world braces itself for a climate emergency that will spur war and economic turmoil – there is no guarantee that we will return to the safe expansion of our living standards and of liberal democracy across the world.

Redistribution should be the guiding ideal of

progressive Britain – calling for higher taxes on the unearned wealth of oligarchs and aristocrats, the devolution of political power away from a corrupt establishment in Westminster, valuing housing as a social good (and a human right) rather than a tool for wealth extraction, clamping down on the dark money interests that polarise and pollute political discourse for their own financial gain, and ending the centuries-old hierarchy in our education system.

This will require bold, capable, radical reforms – tapping into the decency of the British public and their rightful indignation towards the status quo. And this endeavour has to gather momentum before the illiberal elite reorganises, reboots and mounts another well-funded assault on the common good.

It's high time that Britain is seen once again as a nation – a curious, beguiling blend of regions, nations, accents, classes and cultures, all with a stake in our collective prosperity – rather than a corporation owned and controlled by a few all-powerful shareholders.

For this is our country, too.

ENDNOTES

FOREWORD

1 John Arlidge, 'Guppy "going to prison for a very long time" in £1.8m gems fraud', *The Independent* (February 1993).

1 THE STATE WE ARE IN

2 Harry Mount, 'Who was Cincinnatus - and why does Boris use so many Latin words?', *The Oldie* (September 2022).
3 Sangarika Jaisinghani, 'UK Markets Have Lost $500 Billion Since Liz Truss Took Over', *Bloomberg* (27 September 2022).
4 Jasper Jolly, 'Number of billionaires in UK reached new record during COVID crisis', *The Guardian* (May 2021).
5 Haroon Siddique, 'Douglas Hogg becomes first politician to step down over expenses', *The Guardian* (May 2009).
6 Sam Coates, Jennifer Scott, 'Westminster Accounts: MPs earn £17.1m on top of their salaries since the last election – with Tories taking £15.2m', Sky News (January 2023).
7 Sam Bright et al., 'Mapping the Pandemic: £2 Billion in Contracts Awarded to Conservative Associates', *Byline Times* (March 2021).
8 Ephraim Hardcastle, 'Oxford Bullingdon Club's distasteful initiation ceremony', *Daily Mail* (December 2012).
9 Harriet Sherwood, 'Sexism, vandalism and bullying: inside the Boris Johnson-era Bullingdon Club', *The Observer* (July 2019).
10 Tom Mutch, 'Breaking the Bullingdon Club Omertà: Secret Lives of the Men Who Run Britain', the *Daily Beast* (January 2016).
11 'Boris Johnson: The Irresistible Rise', BBC (November 2013).
12 Sherwood, 'Sexism, vandalism and bullying: inside the Boris Johnson-era Bullingdon Club', *The Observer*.
13 Mutch, 'Breaking the Bullingdon Club Omertà: Secret Lives of the Men Who Run Britain', the *Daily Beast*.

14 'Wales in Trouble Over Club Supper; Queen Mary Orders the Prince to Resign from the Lively Bullingdon at Oxford', the *New York Times* (May 1913).
15 Asher Weisz, 'A Day in the Lockdown Life of: a Bullingdon Club member', the *Oxford Student* (February 2021).
16 Tom Nichols, 'The New Era of Political Violence Is Here', *The Atlantic* (August 2022).
17 Patrick Butler, 'Over 330,000 excess deaths in Great Britain linked to austerity, finds study', *The Guardian* (October 2022).
18 Sonia Purnell, *Just Boris: A Tale of Blond Ambition*, (Aurum, 2011).
19 'The Cameron Illusion', Mile End Institute, Queen Mary University of London (June 2016).
20 Simon Kuper, *Chums: How a Tiny Caste of Oxford Tories Took Over the UK* (Profile, 2022).
21 Andrew Rawnsley, 'Boris Johnson, the party animal, has vomited over standards in public life', The Guardian (May 2022).
22 Lucy Pasha-Robinson, 'Grenfell: Police say they have "reasonable grounds" to suspect Kensington council and TMO committed corporate manslaughter', *The Independent* (July 2017).
23 Emma Dent Coad, *One Kensington: Tales from the Frontline of the Most Unequal Borough in Britain*, (Quercus, 2022).
24 'Nearly two-thirds of new Cabinet attended independent schools and almost half attended Oxbridge', Sutton Trust (October 2022).
25 Valentina Romei, 'Living standards grow at slowest rate since second world war', *Financial Times* (January 2020).
26 Liz Truss and others, *Britannia Unchained: Global Lessons for Growth and Prosperity*, (Palgrave Macmillan, 2012).

2 THE GREAT PROCUREMENT SCANDAL

27 Sam Bright and Max Colbert, 'Who Are Johnson's 22 Big Money Backers? And Did They Influence the No Confidence Vote?', *Byline Times* (June 2022).
28 Henry Zeffman, 'JCB chairman dug deep to pay for Boris Johnson's wedding', *The Times* (September 2022).
29 Heather Stewart, 'Outcry in India as Boris Johnson visits JCB plant amid demolitions row', *The Guardian* (April 2022).
30 George Arbuthnott and Jonathan Calvert, *Failures of State: The Inside Story of Britain's Battle with Coronavirus*, (HarperCollins, 2021).
31 Sam Bright, 'Frontline Workers Failed by Wasteful, Inefficient

£15 Billion PPE Procurement Effort, Report Reveals', *Byline Times* (November 2020).
32 Sam Bright, 'Government Ignored PPE Warnings in December 2019, Supplier Tells MPs', *Byline Times* (May 2021).
33 Bright, 'Frontline Workers Failed by Wasteful, Inefficient £15 Billion PPE Procurement Effort, Report Reveals', *Byline Times*.
34 Sarah Marsh, 'Hancock criticised for claim there was never a national PPE shortage', *The Guardian* (February 2021).
35 Richard Vaughan, 'Coronavirus in the UK: Doctors lacking even most basic personal protective equipment, BMA warns', *iNews* (March 2020).
36 Sam Bright, 'Another Strange Trio of PPE Contracts Emerge', *Byline Times* (July 2020).
37 Sam Bright, 'Anatomy of the PPE Procurement Scandal', *Byline Times* (November 2022).
38 Richard Adams, 'David Meller, the Tory donor "desperate to be part of the establishment"', *The Guardian* (January 2018).
39 Department of Health and Social Care, 'PPE procurement in the early pandemic', (November 2021).
40 David Conn, Rowena Mason, Rob Evans, and Joseph Smith, 'Michael Gove backer won £164m in PPE contracts after "VIP lane" referral', *The Guardian* (November 2021).
41 Sam Bright, '"VIP" Firms Referred by Tory MPs and Peers for PPE Deals See Profits Soar', *Byline Times* (November 2022).
42 Sam Bright, 'Minister's Meetings Fuel the Conservative Procurement Scandal', *Byline Times* (November 2020).
43 Sam Bright, '"Informal Arrangements" Used for Government PPE Procurement, Says Health Minister', *Byline Times* (November 2020).
44 Sam Bright, 'Owner of Firm Awarded £275 Million in COVID Contracts Makes Donation to Conservatives', *Byline Times* (March 2021).
45 Sam Bright, 'Friend of Matt Hancock Wins £14.4 Million PPE Contract', *Byline Times* (February 2021)/
46 Sam Bright, 'The Anatomy of a PPE Deal to a Matt Hancock Associate', *Byline Times* (June 2021).
47 David Conn, 'Horse racing, Tory donations and a swift return from lockdown', *The Guardian* (June 2020).
48 Sam Bright, 'Randox Releases Private Messages Between Owen Paterson and Matt Hancock Over Randox Contracts', *Byline Times* (February 2022).

49 Bright, 'Randox Releases Private Messages Between Owen Paterson and Matt Hancock Over Randox Contracts', *Byline Times*.
50 Sam Bright, 'News in Brief: Undisclosed Insights from the Corridors of Power: Randox and Turing', *Byline Times* (28 January 2022).
51 Sam Bright, 'Health Department Failed to Declare Minister's 27 Meetings Held at Outset of Pandemic', *Byline Times* (June 2021).
52 Sam Bright, 'Hancock Meeting with Tech Giants That Won £1.3 Billion in COVID Contracts Declared 21 Months Late', *Byline Times* (May 2022).
53 Sam Bright, 'Very Inefficient Process: Watchdog Exposes Government's PPE Failures', *Byline Times* (March 2022).
54 Tom Clark, 'How the rich ate us', *Prospect* (June 2022).
55 Byline Times Team, '£400 Million COVID Contract Winners Go On to Donate £615,000 to Conservatives', *Byline Times* (June 2021).
56 'Yarl's Wood: undercover in the secretive immigration centre', Channel 4 News (March 2015).
57 John Lubbock and Sian Norris, 'Meet the Companies for Which Asylum Policy is Big Business', *Byline Times* (December 2021).
58 Sam Bright, 'Government Reveals Total Number of Private Sector Consultants Working for 'Test and Trace'", *Byline Times* (January 2021).
59 Sam Bright, 'Concierge Capitalism: The Conservative Free Market Myth', *Byline Times* (July 2022).
60 Daniel Markovits, 'How McKinsey Destroyed the Middle Class', *The Atlantic* (February 2020).
61 Sam Bright and Sian Norris, 'Big COVID Management Consultancy Winners Fined £101 Million Since 2010', *Byline Times* (October 2021).
62 Aeron Davis, *Reckless Opportunists: Elites at the End of the Establishment*, (Manchester University Press, 2018).
63 Graeme Paton, '£43m of public cash for a garden bridge that was never built', *The Times* (February 2019).

3 FLOREAT ETONA!

64 Purnell, *Just Boris*.
65 Conrad Duncan, 'Eton College exam question asking students to justify the Army killing protesters resurfaces', *i100* (September 2019).

66 Richard Beard, *Sad Little Men: Private Schools and the Ruin of England*, (Harvill Secker, 2021).
67 Iain Overton, 'Etonocracy: How One Public School Came to Dominate Public Life', *Byline Times* (August 2021).
68 Purnell, *Just Boris.*
69 Simon Kuper, '"A nursery of the Commons": how the Oxford Union created today's ruling political class', *The Guardian* (April 2022).
70 Beard, *Sad Little Men.*
71 Kuper, *Chums.*
72 Ruby Lott-Lavigna, 'Where has Boris Johnson Gone on Holiday?', *VICE* (April 2020).
73 Sam Bright, *Fortress London: Why We Need to Save the Country from its Capital*, (Harper North, 2022).
74 Truss and others, *Britannia Unchained.*
75 Michael Young, *The Rise of the Meritocracy: 1870-2033*, (Thames and Hudson, 1958).
76 Peter Hennessy, *Establishment and Meritocracy*, (Haus, 2014).
77 Aubrey Allegretti, 'A-level results: Government accused of "baking in" inequality with "boost" for private schools', Sky News (August 2020).
78 Akala, Natives: *Race and Class in the Ruins of Empire*, (John Murray, 2018).
79 'Access to Advantage', Sutton Trust (December 2018).
80 Sam Bright, 'Elite Rule: Liz Truss' Socially Exclusive Cabinet', *Byline Times* (September 2022).
81 'Parliamentary Privilege 2019', Sutton Trust (December 2019).
82 'Nearly two-thirds of new Cabinet attended independent schools and almost half attended Oxbridge', Sutton Trust.
83 Geoffrey Wheatcroft, 'The Making of the English Middle Class', *The Atlantic* (July 1999).
84 Nick Fraser, 'You can take the boy out of Eton...', *The Guardian* (November 2005).
85 Patrick Wintour, 'Gove attacks "preposterous" number of Old Etonians in Cameron's cabinet', *The Guardian* (March 2014).
86 Matthew Weaver and Henry Dyer, 'Boris Johnson gives peerages job to author of book on his "wit and wisdom"', The Guardian (September 2022).
87 John Harris, 'Forget "levelling up" – Liz Truss isn't even pretending to care about inequality', *The Guardian* (September 2022).

88 Pippa Crerar, 'Leaked audio reveals Liz Truss said British workers needed "more graft"', *The Guardian* (August 2022).
89 Sam Bright, 'Charity Fallacy: Private Schools Estimated to Get £3 Billion a Year from Tax Exemptions', *Byline Times* (June 2022).
90 Jacob Dirnhuber, 'Overseas satellite colleges rake in millions tax-free for private schools including Harrow', *The Times* (October 2021).
91 Bright, 'Charity Fallacy: Private Schools Estimated to Get £3 Billion a Year from Tax Exemptions', *Byline Times*.
92 'Household total wealth in Great Britain: April 2018 to March 2020', ONS (January 2022).
93 Ben Ellery and George Greenwood, 'Dirty cash pays fees at top private schools', The Times (February 2022).
94 Beard, *Sad Little Men*.
95 Sascha Lavin and Iain Overton, 'Elite Private Schools Increase Assets by More than Half a Billion Pounds in Six Years', *Byline Times* (November 2021).
96 Lavin and Overton, 'Elite Private Schools Increase Assets by More than Half a Billion Pounds in Six Years', *Byline Times*.
97 'Findings of the Second Permanent Secretary's investigation into alleged gatherings on government premises during COVID restrictions', Cabinet Office (May 2022).
98 Lizzy Buchan, 'Shameless Boris Johnson "takes responsibility" for Partygate – then promptly blames his staff", *The Mirror* (May 2022).
99 India McTaggart, 'Rachel Johnson: My brother Boris dreamt of being world king – and he almost achieved it', *The Telegraph* (July 2022).
100 Musa Okwonga, *One of Them: An Eton College Memoir*, (Unbound, 2021).
101 Kuper, *Chums*.
102 Daisy Stephens, 'PM refers to Telegraph as his "real boss", Dominic Cummings claims', LBC (July 2021).

4 TUFTON STREET

103 Shahmir Sanni, 'Behind Closed Doors Johnson and his Cabinet Do Not Applaud the NHS – They Ideologically Oppose It', *Byline Times* (March 2020).
104 Peter Geoghegan, *Democracy For Sale: Dark Money and Dirty Politics*, (Apollo, 2020).

105 'Funding', TaxPayers' Alliance.
106 Rob Evans, David Pegg and Felicity Lawrence, 'Taxpayers' Alliance received over £223k in foreign donations', *The Guardian* (November 2018).
107 Owen Jones, *The Establishment: and how they get away with it*, (Allen Lane, 2014).
108 'Who Funds You?', *openDemocracy*.
109 Lawrence Carter and Alice Ross, 'Revealed: BP and gambling interests fund secretive free market think tank', *Unearthed* (July 2018).
110 Max Colbert, 'Is a Big Money Coalition Influencing Liz Truss' Climate Change Policies?', *Byline Times* (October 2022).
111 Robert Booth, 'Rightwing UK thinktank "offered ministerial access" to potential US donors', *The Guardian* (July 2018).
112 'Record-breaking traffic year', Guido Fawkes (December 2017).
113 Jim Waterson, 'Pro-Boris Johnson campaign launched by Guido Fawkes blogger', *The Guardian* (May 2019).
114 Sam Bright, 'Liz Truss: The Tufton Street Candidate', *Byline Times* (January 2022).
115 'Freeports Consultation', Transparency International UK (July 2020).
116 Byline Intelligence Team, 'The Truss Network: Who are the New Prime Minister's Donors and Advisors?', *Byline Times* (September 2022).
117 Sam Bright, 'The Tentacles of Tufton Street: Think Tank Alumni Handed Top Government Roles', *Byline Times* (October 2022).
118 Matt Honeycombe-Foster, 'London Influence: IEA way or the highway – SpAd advice – Give (time) generously', *Politico* (September 2022).
119 Adam Bychawski, 'Will think tanks be kicked out of Downing Street after the Truss disaster', openDemocracy (October 2022).
120 'British Social Attitudes 39', NatCen Social Research (2022).
121 'About the 2020 Tax Commission', TaxPayers' Alliance.
122 Sam Bright, 'The Tufton Street Elite Takes Back Control of the Brexit Project', *Byline Times* (September 2022.
123 Bright, 'The Tufton Street Elite Takes Back Control of the Brexit Project', *Byline Times*.
124 Truss and others, *Britannia Unchained*.
125 Sam Bright, 'Overseas Assistance Austerity: Government's

Drastic Cuts to Foreign Aid, Health, Climate and Gender Equality Revealed', *Byline Times* (September 2021).
126'Yemen on the brink: conflict is pushing millions towards famine', Oxfam International.
127 Andrew Woodcock, 'UK slashes aid to Commonwealth countries by "staggering" £500m', *The Independent* (October 2021).
128 Jacob Thorburn, 'Foreign Office to cut staff by 20%: Civil servants told their jobs could be at risk over the next four years as ex-ambassadors warn cuts will "severely damage UK's global reputation"', *Daily Mail* (December 2021).
129 Johann Tasker, 'Defra can deal with budget cuts, says Truss', *Farmers Weekly* (October 2015).
130 Pippa Crerar and Helena Horton, 'Liz Truss "has sewage on her hands" over Environment Agency cuts, *The Guardian* (August 2022).
131 George Monbiot, 'Toothless Environment Agency is allowing the living world to be wrecked with impunity', *The Guardian* (November 2015).
132 Emilio Casalicchio, Graham Lanktree and Cristina Gallardo, 'Everything you need to know about Liz Truss', *Politico* (September 2021).
133 Clark, 'How the rich ate us', *Prospect.*
134 'From the doom loop to an economy for work not wealth', Trades Union Congress (February 2023).
135 James Meadway, 'The left shouldn't rush to blame Liz Truss for Britain's woes', *New Statesman* (February 2023).
136 Tony Diver, 'David Frost brands COVID lockdowns a "serious mistake"', *The Telegraph* (January 2022).
137 'Large scale lockdowns in Europe saved millions of lives', National Institute for Health and Care Research (June 2020).
138 David Wilcock, 'Could a regional "circuit breaker" STILL happen at half-term? Claims Dominic Cummings and Michael Gove are backing a broad crackdown in badly-affected "urban areas"', Daily Mail (October 2020).
139 Sam Bright, 'Records Confirm Johnson Met with Lockdown-Sceptics at Key COVID Turning Point', *Byline Times* (February 2021).
140 Karl McDonald, 'Second lockdown: why an Oxford expert thinks it might be better to wait until Christmas for a "circuit break"', *iNews* (September 2020).

141 Sunetra Gupta, Carl Heneghan and Karol Sikora, 'Boris must urgently rethink his COVID strategy', *The Spectator* (September 2020).
142 Nafeez Ahmed, 'Climate Science Denial Network Behind Great Barrington Declaration', *Byline Times* (October 2020).
143 'Bloomberg Billionaires Index: Charles Kock', *Bloomberg*.
144 'UK PM's former adviser confirms Johnson said "let the bodies pile high"', *Reuters* (May 2021).
145 Sam Bright, 'Cummings Exposes More Details of Boris Johnson's Pact With Right-Wing Press Proprietors', *Byline Times* (May 2022).
146 'Carole Cadwalladr Archives', *Guido Fawkes*.
147 Sam Bright, 'Alt-Right Ecosystem: Steve Bannon Tried to Buy Guido Fawkes', *Byline Times* (February 2021).
148 Nicky Woolf, 'The rise and fall of Breitbart', *New Statesman* (July 2019).
149 Carole Cadwalladr and Emma Graham-Harrison, 'Revealed: 50 million Facebook profiles harvested for Cambridge Analytica in major data breach', *The Observer* (March 2018).
150 Peter Jukes, 'The Transatlantic Triumph of Trumpism: Boris Johnson, a Plan Years in the Making', *Byline Times* (June 2019).
151 'Data, Democracy and Dirty Tricks', Channel 4 (March 2018).
152 Carole Cadwalladr, 'Revealed: how US billionaire helped to back Brexit', *The Observer* (February 2017).
153 Carole Cadwalladr, and Mark Townsend, 'Revealed: the ties that bound Vote Leave's data firm to controversial Cambridge Analytica', *The Guardian* (March 2018).
154 Channel 4 News Investigations Team, 'Exposed: Undercover secrets of Trump's data firm', Channel 4 (March 2018).
155 Carole Cadwalladr, 'Video reveals Steve Bannon links to Boris Johnson', *The Observer* (June 2019).
156 Geoghegan, *Democracy For Sale*.
157 Jane Mayer, *Dark Money: The Hidden History of the Billionaires Behind the Rise of the Radical Right*, (Doubleday, 2016).
158 Adam Bychawski, 'Exclusive: US climate deniers pump millions into Tory-linked think tanks', *openDemocracy* (June 2022).
159 Kate Nicholson, '6 Times Boris Johnson Revealed His Climate Change Scepticism', the *Huffington Post* (September 2021).
160 Sascha Lavin, 'The Conservative Party's Climate Climbdown', *Byline Times* (July 2022).

161 Adam Barnett and Damien Gayle, 'GB News chairman has history of dismissing threat of climate crisis', *The Guardian* (May 2022).
162 Adam Forrest, 'One in 15 Conservative MPs believe climate change is a "myth", poll finds', *The Independent* (November 2021).
163 Colbert, 'Is a Big Money Coalition Influencing Liz Truss' Climate Change Policies?', *Byline Times*.
164 Colbert, 'Is a Big Money Coalition Influencing Liz Truss' Climate Change Policies?', *Byline Times*.
165 'Fracking is the "moral and economic choice", says IEA energy analyst', Institute of Economic Affairs (April 2022).
166 Robert Colvile, 'Green politics with a big splash of blue', the *Sunday Times* (January 2020).
167 Christopher Deane and Adam Barnett, 'UK Minister Steve Baker Receives £10k from Chair of Tufton St. Climate Denial Group', *DeSmog* (February 2023).
168 Sam Bright and Max Colbert, 'The Hardline Forces Shaping the Conservative Leadership Contest', *Byline Times* (July 2022).
169 Helena Horton, 'Green Tories fear next party leader could ditch net zero strategy', *The Guardian* (July 2022).
170 Luke Murphy and Becca Massey-Chase, 'As some politicians seek to divide on climate change, the public remain united', IPPR (July 2022).

5 POLITICS, PRIVATISED

171 Lukas Audickas, 'General Election 2019: Which party received the most donations?', House of Commons Library (January 2020).
172 Peter Geoghegan, Seth Thévoz and Jenna Corderoy, 'Revealed: The elite dining club behind £130m+ donations to the Tories', *openDemocracy* (November 2019).
173 Geoghegan, *Democracy For Sale*.
174 Gabriel Pogrund and Henry Zeffman, 'The Tory donors with access to Boris Johnson's top team', the *Sunday Times* (February 2022).
175 Martin Williams, '20% of Tory donations come from property tycoons', *openDemocracy* (July 2021).
176 Byline Intelligence Team,'The Truss Network: Who are the New Prime Minister's Donors and Advisors?', *Byline Times*.

177 Brigid Francis-Devine, 'Household Debt: Key Economic Indicators', House of Commons Library (January 2023).
178 Sascha Lavin, '"A Haven for Dirty Money": Nearly Half of All Corporate Violations in the Past Decade Committed by Financial Sector', *Byline Times* (October 2021).
179 Seth Thévoz, 'Tories rake in £11m from hedge funds and finance tycoons', *openDemocracy* (September 2021).
180 Sam Bright, 'The Tories' Big Money "Summer Party": What We Know and Don't Know', *Byline Times* (June 2022).
181 Melanie Newman, Robert Booth, Nick Mathiason and Luke Harding, 'Tennis with Cameron and Johnson sells for £160,000 at Tory fundraiser', *The Guardian* (July 2014).
182 Max Colbert, 'Conservative Party Dodges Questions About Vetting of Russian-Linked Donors', *Byline Times* (February 2022).
183 'Russia', Intelligence and Security Committee of Parliament (July 2020).
184 Sam Bright and Max Colbert, 'Black Ties and Dark Money: The Conservative-Cash-for-Access Machine', *Byline Times* (June 2020).
185 'Membership FAQs – Conservatives', Conservative Party website (2023).
186 Sam Bright, 'Concern Over Foreign Interference and Conservative Membership Rules', *Byline Times* (July 2022).
187 Rajeev Syal, 'Brexit party at high risk of accepting illegal funds, says watchdog', *The Guardian* (June 2019).
188 Victoria Young, 'London Paper Tries to Decipher a Russian Owner', *New York Times* (February 2009).
189 Sam Bright, 'Government Didn't Record Minutes of Meeting Between Lebedev and Johnson', *Byline Times* (March 2022).
190 'Evening Standard comment: Vote for Boris – Corbyn is unfit to lead Britain', *Evening Standard* (December 2019).
191 Luke Harding and Dan Sabbagh, 'Johnson visit to Lebedev party after victory odd move for "people's PM"', *The Guardian* (December 2019).
192 Gabriel Pogrund and Harry Yorke, 'Boris Johnson's Russian crony Evgeny Lebedev got peerage after spies dropped warning', the *Sunday Times* (March 2022).
193 John Sweeney, 'Lebedev: The KGB Spy Who Helped Put Putin in the Kremlin', *Byline Times* (March 2022).
194 Luke Harding, 'Alexander Lebedev: an oligarch we could

learn to love', *The Observer* (January 2009).
195 Samuel Stolton, 'UK-linked media magnate Lebedev hit by Canada sanctions', *Politico* (May 2022).
196 Nick Hopkins, 'Morning after: Boris Johnson recovers from Lebedev's exotic Italian party', *The Guardian* (July 2019).
197 Gemma Newby, Karla Patella and Paul Caruana Galizia, 'Lebedev: Lord of Siberia', *Tortoise* (February 2022).
198 Alexandra Hall Hall, 'Johnson's Visit to the Lebedevs: A Dire State Not a "Deep State"', *Byline Times* (July 2022).
199 Adam Bienkov, 'The Johnson-Lebedev Letters: A Back-Channel to Vladimir Putin?', *Byline Times* (March 2022).
200 Sam Bright, 'Lord Evgeny Lebedev Joins Enterprise Run by Saudi Ruler Accused of Approving Killing of Journalist Khashoggi', *Byline Times* (July 2022).
201 Stephanie Nebehay and Stephen Kalin, 'Saudi crown prince linked to Khashoggi murder in UN report', *Reuters* (June 2019).
202 Jim Waterson, 'Lebedev dinner with Mohammed bin Salman raises questions over Saudi links', *The Guardian* (September 2019).
203 Mark Sweney, 'Sale of Standard and Independent stakes to Saudi investor investigated', *The Guardian* (June 2019).
204 Byline Times Team, 'UK Newspapers Accepted Money to Publish Positive Environmental Stories About Saudi Arabia Around COP26', *Byline Times* (November 2021).
205 'UK PM Johnson defends Saudi visit after mass execution', *Reuters* (March 2022).
206 'Saudi Arabia: Events of 2021', Human Rights Watch.
207 Byline Intelligence Team, 'Tory Entitlement: Quarter of Top Conservative Donors have Received Honours or Peerages', *Byline Times* (September 2021).
208 Sebastian Payne and Daniel Thomas, 'Hancock affair highlights opaque world of Whitehall non-execs', *Financial Times* (July 2021).
209 Martin Williams and Peter Geoghegan, 'At least 16 Tory allies given paid "independent" roles in government', *openDemocracy* (June 2021).
210 Sam Bright, 'Chumocracy: Jacob Rees-Mogg's Business Partner Appointed to Senior Trade Role', *Byline Times* (December 2020).
211 Ian Lucas, 'The Populist Alliance: How Vote Leave Came to Rule British Politics', *Byline Times* (December 2021).

212 'Committee on Standards publish report on the conduct of Rt Hon Owen Paterson', UK Parliament (October 2021).
213 Aubrey Allegretti, 'MP Owen Paterson faces suspension for breaking lobbying rules', *The Guardian* (October 2021).
214 Sam Bright, 'Conservative MPs Opposing Lobbying Suspension have Second Jobs Worth £1 Million', *Byline Times* (November 2021).
215 Jon Stone, 'Tory MP voted in parliament while doing £1m second job from Caribbean island tax haven' *The Independent* (November 2021).
216 Arj Singh, 'Sir Geoffrey Cox: Tory MP defends his legal work for British Virgin Islands and lockdown trip to Caribbean', *iNews* (November 2021).
217 Sam Bright and Sascha Lavin, '20% Increase in Child Poverty in Constituencies Represented by MPs Who Have Earned £6 Million', *Byline Times* (17 November).
218 Sam Bright, '£60,000 Contract Between MP and Firm Begins Weeks After Constituency Meeting', *Byline Times* (June 2021).
219 'Meeting with MHR', Ruth Edwards website (March 2021). Retrieved via the WayBack Machine (February 2023).
220 Jessica Elgot and Helen Pidd, '"It feels gruelling": new Tories reflect on difficult year', *The Guardian* (December 2020).
221 Joe Pike and Alan McGuinness, 'David Cameron: Financier Lex Greensill claimed to be "senior adviser" to David Cameron, business card handed to Labour shows', Sky News (April 2021).
222 Robert Smith and Jim Pickard, 'Greensill Capital paid Cameron salary of more than $1m a year', *Financial Times* (July 2021).
223 'Tony Blair makes £1m a month from private speeches as offers flood in for the former PM', *Evening Standard* (April 2012).
224 John Siddle, 'Ex-PM Theresa May gets £2m for speeches, including £1m for just 70 hours of work', *The Mirror* (November 2022).
225 Liam James, 'Boris Johnson to publish memoir "like no other" after signing book deal', *The Independent* (January 2023).
226 Ben Quinn and Alison Flood, 'For the Record: signs of trouble before David Cameron book hits shelves', *The Guardian* (September 2019).
227 David Hencke, 'Former Prime Ministers Receive £6 Million from Taxpayer in 13 Years for Expenses', *Byline Times* (December 2022).

228 'Gordon Brown earns £1.4m since leaving Number 10', BBC News (February 2012).
229 'Former UK PM Johnson has earned £1m for speeches since quitting', *Reuters* (December 2022).
230 Isabel Hardman, *Why We Get the Wrong Politicians*, (Atlantic Books, 2018).
231 Suzanne Moore, 'Dominic Cummings: "I don't like parties"', Unherd (May 2022).
232 Jones, *The Establishment.*
233 Katy Balls, 'Could Liz Truss's cabinet cull come back to haunt her?', *The Spectator* (September 2022).
234 'Chancellor Rishi Sunak held US green card until last year', BBC News (April 2022).
235 Sam Bright, 'Britain's Foreign Media Oligarchy', *Byline Times* (April 2022).
236 'The Sunday Times Rich List 2022', the *Sunday Times* (May 2022).
237 Rosaleen Fenton, 'Chancellor's sprawling £100m property empire – including high-street supermarket', *The Mirror* (July 2022).
238 Martin Williams, 'A quarter of Tory MPs are private landlords', *openDemocracy* (July 2021).
239 Rupert Neate, 'Who is Lord Brownlow, the man who helped pay for Downing Street refurb?', *The Guardian* (April 2021).
240 Tom Ambrose, 'Boris Johnson wanted £150,000 treehouse at Chequers, say reports', *The Guardian* (June 2022).

6 THE GAME

241 Davis, *Reckless Opportunists.*
242 Chris Grey, '"Fundamentally Meaningless: The Government's Brexit Benefits Paper', *Byline Times* (February 2022).
243 David Conn, Peter Geoghegan, Rob Evans and Russell Scott, 'Tory-linked PR firm granted £3m Covid-19 contract without tender', *The Guardian* (August 2020).
244 Sam Bright, 'How Two Right-Wing Meme Merchants Scored a £3 Million Government Coronavirus Contract', *Byline Times* (July 2020).
245 Jim Waterson, 'Tories hire Facebook propaganda pair to run online election campaign', *The Guardian* (October 2019).

246 Daniel Finkelstein, 'If Boris Johnson's magic has gone, it won't come back', *The Times* (February 2022).
247 Alex Hern, '"Eat out to help out" may have caused sixth of COVID clusters over summer', *The Guardian* (October 2020).
248 Aletha Adu, 'Flashy Rishi Sunak's Treasury communications budget soars to £3.4 million', *The Mirror* (May 2022).
249 Rob Merrick, 'Rishi Sunak spends £500,000 of taxpayers' cash on focus groups 'to repair his image', *The Independent* (May 2022).
250 'What Liz Truss's Instagram account reveals about her', Sky News (September 2022).
251 Aubrey Allegretti, 'Millions in UK face disenfranchisement under voter ID plans', *The Guardian* (July 2021).
252 Caroline Wheeler, 'Dirty dossiers on S&M and affairs as Tory rivals turn on each other', the *Sunday Times* (July 2022).
253 Andrew Prokop, 'The "pee tape" claim, explained', *Vox* (April 2018).
254 'Boris Johnson's personal mobile phone number available online for 15 years', BBC News (April 2021).
255 'Supreme Court: Suspending Parliament was unlawful, judges rule', BBC News (September 2019).
256 Alix Culbertson, 'Boris Johnson changes ministerial code so those who breach it don't have to quit or face sack', Sky News (May 2022).
257 Jessica Elgot, '"Reasonable" to suggest PM may have broken code over Partygate, says ethics adviser, *The Guardian* (June 2022).
258 Kate Proctor and John Johnston, 'An Inquiry Found Priti Patel Broke The Ministerial Code But Boris Johnson Will Take No Further Action', *PoliticsHome* (November 2020).
259 Sam Bright, 'Where is the Government's Anti-Corruption "Champion"', *Byline Times* (November 2021).
260 Andrew Woodcock, 'No inquiry into claims Boris Johnson proposed partner for £100k government job, says civil service chief', *The Independent* (June 2022).
261 Rupert Neate, 'Sunak under pressure to reveal whereabouts of his own investments', *The Guardian* (October 2020).
262 Tom Pettifor, 'Tory minister Nadhim Zahawi pockets fortune from second job at oil company', *The Mirror* (November 2021).
263 Greg Heffer, 'Boris Johnson offers "humble" apology and blames new phone for failing to release messages to Downing

Street flat probe', Sky News (January 2022).
264 Sam Bright, 'Minutes of Boris Johnson Meeting with Cambridge Analytica "Would Directly Undermine Trust Between the UK and US"', *Byline Times* (January 2023).
265 Jenna Corderoy, 'Government's "Orwellian" unit to be disbanded after openDemocracy revelations', *openDemocracy* (August 2022).
266 'Dawn Butler thrown out of Commons for PM lie accusation' BBC News (July 2021).
267 Chris Giles and Nick Peterson, 'UK trade performance falls to worst level on record in first quarter', *Financial Times* (June 2022).
268 Sam Bright, 'Dover Insider: "95% of Problems Caused by Brexit"', *Byline Times* (January 2022).
269 Georgia Lee, 'How many bankers were jailed for their part in the financial crisis?', Channel 4 FactCheck (November 2017).
270 Zamira Rahim, 'Boris Johnson showed "disgracefully cavalier" attitude to studies, school letter reveals', *The Independent* (October 2019).
271 Oliver Browning, 'Boris Johnson discusses his "brilliant strategy for confusing media" in resurfaced clip', *The Independent* (January 2022).
272 Brian Stelter, 'This infamous Steve Bannon quote is key to understanding America's crazy politics', CNN (November 2021).

7 THE PROTECTION RACKET

273 Aisha Majid, 'Top 50 biggest news websites in the world', *Press Gazette* (January 2023).
274 'Annual Report on the BBC 2021-22', Ofcom (November 2022).
275 Bright, 'Cummings Exposes More Details of Boris Johnson's Pact With Right-Wing Press Proprietors', *Byline Times*.
276 Simon Bowers and Helen Pidd, 'Brecqhou: how windswept eyesore became Barclays' getaway', *The Guardian* (June 2012).
277 Sam Bright, "'Relationship Management": Daily Mail Pressured Government to Delete Tweet Criticising "Misleading" COVID Article', *Byline Times* (April 2021).
278 Bright, "'Relationship Management": Daily Mail Pressured Government to Delete Tweet Criticising "Misleading" COVID Article', *Byline Times*.

279 David Churchill, 'Department of Health in climbdown after online swipe at The Mail's analysis of Covid-19 facts and figures', *Daily Mail* (November 2020).
280 Nick Evershed, 'Australia's newspaper ownership is among the most concentrated in the world', *The Guardian* (November 2020).
281 Sam Bright, 'Rupert Murdoch in Series of Meetings With Boris Johnson and High-Profile Ministers', *Byline Times* (February 2021).
282 Jane Martinson, 'Rupert Murdoch was in room for Michael Gove's Donald Trump interview', *The Guardian* (February 2017).
283 Aisha Majid, 'Analysis: Daily Mail Partygate front pages overwhelmingly supportive of Boris Johnson', *Press Gazette* (May 2022).
284 Sam Bright, '"We're Living in a Bizarre Fantasy World": Alastair Campbell on Boris Johnson, Brexit and Labour', *Byline Times* (April 2021).
285 Peter Oborne, 'British journalists have become part of Johnson's fake news machine', *openDemocracy* (October 2019).
286 John Plunkett and Ben Quinn, 'Telegraph's Peter Oborne resigns, saying HSBC coverage a "fraud on readers"', *The Guardian* (February 2015).
287 Dan Milmo, 'Twitter admits bias in algorithm for rightwing politicians and news outlets', *The Guardian* (October 2021).
288 George Grylls, 'The radicalisation of Laurence Fox shows the worrying power of right-wing YouTube', *New Statesman* (January 2020).
289 Haroon Siddique, 'Laurence Fox says he has coronavirus and is taking ivermectin', *The Guardian* (January 2022).
290 Otto English, 'The Dangers of Politainment: The Laurence Fox Affair', *Byline Times* (January 2020).
291 Gemma Parry, 'Watch as Extinction Rebellion eco-zealots storm House of Lords as peers debated new protest laws to crackdown on guerrilla tactics used by climate activists', *Daily Mail* (January 2023).
292 Charlotte Tobitt, 'GB News secures £60m investment amid WarnerBros Discovery buyout', *Press Gazette* (August 2022).
293 Sam Bright, 'GB News Part-Owned by Two Conservative Lords', *Byline Times* (June 2021).
294 Conrad Duncan, 'Andrew Neil says he quit GB News because he didn't want to work for "British Fox"', *The Independent*

(September 2021).
295 Sam Bright, '"Gold Standard of Broadcasting Impartiality?" New BBC Board Member Sir Robbie Gibb Recently Championed Boris Johnson', *Byline Times* (April 2021).
296 Sam Bright, 'The New BBC Chairman has Donated Over £400,000 to the Conservatives', *Byline Times* (January 2021).
297 Luke Harding, 'Roman Abramovich settles libel claim over Putin biography', *The Guardian* (December 2021).
298 Dominic Casciani, 'Journalist wins "kleptocrat" book High Court libel case', BBC News (March 2022).
299 Ben Quinn, 'British law firms help oligarchs avoid legitimate media scrutiny, MPs told', *The Guardian* (March 2022).
300 Byline Intelligence Team, 'Legal Threats to Byline Times' Reporting on the PPE Procurement Scandal', *Byline Times* (May 2022).
301 Anna Gross and Jemima Kelly, 'Leaked government email reveals Tory peer's anger at treatment of PPE company', *Financial Times* (November 2021)
302 'PPE procurement in the early pandemic', Department of Health and Social Care.
303 David Conn, Paul Lewis and Rob Evans, 'Private emails reveal Gove's role in Tory-linked firm's PPE deals', *The Guardian* (March 2022).
304 Dipesh Gadher, Harry Yorke and Jim Armitage, 'Michelle Mone's husband admits he has financial interest in PPE firm', the *Sunday Times* (May 2022).
305 David Conn, 'Revealed: Tory peer Michelle Mone secretly received £29m from 'VIP lane' PPE firm', *The Guardian* (November 2022).
306 'Strategic Lawsuits Against Public Participation (SLAPPs)', Ministry of Justice (March 2022).
307 Billy Kenber, George Greenwood, 'Nadhim Zahawi sends "threatening" letters to online tax critic', *The Times* (July 2022).
308 Anna Isaac, 'Nadhim Zahawi "agreed on penalty" to settle tax bill worth millions', *The Guardian* (January 2023).

8 THE CULTURE WAR

309 Maria Sobolewska and Rob Ford, *Brexitland. Identity, Diversity and the Reshaping of British Politics*, (Cambridge University Press, 2020).

310 Alex Hern, 'Older people more likely to share fake news on Facebook, study finds', *The Guardian* (January 2019).
311 Julia Manchester, 'Nigel Farage to Zuckerberg: Brexit, Trump wouldn't have happened without Facebook', *The Hill* (May 2018).
312 Sobolewska and Ford, *Brexitland.*
313 'British Social Attitudes 39', NatCen Social Research.
314 Nichols, 'The New Era of Political Violence Is Here', *The Atlantic*.
315 Jack Montgomery, 'Farage at CPAC: Western universities have become "madrasas of Marxism"', Breitbart (August 2022).
316 Joshua Green, *Devil's Bargain: Steve Bannon, Donald Trump and the Storming of the Presidency*, (Penguin Press, 2017).
317 Peter Walker and Paul Lewis, 'Nigel Farage discussed fronting far-right group led by Steve Bannon', *The Guardian* (May 2019).
318 Greg Evans, 'Steve Bannon was interviewed on BBC Radio 4 and people are furious', *i100* (July 2019).
319 Sally Weale, 'UK's "strictest headmistress" fears schools will stop teaching Shakespeare', *The Guardian* (May 2022).
320 Paul Morgan-Bentley and James Beal, 'Censorship on campus: universities scrap "challenging" books to protect students', *The Times* (August 2022).
321 Martin Pengelly, 'I grew up where Liz Truss did, attended the same school. She's not telling you the truth', *The Guardian* (July 2022).
322 Toby Young, 'Rise of the New Puritans', the *Daily Sceptic* (August 2022).
323 Gideon Rachman, *The Age of The Strongman: How the Cult of the Leader Threatens Democracy around the World*, (Bodley Head, 2022).
324 Jon Greenberg, 'Most Republicans still falsely believe Trump's stolen election claims. Here are some reasons why', *Poynter* (June 2022).
325 Nadeem Badshah, 'Liz Truss rebuked for "cheap" jibes at hustings after criticising media', *The Guardian* (August 2022).
326 Arbuthnott and Calvert, *Failures of State*.
327 Sam Bright, 'The "Phantom Threat": Government Admits Its University Free Speech Policy Only Based on "Small" Amount of Evidence', *Byline Times* (March 2021).
328 Bright, 'The "Phantom Threat": Government Admits Its University Free Speech Policy Only Based on "Small" Amount of Evidence', *Byline Times*.

329 Mark Smulian, 'Networks banned from inviting speakers critical of government', *Civil Service World* (November 2021).
330 'Katie Hopkins compares migrants to "cockroaches" and suggests using gunships to stop them crossing the Mediterranean', ITV News (April 2015).
331 Lawler Kang, '"Would You Rather Your Kids Had Feminism or Cancer?"', *Good Men Project* (November 2018).
332 Claire Phipps, Kevin Rawlinson and Rowena Mason, 'Toby Young resigns from the Office for Students after backlash', *The Guardian* (January 2018).
333 Ben Chapman, 'FTSE 100 has more CEOs called Steve than from ethnic minorities, research finds', *The Independent* (February 2019).
334 Rowena Mason, Aamna Mohdin and Emine Sinmaz, 'Police in England and Wales to get new powers to shut down protests before disruption begins', *The Guardian* (January 2023).
335 David Goodhart, *The Road to Somewhere: The Populist Revolt and the Future of Politics*, (Hurst, 2017).
336 Sam Bright, 'Criticise Lee Anderson – but don't be anti-northern', *New Statesman* (February 2023).
337 Michael McQuarrie, 'Trump and the Revolt of the Rust Belt', *LSE Blogs* (November 2016).

9 ETONOMICS

338 Nadine Batchelor-Hunt, 'The chart that shows the UK's 14-year "economic disaster"', *Yahoo News* (October 2022).
339 Jonathan Cribb and Paul Johnson, '10 years on – have we recovered from the financial crisis?', IFS (September 2018).
340 'Household total wealth in Great Britain: April 2018 to March 2020', Office for National Statistics (January 2022).
341 'Brexit: Northern votes not as decisive as assumed', Manchester Metropolitan University (June 2019).
342 Jannick Damgaard, Thomas Elkjaer, and Niels Johannesen, 'Piercing the well', International Monetary Fund (June 2018).
343 Sian Norris, 'Justice System "Inadequate" In Face of Rising Fraud', *Byline Times* (October 2022).
344 'Cities Outlook 2019', Centre for Cities (January 2019).
345 Brigid Francis-Devine, 'Constituency data: Child poverty', House of Commons Library (May 2022).
346 'Suicides in England and Wales: 2021 registrations', Office

for National Statistics (September 2022).
347 Yanis Varoufakis, 'Rishi Sunak's "grown-up" austerity is a gift to the wealthy', *New Statesman* (October 2022).
348 'What is universal credit and who qualifies for it?' BBC News (September 2022).
349 'English Private Landlord Survey 2021', Department for Levelling Up, Housing and Communities (May 2022).
350 Rupert Jones, 'Private rents in Britain hit record highs, with 20% rise in some areas', *The Guardian* (October 2022).
351 'Housing tenure over time', Trust for London.
352 George Hammond, 'How London's property market became an inheritocracy', *Financial Times* (January 2023).
353 Oliver Bullough, *Butler to the World*, (Profile, 2022).
354 Dominic Cummings, 'The Hollow Men II: Some reflections on Westminster and Whitehall dysfunction', Dominic Cummings's Blog (October 2014).
355 Davis, *Reckless Opportunists.*
356 Guy Standing, *The Corruption of Capitalism: Why Rentiers Thrive and Work Does Not Pay*, (Biteback, 2016).
357 Sam Bright, 'The Financial Takeover of Government', *Byline Times* (November 2020).
358 Ha-Joon Chang, *23 Things They Don't Tell You About Capitalism*, (Penguin, 2011).
359 FW Reporter, 'UK should "do a Singapore", says former DEFRA secretary', *Farmers Weekly* (November 2017).
360 Tan Kim Song and Manu Bhaskaran, 'The Role of the State in Singapore: Pragmatism in Pursuit of Growth', *World Scientific* (2016).
361 Arj Singh, 'UK fishermen "sacrificed" by Boris Johnson to win Brexit deal, industry chief says', *iNews* (July 2021).
362 Standing, *The Corruption of Capitalism.*
363 'The Prime Minister's Levelling Up speech: 15 July 2021', Prime Minister's Office (July 2021).
364 John Harris, 'Want to see where Britain's political future will be decided? Head to Milton Keynes', *The Guardian* (May 2022).
365 Bright, *Fortress London.*
366 Larry Elliott, 'Average UK household £8,800 a year worse off than those in France or Germany', *The Guardian* (July 2022).
367 Sian Norris, 'Drop in Life Expectancy Due to Poor Pandemic Management "Chilling" Says Sir Michael Marmot', *Byline Times* (April 2022).

368 Sarah Boseley, 'Austerity blamed for life expectancy stalling for first time in century', *The Guardian* (February 2020).
369 Sam Bright, 'Healthy Life Expectancy Has Fallen in 80% of Red Wall Areas Since Conservatives Took Power', *Byline Times* (October 2021).
370 Sam Bright, '"Our Economic Masters Failed on Their Own Terms": Health of Deprived Areas Stuck in Previous Decades', *Byline Times* (January 2023).
371 'End of Year Stats', the Trussell Trust.
372 David Smith, 'Steve Bannon: "We've turned the Republicans into a working-class party"', *The Guardian* (December 2019).
373 'Can Liz Truss fix Britain?', *The Economist* (September 2022).
374 Michael Savage, 'Revealed: top 10 children's care providers made £300m profits', *The Guardian* (March 2022).
375 Standing, *The Corruption of Capitalism.*
376 '70% of UK rail routes now owned by foreign states', RMT (January 2017).
377 Laurie MacFarlane, 'Our railways have failed – what next?', New Economics Foundation (January 2017).

10 THE NEW ARISTOCRACY

378 Rowena Mason, 'Starmer calls on Tories to sack co-chair Ben Elliot over party links to Russia', *The Guardian* (March 2022).
379 Gabriel Pogrund, and Henry Zeffman, 'Tory chairman Ben Elliot "peddled access to Prince Charles"', the *Sunday Times* (July 2021).
380 Gabriel Pogrund, and Dipesh Gadher, 'Prince Charles aides fixed CBE for Saudi tycoon who gave £1.5m', the *Sunday Times* (September 2021).
381 Gabriel Pogrund, 'Prince Charles accepted €1m cash in suitcase from sheikh', the *Sunday Times* (June 2022).
382 Alice Thompson, 'I talk to my dead wife all the time – Maurice Saatchi on grief', *The Times* (October 2022).
383 Sam Bright, 'A Golden Ticket: 2,000 Oligarchs from Countries with Human Rights Concerns "Buy" Permanent Right to Live in UK', *Byline Times* (March 2022).
384 Paul Caruana Galizia, 'Londongrad: How the Lebedevs partied their way to power', *Tortoise.*
385 'The UK Tier 1 Visa: The dangers of blind faith', Transparency International (December 2018).

386 Rajeev Syal, 'Ten oligarchs who used "golden visa" route to UK are on sanctions list', *The Guardian* (January 2023).
387 Bright, 'A Golden Ticket: 2,000 Oligarchs from Countries with Human Rights Concerns "Buy" Permanent Right to Live in UK', *Byline Times*
388 'Russia', Intelligence and Security Committee of Parliament.
389 Rupert Neate, 'More than 138,000 properties in England and Wales owned by offshore companies', *The Guardian* (November 2022).
390 Damian Shepherd, 'Foreign Grip on London Property Is Easing on a Cocktail of Risks', *Bloomberg* (December 2022).
391 Alex Ralph, 'Malaysian funds take £1.6bn stake in Battersea power station', *The Times* (December 2018).
392 Rob Davies and Joseph Smith, 'How Qatar bought up Britain', *The Observer* (November 2022).
393 'Stats reveal extent of suspect wealth in UK property and Britain's role as global money laundering hub', Transparency International (February 2022).
394 Sam Bright, 'Startling Facts About London: The Oligarch's Paradise', *Byline Times* (February 2022).
395 Nassos Stylianou, Will Dahlgreen, and Alison Benjamin, 'UK property register: What three luxury homes reveal about who owns UK real estate', BBC News (7 February).
396 Patrick Wintour, 'No 10 pressured me to drop anti-money laundering measures, says ex-minister', *The Guardian* (February 2022).
397 'The UK's kleptocracy problem', Chatham House (December 2021).
398 Nafeez Ahmed, 'UK Sanctions Will "Flop" Because City of London Is Compromised by Russian Money', *Byline Times* (February 2022).
399 Sam Bright, 'The Ukraine War Has Exposed the UK's Russia Delusion', *Byline Times* (March 2022).
400 Nafeez Ahmed, 'Ukraine is Just the Beginning: Secret Document Reveals Vladimir Putin's Long War in Europe', *Byline Times* (March 2022).
401 Simon McGee, 'Cameron told to get tough with Russia', *The Times* (September 2011).
402 Sam Bright, 'UK Approved Military Exports to Russia Exceed Ukraine by £18 Million Since 2010', *Byline Times* (February 2022).
403 'Russia', Intelligence and Security Committee of Parliament.

404 'UK-based Russians donating large sums to Tories', BBC News (July 2014).
405 Peter Jukes, 'Putin's Plot Against "Great" Britain and How He Got Away With It', *Byline Times* (March 2022).
406 Bright, 'The Ukraine War Has Exposed the UK's Russia Delusion', *Byline Times.*
407 Luke Harding, *Shadow State: Murder, Mayhem, and Russia's Remaking of the West*, (Guardian Faber, 2020).
408 Sam Bright, 'Human Rights Problem Countries Receive Two-Thirds of UK Military Export Licences Since 2010', *Byline Times* (March 2022).
409 'Yemen war will have killed 377,000 by year's end: UN', *France24* (November 2021).
410 Tom Ambrose, '16 million in Yemen "marching towards starvation" as food rations run low – UN', *The Guardian* (September 2021).
411 Byline Intelligence Team, 'Conflict and Complicity: 11,000 Civilian Casualties Caused by Saudi Coalition's Use of Explosive Weapons in Yemen Since 2015', *Byline Times* (March 2022).
412 Sam Bright, and Sascha Lavin, 'How Johnson's Government is Using Oligarchs In Its Attempt to Rebuild the "Red Wall"', *Byline Times* (April 2022).
413 Molly Blackall, Ben Gartside, and David Connett, 'Sizewell C: UK tapping up Saudi and UAE investors as it struggles to bring in nuclear investment funds', *iNews* (September 2022).
414 Dylan Donnelley, 'Tory MP calls for "key" foreign investment to "level up" the North of England', *Daily Express* (June 2021).
415 Bright and Lavin, How Johnson's Government is Using Oligarchs In Its Attempt to Rebuild the "Red Wall"', *Byline Times.*
416 'Revealed: 6,500 migrant workers have died in Qatar since World Cup awarded', *The Guardian* (February 2021).
417 'Qatar: Security Forces Arrest, Abuse LGBT People', Human Rights Watch (October 2022).
418 'World Report 2022: Kuwait', Human Rights Watch.
419 Stanley Reed, 'In Rebuke to West, OPEC and Russia Aim to Raise Oil Prices With Big Supply Cut', the *New York Times* (October 2022).
420 Cristobal Young, *The Myth of Millionaire Tax Flight: How Place Still Matters for the Rich*, (Stanford University Press, 2017).